D0871716

1. Integral Formation of Catholic Priests

INTEGRAL FORMATION OF CATHOLIC PRIESTS

INTEGRAL FORMATION
OF
CATHOLIC PRIESTS

MARCIAL MACIEL, L.C.

ALBA · HOUSE   NEW · YORK

SOCIETY OF ST. PAUL, 2187 VICTORY BLVD., STATEN ISLAND, NY 10314

Original title: "La formación integral del sacerdote católico."
Translated by Stephen Fichter, L.C. and Francis Snell, L.C.
Revised Translation

ALL RIGHTS RESERVED

Library of Congress Cataloging-in-Publication Data

Maciel, Marcial, 1920-
      [Formación integral del sacerdote católico. English]
      Integral formation of Catholic priests / Marcial Maciel;
   [translated by Stephen Fichter and Francis Snell]. — Rev.
   translation.
            p.   cm.
      Includes bibliographical references and index.
      ISBN: 0-8189-0629-4
      1. Catholic Church — Clergy — Training of.   I. Title.
BX900.M2713   1992
207 '.1 ' 12 — dc20   92-7349
                                                                       CIP

Produced and designed in the United States of America by the
Fathers and Brothers of the Society of St. Paul,
2187 Victory Boulevard, Staten Island, New York 10314,
as part of their communications apostolate.

Printing Information:

Current Printing - first digit	1	2	3	4	5	6	7	8	9	10

Year of Current Printing - first year shown

1992	1993	1994	1995	1996	1997	1998	1999

CONTENTS

Biblical Abbreviations

OLD TESTAMENT

Genesis	Gn	Nehemiah	Ne	Baruch	Ba
Exodus	Ex	Tobit	Tb	Ezekiel	Ezk
Leviticus	Lv	Judith	Jdt	Daniel	Dn
Numbers	Nb	Esther	Est	Hosea	Ho
Deuteronomy	Dt	1 Maccabees	1 M	Joel	Jl
Joshua	Jos	2 Maccabees	2 M	Amos	Am
Judges	Jg	Job	Jb	Obadiah	Ob
Ruth	Rt	Psalms	Ps	Jonah	Jon
1 Samuel	1 S	Proverbs	Pr	Micah	Mi
2 Samuel	2 S	Ecclesiastes	Ex	Nahum	Na
1 Kings	1 K	Song of Songs	Sg	Habakkuk	Hab
2 Kings	2 K	Wisdom	Ws	Zephaniah	Zp
1 Chronicles	1 Ch	Sirach	Si	Haggai	Hg
2 Chronicles	2 Ch	Isaiah	Is	Malachi	Ml
Ezra	Ezr	Jeremiah	Jr	Zechariah	Zc
		Lamentations	Lm		

NEW TESTAMENT

Matthew	Mt	Ephesians	Ep	Hebrews	Heb
Mark	Mk	Philippians	Ph	James	Jm
Luke	Lk	Colossians	Col	1 Peter	1 P
John	Jn	1 Thessalonians	1 Th	2 Peter	2 P
Acts	Ac	2 Thessalonians	2 Th	1 John	1 Jn
Romans	Rm	1 Timothy	1 Tm	2 John	2 Jn
1 Corinthians	1 Cor	2 Timothy	2 Tm	3 John	3 Jn
2 Corinthians	2 Cor	Titus	Tt	Jude	Jude
Galatians	Gal	Philemon	Phm	Revelation	Rv

ABBREVIATIONS

CD   Vatican Council II, Decree *Christus Dominus*, 1965.

CIC   *Code of Canon Law*, 1983.

CL   John Paul II, Apostolic Exhortation *Christifideles laici*, 1988.

DS   Denzinger-Schönmetzer, *Enchyridion Symbolorum...*, 1965.

EN   Paul VI, Apostolic Exhortation *Evangelii Nuntiandi*, 1976.

FC   John Paul II, Apostolic Exhortation *Familiaris Consortio*, 1982.

GS   Vatican Council II, Pastoral Constitution *Gaudium et Spes*, 1965.

LE   John Paul II, Encyclical Letter *Laborem Exercens*, 1981.

LG   Vatican Council II, Dogmatic Constitution *Lumen Gentium*, 1964.

LC   Congregation for the Doctrine of the Faith, Document *Libertatis Conscientia*, 1986.

LN   Congregation for the Doctrine of the Faith, Document *Libertatis Nuntius*, 1984.

OT   Vatican Council II, Decree *Optatam Totius*, 1965.

PO   Vatican Council II, Decree *Presbyterorum Ordinis*, 1965.

PP   Paul VI, Encyclical Letter *Populorum Progressio*, 1967.

RFIS   Congregation for Catholic Education, *Ratio Fundamentalis Institutionis Sacerdotalis*, 1970 (1983).

SC   Vatican Council II, Constitution *Sacrosanctum Concilium*, 1963.

SRS   John Paul II, Encyclical Letter *Sollicitudo Rei Socialis*, 1988.

PREFATORY NOTE

A priest is a man chosen and called by Christ from among God's faithful people to serve them in the person of Christ, head of the Church, by forming, leading, teaching and sanctifying them as a community. To do this, a priest receives the sacrament of holy orders which permanently configures him to Christ. All priestly formation must rest upon a clear concept of the priesthood and particularly how it is differentiated from other ministries within the Church. Otherwise there is the temptation, in the noble effort to highlight other ministries and their value, to downplay the profound theological reality that is the Catholic priesthood.

I underline the definition of Catholic priesthood because there cannot be a renewal and a sustained development of priestly spirituality cut off from a clear and cohesive recognition and acceptance of the identity of the priest. If I am to believe the voices of many many priests, which I do, there is a strongly felt and articulated need among our priests today for the ongoing spiritual renewal that is necessary to sustain daily ministry.

This attention to the spiritual dimension of life mirrors what is taking place all around us. I am convinced from what I hear and learn from those with whom I meet every day, both within and outside our faith family, that a real and true thirst for the things of the spirit exists in our day. Every segment of our society, with few exceptions, seems to recognize, whether in an articulated manner or not, that we do not live by bread alone. We need the Spirit and the hope that the Spirit brings. For too long, too many have accepted the secular gospel that "It doesn't get any better than this." The basic emptiness of the "what-you-see-is-what-you-get" theologies has been recognized by the people of our day. The very addiction of our society to chemicals, fads and self-indulgence challenges us to look more closely at the ultimate meaning of life. Perhaps we are recognizing the human phenomenon that St. Augustine described over fifteen hundred years ago: "You have made us for Yourself, and our heart is restless until it rests in You" (*Confessions,* 1.1.1., PL 32 661).

A priest is a living witness to the realm of the Spirit. He is a special instrument of the presence of God's kingdom in our midst. For that reason the formation, life and ministry of the priest must find its roots and renewal in a re-affirmation of the spiritual dimension of priestly life and ministry.

To address priestly formation necessitates an understanding of the Church and to speak of the Church as the context of priesthood today requires us also to recognize the wider reality in which the Church exists — the world around us. The first of the dual realities in which the priesthood is asserted is the increasingly secular world that is particularly identified with the materially rich and technologically advanced societies of North America, Western Europe and parts of Asia. There is an increasing sector in this "secular city" that does not share our vision of the spiritual reality and dimension of life that for us involves the Kingdom of God — a life everlasting — the possibility of the Church that is somehow a presence in this life of a reality that transcends the physical limitations of which we have become so aware and in which we are enmeshed. This should not be misconstrued as "progress bashing" or a rejection of the scientific and technological advances from which we all so richly benefit. Rather, the focus should be on the increasingly recognized fact that our preoccupation and satisfaction with the City of Man has strongly distracted us from that concentration necessary to focus on the City of God.

The second context is the more immediate spiritual reality of the Church itself as the sacrament of God's presence in the world and a sign of contradiction to the world. It is within the context of this wider reality of the sacramental presence of the body of Christ, in the midst of a world ill at ease with that body, that the priesthood finds its reality and explanation.

When, therefore, we speak of formation leading to ordination into the priesthood of Christ, we have before our eyes a unique and incomparable reality which includes the prophetic and royal office of the Incarnate Word of God. Christ is the image of God breaking into our world to announce that to believe is to walk in the light. To walk in the light is to live in the kingdom. To live in the kingdom is to build up the kingdom which in its fullness is God's new creation.

To serve this community of elect, the Church, Christ set aside those who would devote their energies not only to the task that is shared by all the baptized (to proclaim the Good News and bring about the new creation through the celebration and living out of the paschal mystery) but also to the specific task of serving the whole Body of Christ. This service is rooted in a unique and profound conformation to Christ Himself in such a way that Christ, in glory, continues to be present and to minister to His struggling pilgrim people.

Thus the sacrament of holy orders takes its place as the second great differentiation within Christ's Church. Some are ordained by God to participate uniquely in the priesthood of Christ so that they might more specifically minister to the rest of the body. The Second Vatican Council points out that the sacrament of orders differentiates members of the community and sets them apart for ministerial, priestly works. By baptism, one is distinguished from the world and made a Christian; by orders, one is set apart for the Christian community and made a priest.

Yet this "setting apart" or "differentiation" is not meant to divide or establish a class system within Christ's Body. It is meant to facilitate the life and function of the body. The priest is no more separated from the lay person than the lay person is separated from the world in which he or she lives. The common priesthood of the faithful, conferred in baptism, is interrelated with the ministerial priesthood because each, in its own special way, is a participation in the one priesthood of Christ. Each is unintelligible without the other.

The function of the priest is to lead or shepherd the faithful. In this area we have witnessed the most notable changes in how the priesthood is articulated. Today there is an increased emphasis on the role of the laity, their gifts and the various ministries to which they are called. The priest as leader of the faith community today exercises that role by encouraging others in the community to do the tasks that their own baptism empowers them to do while at the same time coordinating for the good of the whole community the exercise of various gifts that serve the Church. Increasingly as more and more people recognize their own calling and respond to it, the tasks of the priest as leader of the faith community will more and more center on his ability to coordinate, oversee and enable all of the members of the faith community to participate in the building up of the Church.

Our Holy Father's apostolic exhortation, *Christifideles Laici,* speaks to this unity and diversity within the local Church. "In fact, at one and the same time it is characterized by a diversity and a complementarity of vocations and states in life, of ministries, of charisms and responsibilities. Because of this diversity and complementarity, every member of the lay faithful is seen in relation to the whole body and offers a totally unique contribution on behalf of the whole body" (20).

Because of the service that only a priest can render, priestly formation necessarily concentrates on providing the personal, academic, spiritual and pastoral development required to enable the ordained priest to respond faithfully and effectively both to God's call and the needs of the Church.

The priest is first of all a disciple. Therefore, priestly formation must provide the spiritual guidance and personal growth that elicits from the candidate for priesthood a prayerful and mature commitment to the way of Christ, his Lord and Master.

A priest shares in the apostolic mission of the Church. Intellectual and academic preparation allows the priest to speak from the context of the Church's faith tradition so that he articulates fully and authentically the gospel, which has been handed down in the lived tradition of the Church. In this way, the salvific voice of Christ is clearly heard in our day.

This process of formation enables the candidate for priesthood fully to appreciate the power of God's word and the efficacy of the sacramental life of the Church, especially as he re-presents in the Eucharistic liturgy the paschal mystery of the death and resurrection of the Lord. Such formation prepares a priest for a pastoral ministry so that he can stand in the midst of God's people as one who serves, as one who confidently guides them on the spiritual pilgrimage that leads them eventually to the fullness of the kingdom — their heavenly home.

Most Reverend Donald W. Wuerl
Bishop of Pittsburgh
November 5, 1991

INTRODUCTION

This book is a tribute to God's love. It is a response to his tenacious love, which continues sending workers to the harvest. Statistics reveal a new surge in the number of vocations to the priesthood, especially in certain countries. Indifference or passive gratitude to the Lord for this new manifestation of his perennial, living presence in the Church is out of the question. True thankfulness calls for an active response. We must respond to God by attempting to form as well as possible these young men whom He is calling into his service for the good of all humanity.

An awareness is growing in the Church that we need holy, well-prepared priests who can truly serve the people of God as the faithful seek holiness and give themselves to the apostolic task of announcing the Gospel. This awareness is growing, perhaps in a special way among Catholic lay people. In the previous synod of bishops, dedicated to the laity, it was a lay participant who appealed for an in-depth consideration of the theme of the priesthood. He commented: "An essential witness in the life of the Church would be missing if we don't have priests who can call lay people to fulfill their role in the Church and in the world, who can help form them for the apostolate, supporting them in their difficult vocation."

It is clearly not enough for the Church merely to have a great number of priests. If they are to "call" lay people and "help form them," they must first of all be well formed in their own vocation. This explains why such universal interest has been focused on the theme of the upcoming synod: priestly formation.

Since the Second Vatican Council, a general consensus has emerged that we need to renew programs of priestly formation "in present-day circumstances." Continuous transformations in the world and the Church also touch priests, and oblige us to reflect carefully on a more adequate preparation for them. The ecclesiology of Vatican II sheds new light on the preparation of those men whose ministry it is to serve the people of God, the Church, sacrament of salvation in the world. This light is also reflected in other conciliar documents, and has yet to be applied to many areas.

The theme of priestly formation includes many varied and complex elements. Not only that, these elements must be analyzed from different points of view, from diverse experiences and cultures. An open and frank dialogue in which each of us shares his knowledge and experiences in this field can only help enrich the collective reflection of the Church.

We exchange our knowledge and experience... above all our experience. We need specific courses of action in order to draw up truly effective programs of formation. This is a real challenge. We all know the difficulty of communicating our own experience with its many nuances and particular applications. Throughout my nearly fifty year experience as a formator of priests, I have often been questioned about specific aspects. At times the question is easy to answer. But it is not so simple when the question is a global one, "How do you form your priests?" There is so much to explain, so many fine points to distinguish...

For the past few years I have been working with my team of educators and formators to systemize our formative experience. This effort has enabled me to put together an overall program and offer it in all humility as one more contribution to the open dialogue that enriches ecclesial reflection on the formation of priests.

The pages which follow seek primarily to express a living experience. They are meant to be an aid and a support to those who are called to direct seminaries and centers of formation. Forming priests is an art practiced every day as we walk with each candidate on his road to the altar. As a result, this book deals largely with reflections and suggestions of a practical and lived nature. The doctrinal and theoretical elements which have been incorporated are in function of pedagogical practice, providing its light and its strength.

I mentioned earlier that different points of view, experiences and cultures must converge on the topic of priestly formation. This book's perspective is grounded fundamentally in western culture. Some elements could and perhaps should necessarily be interpreted and adapted to other environments through the principles of a correct inculturation.

The same should be said regarding institutional aspects: there are obvious differences between forming diocesan priests and forming religious aspirants to the priesthood. This book refers primarily to the first group. Doubtless, the priestly formation of religious varies in each institute according to the traits of its own charism: its spirituality and apostolate, customs and lifestyle. Still, the most essential aspects of priestly formation are equally valid for diocesan and religious priests.

At the beginning I spoke of renewing priestly formation. Renew does not necessarily mean innovate. Changing circumstances in the world and the Church demand revision, adaptation and, at times, change in certain outlooks and methods, but this will mainly be in elements that are accidental to the priesthood itself. What is essential and constitutes the very marrow of the ministerial priesthood instituted by Christ, cannot change. To renew is to adapt accidental elements so that the essential aspects of the priesthood will be more fully realized under new circumstances.

In this sense, renewal is not at odds with tradition. It is true that there are some traditions which are no longer valid (or perhaps never really were). But at times, renewal consists in rescuing values which have been lost along the way. This is the meaning, for example, of the current patristic renewal. It is not a question of returning to the past, but of recovering elements which will enrich our present and our future. In the field of priestly formation there are treasures forged in the millinery experience of the Church, which on occasion have been too quickly thrown overboard. Renewal also means rediscovering their richness, scouring away possible tarnish and adapting them to the present.

Priestly formation covers a variety of aspects. At a given moment we may have to insist on one facet of formation more than another. But we should keep the overall image of the priest always before our eyes. Efforts to achieve individual aspects should be carried out within the framework of an integral formation of our catholic priests. Our work has to revolve around an essential nucleus if we don't want its multiplicity of elements to degenerate into fragmentation. For priests, men who participate sacramentally and existentially in the eternal priesthood of Christ, the nucleus of their integral formation has to be their spiritual formation. If we forget this or accept it only in theory, we might reduce the preparation of our priests to a more-or-less intense academic curriculum. Young men would then emerge from our seminaries as intellectuals or as specialists well-versed in pastoral techniques. We need that... but we need more than that. The laity has asked for "an essential witness in the life of the Church."

This witness springs from the very nature of the Catholic priesthood. And so, we dedicate the first part of this work to the priest's identity and mission. Based on this, we outline some educative principles which stand as pillars or fundamental principles of priestly formation. Upon these we build the integral preparation of our priests, which can be divided into four areas of formation: spiritual, human, intellectual and pastoral. But all of this is a dream if we don't have the men to help realize the project. Once again, these ideas are directed especially to them. Therefore, we must speak about formators, what they should be and how they should act. And since the candidates are normally trained in a center for formation we will examine the conditions that have to exist for a truly formative environment. Finally, forming a priest is a slow, gradual process spanning a variety of steps. We must be able to adapt the whole educational system to the different stages of priestly formation.

Reading through these pages, it might appear that we offer too wishful a portrait of the priest, too ambitious an ideal of formation. Today's priest lives immersed in difficult social, cultural and ecclesial situations. He can easily feel as if he were lost in a hostile jungle. He doesn't have all the answers for others, and finds it difficult to bear the weight of his own consecration to God and the apostolate. Shouldn't we just try to save what we can?

It is one thing to speak about forming priests, quite another to form them. At times it seems impossible. Perhaps we don't have competent formators, adequate programs, financial resources... or vocations. Aspiring to so high an ideal could seem unrealistic, and therefore not worth the effort.

Nevertheless, I'm convinced that if we work enthusiastically, if we use all the resources at our disposal, we can achieve much more than we might expect. Most of all we need clear ideas and sufficient determination to achieve our goals. We can't afford to get discouraged.

The effort is worth it. It is our best response to the love of God, who continues to call workers to the harvest.

CHAPTER ONE

IDENTITY AND MISSION OF THE PRIEST

On the surface, the formation of priests appears to be a clearly defined field. The specific nature and qualities of the priesthood seem to impose a very particular formation program. But we have to ask ourselves if we have in our minds a clear and in-depth understanding of what the priest we want to form is. When we find difficulty in defining a plan of formation or when our plans do not give the results we hoped for, we have to ask ourselves if the true image of the priest which we sometimes may take for granted has not become somewhat vague in our minds.

It is evident, then, that the formation of priests is intimately related to the question of *priestly identity and mission*. This is the fundamental question that determines the type of formation that we will offer to candidates for the priesthood.

No less important for our task as formators is the fact that the priest, with his identity and mission, is first and foremost a *man*. The human element is essential to his identity and evidently our concept of man plays a key role in our plans for the formation of priests.

What is a priest? It seems a simple question yet for the past three decades, deep uncertainty has assailed most attempts at a serious answer. Different models of the priest have come to the fore one after another, each seeming to disqualify the other, from the worker priest to the political activist, from the social worker to community representative... As von Balthasar puts it, it was easy to run into priests who were inventing ways to attract people, who tried to speak about God using modern slang in the hopes of getting their attention; having been called to the lifestyle of Jesus Christ, they were afraid of not finding a warm welcome among their fellow men and allowed their love for God to dry up in a horizontal love for

1

neighbor. They were priests who lost themselves in the anonymity of what is 'human.'[1] Talk of the crisis of priestly identity was already common-place.

Actually, any response to the question about the identity of the priest leaves a certain dissatisfaction, the element of uncertainty you experience before a mystery.

> When a priest, trembling at the sight of his unworthiness and the sublimity of his ministry, places his consecrated hands on our heads; when, in his amazement at being made dispenser of the Blood of the Testament and his surprise at being able to infuse life with his words, a priest forgives a sinner being himself a sinner, we rise to our feet with great confidence... We have been at the feet of a man, but a man who took Christ's place.[2]

These words of Manzoni profess a mystery that conceals all of the world's insignificance and all of heaven's splendor in the reality of one man: the Catholic priest. A man certainly, but one who embodies the presence of God, the Redeemer, on the streets of our cities and in the midst of our lives.

It is necessary, however, to try to penetrate this mystery. The author of the letter to the Hebrews gives us a good starting point when he presents the figure of the high priest which culminates in Jesus Christ: "For every high priest chosen from among men is appointed to act on behalf of men in relation to God, to offer gifts and sacrifices for sins" (Heb 5:1).

First, then, we should consider that the priest is *chosen* or, in other words, the priest is *called*. He does not call himself, he does not invent his own path in life. His identity and his mission are born of a *vocation*.

In the second place it is necessary to reflect upon the meaning and purpose of this call. The priest is chosen *to act on behalf of men*... but not in the same way as an engineer or policeman. He exists in order to serve men *in relation to God* and, specifically, *to offer gifts and sacrifices for*

---

[1] Cf. H.U. Von Balthasar, *The priest that I seek,* in Ecclesia, 1 (1987), p. 12.
[2] A. Manzoni, *Observations of Catholic morality,* ch. XVIII.

sins. He is a bridge between God and men by the ministry of the word and the sacraments.

Finally, it is important to comprehend who this person, chosen and appointed to act on behalf of others, really is. We are dealing with someone who has been chosen *from among men.* A man like the rest, with the same capacity for greatness and misery. In the next few pages the human make-up of the priest, with all its possibilities and limitations will be at the heart of our reflection.

As we measure the distance separating the human reality of the man who has been "chosen" from the ideal for which he has been "appointed," the need to help him effectively to *form himself* should impress itself on our hearts. We should better understand the model to which all of his efforts, and ours, have to be oriented... "until Christ is formed in you" (Gal 4:19).

Called by God

Every year pontifical and episcopal annual reports give an account of a phenomenon which has uninterruptedly repeated itself since the origin of the Church: a certain number of men, most of them young, embrace the priestly life. Each one of them carries with him an unrepeatable personal history. Their nationality, culture, social environment, family and temperament define them in a unique way. Nevertheless, there is something they all bear in common even before they begin to consider the idea of entering the seminary: the vocation.

The first thing we must understand and always remember when we talk about candidates for the priesthood and their formation is that they have been "chosen" by God. Certainly they have freely and knowingly knocked at the doors of the seminary, but in reality the initiative was not theirs. "One does not take the honor upon himself, but he is called by God" (Heb 5:4). No one creates his own vocation, nor does it depend on his own likes or sensibility. It does not depend on the invitation or the inspiring example of other men. It cannot be reduced to simple chance.

The vocation is God's initiative; it is a very real and objective call from Christ. The story of the disciples of Christ is repeated in each man who perceives the call to the priesthood... disciples with whom the Master did not mince words: "You did not choose me, but I chose you" (Jn 15:16). Each one of them, in various ways, one day heard an interior voice that said, "Follow me" (Mk 10:21).

The whole history of salvation speaks of God's mysterious way of acting: God calls Abraham to found a new people; He calls Moses to free Israel from Egyptian hands; He calls the prophets to be the heralds of truth, witnesses of his divine will; He calls Mary to be the Mother of the Savior. Later, Jesus of Nazareth, the Incarnate Word, called certain men "to be with him, and to be sent out to preach" (Mk 3:14). Throughout the history of the new People of God, Christ has continued to choose and call co-workers who prolong his saving presence among the rest of humanity.

God calls each priest at a very precise moment of the world's history and of his own personal history. But in reality it is a choice He has made from all eternity: "Before I formed you in the womb I knew you, and before you were born I consecrated you; I appointed you a prophet to the nations" (Jr 1:5).

It is not a merely functional and cold choice. It is a declaration of love.[3] With complete liberty, Christ surrounded himself with a group of disciples: "He called those whom he desired" (Mk 3:13). He chose them, looking at each one with love. To the rich young man who fulfilled the commandments but wanted something more, "Jesus looking upon him loved him, and said to him... Come, follow me" (Mk 10:21). To those who followed Him to the end He declared at the Last Supper, "As the Father has loved me, so have I loved you" (Jn 15:9). Although they were his disciples, they were not as servants, rather He called them friends (cf. Jn 15:15).

When Christ focuses his attention on a man to call him to the priesthood, He makes his voice heard through a series of insinuations and beckonings which seep silently, lovingly, into the intimacy of the man's conscience and heart. At times a word or a simple question, a book or a good example is enough for God to reveal his declaration of love to the heart of a young man. In the vastness of his eternal plan, He has foreseen the suitability of the individual He chooses. He has given him the ensemble of qualities he needs to respond fully to the vocation. The official welcome

---

[3] John Paul II, *Message to seminarians in Spain,* November 8, 1982.

of the Church is a seal and a guarantee, and appeals to God's fidelity to his promises: *May God who has begun this good work in you bring it to completion.*[4]

Yet this declaration of love requires a response of love by the one chosen. God's call respects our integrity. God speaks clearly but does not harass or use force. In the depths of the young man's conscience He suggests, prepares his soul, gently calls, but He wants the soul to respond with total freedom and authentic love. The last thing God wants is a priest who follows Him under obligation or "professionally," but without love.

Awareness of the vocation must make way in the heart of the young man who listens. It must enter into his innermost thoughts, sentiments and will in order to influence his moral conduct.[5]

Each vocation is an authentic dialogue of friendship between Christ the Redeemer and a man whom He, from all eternity and out of love, has "chosen" from among men.

Appointed to Act on Behalf of Others...

The priest then is first and foremost a man chosen by God, but the divine choice does not obey some blind whim, nor is its full meaning limited to the priest himself. God calls to a specific mission. He asks for a very particular form of cooperation in his plan of salvation.

The priest "is appointed to act on behalf of men in relation to God, to offer gifts and sacrifices for sins" (Heb 5:1). God has placed him at the service of others: a service which specializes in the things that refer to God and reaches its fullness in the sacramental ministry.

Clearly, it is not enough to be aware of all this in order to define properly the identity and mission of the man called to exercise the priestly ministry. We could come up with different and even contradictory interpretations of what this service to others means or how far "in relation to God" extends. Undoubtedly, there is room for different priestly styles, but we can perfectly well ask ourselves if it is possible to find an essential underlayer which is valid for all places and all times.

---

[4] *Ritual of ordination,* 1978.
[5] Cf. John Paul II, *Angelus,* December 31, 1989.

CHRIST THE PRIEST, PRIESTS OF CHRIST

The same text of the letter to the Hebrews offers us an answer because, in reality, the author has outlined a description of the high priest only in order to present us with the figure of *Christ, the true High Priest.* This is the meaning of the entire letter. "... He was heard for his godly fear. Although He was the Son, He learned obedience through what He suffered; and being made perfect He became the source of eternal salvation for all who obey Him, being designated by God a high priest" (Heb 5:7b-10). Although his entire life, from Bethlehem to Golgotha, was a continuous priestly act, his death on the cross capsulizes in a special way the meaning of his priesthood. On the altar of the cross He offered the sacrifice of Himself. The letter to the Hebrews, contemplating the Passion scene from a priestly standpoint, highlights the role Jesus' humanity played. That afternoon had a climate of petition, of intercession for mankind. The death of the Son of God obtained salvation for his brothers. In this way, the entire regeneration of the human race is the work of the priestly action of Christ, the Son of God made man. "Therefore He is the Mediator of a New Covenant, so that those who are called may receive the promised eternal inheritance, since a death has occurred which redeems them from the transgressions under the first covenant" (Heb 9:15).

Even today, "the one Mediator between God and men" (1 Tm 2:5; cf. Heb 8:6), Jesus Christ, intercedes before the Father for his brothers and sisters, and as God, He brings salvation and grace from heaven. Jesus Christ is, for this reason, *the Priest of the New Covenant.*

The others, all the priests of the new People of God, are but a prolongation of this one priesthood, in which they participate sacramentally, because He so wished it. At the Last Supper He gave them the power to offer the sacrifice of his own body and blood, exactly as He had done. To emphasize the identification He told them, "Do this in memory of me" (Lk. 22:19). Later, He gave them the power to forgive sins, a power that only God could claim and which He had demonstrated in the cure of the paralytic (cf. Lk. 5:21-24). When He conferred the pastoral ministry on Peter, He made it clear that he was to assume and continue the care of the Master's flock: "Feed *my* lambs" (Jn 21:15).

Christ is, then, *the* Priest. And consequently, only Christ can say anything definitive about priestly identity and ministry. There is no other model for the priest except Him. Along these lines we do get an essential outline of the priest which does not change. The priest of tomorrow, no less than the priest of today, has to be similar to Christ. On earth Christ offered himself as the definitive model of the priest, carrying out a ministerial priesthood which the apostles were the first to receive. It is a priesthood that is destined to last, an unending chain throughout history. The priest of the third millennium will, like the priests of the preceding millennia, continue to uplift the life of the Church. In the year 2000, as in any other time, the priestly vocation will continue being the call to live the one and only permanent priesthood of Christ.[6]

The mission of Jesus of Nazareth appears before us as a colorful and varied prism: He cured the sick; He preached in synagogues and town squares; He forgave the sins of adulteresses and tax collectors; He transformed selfish hearts; He reproached the errors and abuses of the false guides of the people; He gathered and shaped a group of intimate collaborators... and, finally, He offered his own life as a victim of Redemption. Yet all of this was born of a single intention: to be the *Glorifier of the Father and the Savior of all men and women.* From Nazareth to Calvary, Jesus' life has meaning solely in relation to these two gravitational points. Although He brought Lazarus back to life out of true love for his friend, He was also conscious that this illness was "for the glory of God" (Jn 11:14). When the hour of his supreme gift of self for the salvation of humanity drew near (cf. Mt 26:28), He explained to his own that the Son of Man would be "glorified," "and God will be glorified in Him" (Jn 13:31). Afterwards, turning to his Father, He clearly summarized the meaning of his entire life: "I glorified you on earth, having accomplished the work which you gave me to do" (Jn 17:4). The angels had already announced this same message at the moment of his birth in Bethlehem: *"Glory to God* in the highest, and on earth *peace among men* with whom he is pleased" (Lk. 2:14).

In the same way as Christ, the priest has to travel, preach, attend the sick, help the needy, celebrate the divine worship, organize... But he knows that, like Christ, he must do everything, from the most sublime act of the Eucharistic celebration down to the most menial task of his day,

---

[6] Cf. John Paul II, *Angelus,* January 14, 1990.

living his priestly vocation as savior of souls and glorifier of the Father, through Jesus Christ, in Jesus Christ and with Jesus Christ.

MINISTERIAL PRIESTHOOD, SACRAMENTAL CHARACTER

It is true that all the baptized share in the priesthood of Christ: "You are a chosen race, a royal priesthood, a holy nation, God's own people" (1 P 2:9). Vatican II reminds us of this very clearly. Yet the Council notes that the common priesthood of the faithful and the ministerial or hierarchical priesthood, although they are ordered one to another, *differ essentially and not only in degree.*[7] For the Lord appointed certain men from among the faithful to be ministers,[8] with the plan that the faithful form one body in which "all the members have not the same function" (Rm 12:4). Thus, in the community of the faithful some men were to hold the sacred power of orders.

This essential difference is determined by the *priestly character.* The effect of any sacramental character is that God's project for an individual does not simply remain as something in God's will, but is impressed indelibly on the most intimate depths of that person's being. This means that God's plan can be carried out not as a divine mandate imposed from above, but rather as something that comes from within the Christian. Thanks to the priestly character, the identity of the priest is not a blueprint which configures him from outside. It is a living force which is grafted to the intimacy of the individual and becomes inseparable from his being.

The seal that the character leaves on the soul of the priest transforms him into God's special property. By exclusive right he is from God and for God. He is thoroughly identified with God. This is due not just to human nature's drive towards God, but is also God, from within the priest, venturing out in search of his people in order to save them.

The priestly character is also a sign of configuration with Jesus Christ.[9] Consequently, when we say that the priest is *alter Christus,* we do

---

[7] Cf. LG 10.
[8] Cf. PO 2.
[9] Cf. PO 12.

not mean just Christ's delegated representative but that the figure of Christ the Priest has been stamped in his soul. Pope Paul VI affirmed: "By virtue of the sacrament of orders, you have been made participants in Christ's priesthood to the point that you not only represent Christ nor merely exercise his ministry, but you live Christ; Christ lives in you."[10]

This configuration extends to the being and the *acting* of the person of the priest. The sacramental character of holy orders empowers the minister to take Christ's place and, as the head, act *in persona Christi*.[11] We can say that through the priest, Jesus renews his Eucharistic sacrifice, forgives sins and administers his grace in the other sacraments. Through the priest He continues to proclaim the Good News to the world. Through the priest He continues to guide and take care of his own flock. This truth has always had a decisive importance in the Church,

> If you do not have faith in the priest, all your hope is in vain. If God does not work through him, you have not been baptized, nor do you participate in the mysteries, nor have you been blessed; that is to say, you are not a Christian.[12]

Herein lies the true foundation of the mission of the priest. He has been chosen to act on behalf of humanity in relation to God... as was Christ. Moreover, he has been chosen as the living extension of Christ's service. The sacramental character has sealed his being, configuring it to Jesus Christ so as to prolong the mission of the Master in his actions.

PROPHET, PRIEST AND KING

Christ has a single mission, yet it unfolds itself in three different though complementary functions: teaching, offering worship and guiding the People of God.[13] The priest, then, also fulfills the threefold role of *prophet, priest and king.*

---

[10] Paul VI, *Discourse to new priests in Manila*, November 28, 1970.

[11] Cf. PO 2.

[12] St. John Chrysostom, Homily on 2 Tm 2:2-4.

[13] Cf. John Paul II, *Letter "Novo Incipiente"* to all priests on Holy Thursday, 1979, n. 3.

As *prophet,* Jesus Christ dedicated his ministry to announcing the Good News (cf. Mk 1:39), and sent his disciples to do the same (cf. Lk 9:6). This was his last command, "Go into all the world and preach the Gospel to the whole creation" (Mk 16:15).

From that moment on, the disciples understood that they were "sent," "apostles" of the Word which had become man. They came to realize that the priestly consecration which they received at the Last Supper was inseparably united to their duty of evangelization.

No differently today, the priest of Christ feels himself urged on by this duty. Within his soul he hears Paul's cry: "Woe to me if I do not preach the Gospel!" (1 Cor 9:16). He too knows that he has been sent, that he is an apostle — an apostle of the Kingdom of Jesus Christ in the world. Preaching and extending Christ's Kingdom constitute the ideal which inspires, directs and unifies all his actions. His only desire is to have Jesus Christ reign in the hearts of all people and families, and in the very life of society. His love for the Kingdom is proven in his sincere love for the Church founded by the Master, presence and promise of Christ's Kingdom.[14] From the moment the priest experiences that God-given mission, he knows that his life is definitively committed. He feels himself completely seized by the mission. It is the cause of his fears and hopes, his sorrows and joys. He is a "prisoner for Christ Jesus" (cf. Ep 3:1). The impetus of the love of Christ towards all men is an uncontainable force in the heart of the priest. It is the passion that unifies his entire life. Therefore everything — every circumstance, every situation, every chance encounter — is an occasion for him to preach Christ. He does not have time for himself, nor time to waste. The mission urges him on. He is aware that souls were bought at the price of the Blood of Christ. Those are not empty words for a priest who truly loves Christ and is completely identified with Him and with his prophetic mission, they are his real-life experience.

The *priestly function* of Jesus Christ, which culminated when He offered Himself as the Paschal Victim (cf. 1 Cor 5:7), is also prolonged by the priestly ministry. The first priests of the New Covenant, to whom the Master entrusted his sacraments (cf. Lk. 22:19; Jn 20:23), understood that their prophetic mission could not be separated from their sacramental function. Therefore the members of the first community "devoted them-

---

[14] Cf. LG 3.

selves to the apostles' teaching and fellowship, to the breaking of bread and the prayers" (Ac 2:42).

What the priest proclaims is what he celebrates and enacts in the liturgy especially when *in the person of Christ he effects the Eucharistic sacrifice and offers it to God in the name of all the people.*[15] The salvation in Christ which he preaches without ceasing, is realized in the pardon of sins and in the other sacraments. The priest knows that he is not simply a "bureaucrat" of the sacred, but a minister and dispenser of the mysteries of God (1 Cor 4:1). When he celebrates the sacraments he does so not as one who receives a command which in his heart seems foreign to him but as one who performs the act for which his entire being has been configured. When he offers the sacrifice on the altar he knows that he must offer himself along with it. This offering sets the stage for his total gift of self in all his daily tasks.

Finally, the priest is also a *shepherd.* By his participation in the royal function of Christ he completely identifies with the Good Shepherd (cf. Jn 10:11-16). His anointing and apostolic mandate make him the guide of a portion of the flock of Christ which he gathers, presides over, directs, unites and organizes in the name of Jesus.

This implies that he has been called to exercise authority. Yet his authority is none other than that of the Son of Man "who came not to be served, but to serve" (Mt 20:28). The office of shepherd requires a shepherd's heart. The most important virtue for a good shepherd is, as it was for the Good Shepherd, charity.

> Ordination confers on the young man a special grace of charity because the life of the priest only has meaning when considered as a practice of this virtue. Christians expect the priest to be a man of God and a man of charity. Since God is love, the priest will never be able to separate the service of God from the love of his brothers. The priest, upon committing himself to the service of the Kingdom of God, firmly sets himself on the road of charity.[16]

---

[15] LG 10.
[16] John Paul II, *Angelus,* February 18, 1990.

Charity, the essential attribute of God Himself (cf. 1 Jn 4:8), becomes the soul of the priesthood which represents Him before the world.

But love only flourishes in the garden of humility. Without it authority would cease to be service. A proud heart is always and everywhere petty, recalcitrant, bitter, cruel. A proud priest is the opposite of the Gospel Christ, he does not draw souls to God, but rather, even unbeknownst to himself, he drives them away.

The functions of prophet, priest, and pastor are distinct but *intimately related to each other, they develop hand-in-hand, they condition each other and explain each other.*[17]

PRIESTLY WITNESS

The priestly mission is born from the configuration of the minister with Christ in virtue of the priestly character which configures both his being and his action. However, that is not enough. To his sacramental identification with Christ the priest must add his vital, experiential and spiritual identification with his Master. The priest will never truly fulfill his mission if he is not a living image of the Good Shepherd. For this reason Vatican II *strongly exhorts all priests to strive... towards that greater holiness that will make them daily more effective instruments for the service of all God's people.*[18] The authenticity of his priestly life and the effectiveness of his ministry depend on his profound union with the Vine, without which "he can do nothing" (cf. Jn 15:5). This existential transformation that makes the priest "another Christ" not only through the sacrament but also in the way he lives is the *sine qua non* for his presence in the world to be, like Christ's, salvific.

The personality of the priest has to be a clear and transparent sign for the world. This is the first condition of the pastoral service of priests. The people from among whom they were chosen and for whom they were appointed priests want more than anything else to see them as that sign. And we cannot deny them that. Despite appearances people seek priests who are aware of the full meaning of their priesthood. People want a priest who believes profoundly, who manifests his faith with courage, who prays

---

[17] John Paul II, *Letter "Novo Incipiente,"* n. 3.
[18] PO 12.

with fervor, who teaches with intimate conviction, who serves, who gives example of the beatitudes in his life, who can love selflessly, who is close to all.

Such a priest, a true priest, is a living witness of eternal values. His person is an undecipherable mystery for many. He is an irrepressible call to things divine, a luminous testimony of the presence and action of God in the world. At a time in which so many men and women desperately seek their existential security in scientific and technical progress, power, money and comfort, the priest witnesses with his life that only Christ is the solution to all the enigmas of humanity, only Christ is capable of satisfying the deepest desires of the human heart, only Christ is worthy of faith.

A truly lofty identity and mission far beyond what anyone could imagine, and yet we are talking about someone as human as everyone else.

Chosen from Among Men

...We have been at the feet of a man, but one who took Christ's place. The words of Manzoni invite us to reflect upon the human reality of one who has been called to priestly dignity and ministry. Perhaps the emphasis is clearer if we turn the phrase around: "We have been at the feet of someone who took Christ's place, but who is a man."

The author of the letter to the Hebrews points out that the high priest has been chosen "from among men." He is a man like the rest. He participates in the greatness of the human race, but "he himself is beset with weakness" (Heb 5:2).

Our desire here is not to develop an anthropology but rather to sketch some features which will help us understand the priest in his human dimension. This should help us appreciate the tremendous need to form and orient the human component of young men destined to be priests. Revelation has the last word on this question, but it is extremely helpful to make use of whatever light philosophy and psychology can offer us.

A Particular Concept of Man

Even a summary philosophical reflection on man is enough to reveal that we are faced with a complex being, made of elements which are not just different but apparently contradictory. He is composed of *spirit* and *matter* and this makes him a genuine enigma.

Man's spiritual nature radically differentiates him and sets him high above all other beings that share his world. His *rationality* gives him the capacity for openness to all reality, including his own, through the act of knowing. This capacity is potentially open to the infinite. He likewise possesses the capacity of *willing with liberty,* and therefore he is master of his own acts. He is responsible. His openness to reality allows him to be open to others. He is a *social being* and he expresses himself *in dialogue.* He finds the fulfillment of his 'I' in his relation to the other, *'you,'* and ultimately, in his relationship with the Infinite You.

But his *corporal dimension* is an integral part of his humanity, and permeates his entire existence. His internal and external senses supply data to his intelligence. His affections prepare the way for the action of his will. His openness to the outside world and his dialogue with others are necessarily mediated by his corporeity.

This blend of contradictory elements makes man a citizen of two worlds; he straddles the border. Radically open to the absolute, he feels limited by the relativity of his actual accomplishments and perceives the weight of his corporeity. He can audaciously look beyond the borders of space and time but is inalterably bound by the chains of history. He ardently desires immortality but finds himself subject to the biological life span of all animals in its rising and falling rhythm from birth to biological maturity and from there to death.

Chosen from among men, the aspirant to the priesthood is also a citizen of two worlds. He has the ability to listen to a divine call, to respond freely and nobly, and to welcome the grace that elevates and even makes him divine. Yet this ability is always affected and conditioned by the limits of his finite existence.

From another perspective, psychology illustrates how opposing forces within a person, much more complex than we usually think, affect his actions and reactions.

Before all else we must recognize that the three levels of the human psychology *(physiological, psycho-social and spiritual)* continually over-lap one another in the unity of the "I," each one with its own influence. On the other hand, human behavior is not based exclusively on visible and definable attitudes. In reality, these *attitudes* are triggered and sustained by the force of *drives* (aggressiveness, autonomy, sexuality...) and by *values* (positive properties that the subject discovers in reality and makes his own). Frequently these two tendencies mix with one another in the formation of attitudes in such a way that it is difficult to know if the behavior of a person, of a seminarian, depends on the one or the other.

The difficulty increases when we consider the influence of the *subconscious,* above all the affective subconscious. The so-called *affective memory* can provoke emotional reactions which are determined not by the effect of a present reality but by an impression received in the past and stored in the subconscious.

Every human subject because of his spiritual nature tends, from the depths of his human nature, to *self-transcendence,* to know and acknowledge what he is and is worth in himself. This tendency, which has the infinite as its ultimate horizon, induces a person to form permanently his ideal of self. Yet his present reality (his tendencies, values, interests, subconscious emotions, etc.) may very easily not coincide with his ideal. Thus *inconsistencies,* conscious or subconscious, can open a gap between what one knows he must be and do, and what he actually is and lives. This possible and frequent dialectic tension, above all when it is not conscious, has a notable influence on human behavior.

Chosen from among men, the aspirant to the priesthood also operates psychologically on these different levels. The diverse forces of his human psyche intervene in his response to the Lord's call and the living of his priestly formation. It is necessary to know them and to take them into account.

Philosophy and psychology have helped us explore the complex enigma of man. Yet ultimately any attempt to understand him using the power of reason and science alone produces incomplete results. In man we perceive a mystery which reason cannot fully unravel. A higher sort of understanding is necessary. Only in the light of Revelation do we discover man's full identity.

Echoing the message of Scripture we can describe the human being as *an image of God that has been disfigured by sin and restored by Jesus Christ.*

Image of God

"Let us make man in our own image, after our likeness... God created man in his own image, in the image of God he created him" (Gn 1:26-27). As a created being, man is the product of an act of the One and Triune God. Freely and out of love he has been given the gift of existence. Every individual is a singular thought and loving act of God; he exists precisely because God in wisdom and love has called him by name.

Yet creation is not locked into one instant of time. It lasts as long as the existence of man. Man's being is permanently in the hand of God without whom he would cease to exist. Thus each moment of his life corresponds to a new creative act.

Without God, Man is an absurdity, ontologically impossible. Hence every human being's undeniable yearning for the Absolute. Even in the most hidden fibers of his being he gives away that he thirsts for the infinite — that he thirsts for God.

Man's creaturehood is not limited to admitting the obvious, that he is not God. It also includes his likeness to his Creator which gives him a dignity above all the rest of creation. He expresses this likeness especially in his liberty and conscience, which allow him to consent responsibly to God's word to him. This is the greatness of man which the Fathers of the Church never tired of proclaiming:

> The sky was not created in the image of God, nor was the moon, nor the sun, nor the beauty of the stars, nor any of the other things which can be observed in nature. Only you. He who is so great that He has all of creation in the palm of his hand is entirely contained in you. He lives in your nature.[19]

But this sublime image of the Creator was created from the dust of the earth (cf. Gn 2:7), insubstantial of itself. And while he most certainly bears within himself the divine breath, it is nevertheless a divine breath that gives life to a piece of clay. He sees that with his liberty he can choose between good and evil, making himself similar to the gods. Yet this is a deceptive temptation, for he has not planted the tree of good and evil (cf.

---

[19] St. Gregory of Nyssa, *Commentary on the Cant. of Cant.*, 2.

Gn 3:1-7). Without God he is worth nothing; he feels naked. He is nothing but transience, death and nothing. His true greatness then rides on his ability and effort to be as close as possible to the One after whose image he is modeled.

Fallen image of God

Scripture speaks to us about another fact of definitive importance for understanding man: he has sinned (cf. Gn 3:1-13). The divine image etched in his being became disfigured from its very beginning. Original sin wounded human nature, leaving in man's soul, according to St. Thomas Aquinas, four scars: ignorance (wounded intelligence), malice (wounded will), fragility (wounded irascible appetite) and concupiscence (wounded concupiscible appetite).[20]

With a glance inside his own heart, man verifies his inclination to evil and he feels weighed down by multiple evils. By often refusing to recognize God as his origin, he breaks his proper subordination to his ultimate end and his natural harmony with the rest of creation (cf. Gn 13). On account of this disorder every human person, including the aspirant to the priesthood, experiences the internal struggle between good and evil in himself. He experiences weakness in overcoming the attacks of evil, the rebellion of the flesh and the slavery of sin which lowers his dignity. Thus burdened, man is a sad reality and shows us the human person burdened with incoherence and contradiction. He cries like a child but feels that his lack of innocence is culpable. Perhaps he raises his eyes to God every day and ends up hiding himself, seeking consolation in created things. Man is a king incapable of not being a tyrant. In his weakness he suffers from the inability to do the good he yearns for. He is the man who one day loves Christ and the next day sells him for thirty pieces of silver.

God's Image Restored by Christ

But to see no more than the fall would consign us to hopeless pessimism. The divine image etched in man and wounded by sin has been restored by Jesus Christ, "the image of the invisible God" (Col 1:15; cf. 2

---

[20] *Summa Theologiae*, I-II, q.85, a.3 c.

Cor 4:4) with the urgency with which an artist repairs a broken sculpture or restores a painting.

The Incarnation of Christ, true God and true man, restores man's true value. He is the foundation of the new creation of humanity because He has become like us in all things, except sin (cf. Heb 4:15). He is the model of the "perfect man."[21] With the perfection and sanctity of his spirit, He reaches the highest peaks of human excellence and nobility. With his corporeity, clothed in humility from the manger to the cross, He has descended to the extremes of human sorrow. With his definitive triumph in his resurrection and his ascension to the right hand of the Father, He has conferred dignity and meaning to the entire human pilgrimage and guaranteed a happy and lasting destiny. In this way He offers us the true figure, dignity and value of man.

Through baptism man is incorporated into the restored humanity in Christ, a new humanity: "Therefore, if anyone is in Christ, he is a new creation; the old has passed away, behold, the new has come" (2 Cor 5:17). Those who grasp this truth are astonished and engrossed by it:

> Let us rejoice and give thanks: we have become not only Christians, but rather Christ. Let us be amazed and rejoice: we have become Christ![22]

But the restoration wrought by Christ and acquired at baptism does not eliminate all the harmful effects of sin. Human nature has remained wounded forever. The new humanity brought about by Christ is a goal and a task for us: "Take off the old man with his works, and clothe yourselves with the new man, who will progress to perfect knowledge, according to the image of its Creator" (Col 3:9-10; cf. Ep 4:24).

The determining factor in this process is the adoption of a new heart that knows, loves and serves God with a filial spirit, following the example of Christ. This new heart also loves, in God, all people and things.

In his new knowledge, love, and service, the new man is driven by an interior dynamism to develop the traits of his religious and moral conduct, in conformity with Christ his model, and to incessantly purify his

---

[21] Cf. GS 38.
[22] St. Augustine, *In Joan. Tract.* 21, 8.

heart of the disordered tendencies of sensuality and pride which continue to afflict him from within.

Thus Revelation offers us a highly realistic view of the human person: the image of God, wounded by sin, restored by Christ the Redeemer, but the restoration becomes a task for us to do. Consequently the Word of the Creator provides the key for understanding his creature. In it we can see the deepest roots of what philosophy and psychology have tried to describe about man.

Until Christ is Formed in You

We have gone over several of the fundamental features of the figure of the priest to set the stage for our program of formation. We can now draw a few preliminary conclusions from these reflections.

The young man who enters the seminary on his way to priesthood is above all *called* by God with an eternal love. We have not called him. Thus, we are not, as formators, the absolute masters of his vocational path. He has been entrusted to us as a lofty and serious responsibility, for which we will be held accountable to the Lord of the harvest.

He has called the seminarians in order to anoint them as *priests in Christ the priest.* Their formation should encompass all the necessary adaptations to our ever-changing times, but it must first of all be geared towards molding the essential priestly identity which stands above all circumstances of time and place. Thus we may not form the priest we please or fashion dictates, but rather the one the Word of God presents to us and the living tradition of the Church has been forging. They are to be priests who, besides acting *in persona Christi* because of the sacramental character, have identified themselves profoundly with their Master and Friend, in whose priesthood they participate and whom they effectively represent before the community.

But He has called men as human as any others. We need a thorough understanding of the human material with which we have to work. We must recognize the greatness, the marvelous possibilities present in every human being: the living image of God, sanctified by Christ; the spiritual being who can grasp the truth of things and open himself to the infinite, endowed with the drive towards self-transcendence and the fulfillment of an ideal which always beckons him to go farther. But we must be also aware of his limitations and weakness. Let us not forget that his nature has been wounded forever by sin, thus producing grave disorder within; that he is not pure spirit but also possesses the energies and limitations of corporeity; that contrasting and sometimes unconscious drives overlap in his psychology which can give rise to inconsistencies between his ideal and his reality, and greatly influence his behavior. Finally, we must see it all through the prism of that hope which comes from Christ, the Redeemer of mankind. He has inaugurated the new man who, as we said above, is given to us as a seed, as a task and goal to achieve.

The formation of priests is a clearly defined task once we understand that we are forming men who have been called by God to the sublime mission of prolonging in history the same priesthood of Christ. As formators, urged on by this awareness, we will welcome with sincere love these young men the Church places in our hands in order to help them walk the path towards the "maturity of the fullness of Christ" (Ep 4:13). With our programs, our guidance and helpful attitude, our understanding and our firmness... we will motivate these young men to form themselves properly, to respond fully to their vocation. With our words and with our deeds we will show them that we are here to help always "until Christ is formed in you" (cf. Gal 4:19).

Chapter Two

FUNDAMENTAL PRINCIPLES OF PRIESTLY FORMATION

The formation of any man and therefore the formation of one preparing for the priesthood is an art. It is the art of helping a person grow from within to his proposed ideal. Never a question of theories or empirical science, to form is to accompany the person in formation on the path of everyday life. It is a task that we perform by paying attention to the present situation, the specific need of each moment and the varied details of daily life which can help the seminarian who is forging in himself the personality of Christ the priest. What we hope above all to offer in this book are some practical reflections and proposals, based on experience.

Proficiency in a field of study naturally calls for an order or a system. So we speak of "educational systems." Before getting involved directly in the intricacies of actual formation we should have a guide to go by, otherwise we can miss our way or go in circles. In some way the introductory chapter has reminded us where we are heading (the identity and mission of the priest) and where we start from (the human material we have to form for the priesthood). We will now examine how and by which path we will travel. To put it another way, we must have some of the *fundamental principles* of priestly formation, columns on which to build the edifice of priestly formation. Naturally, some principles are common to formation in general, but they are applied here specifically to priestly formation.

Many of the practical pedagogical reflections of this book may ultimately have to be disregarded or adapted depending on particular circumstances. Yet we do not think it presumptuous to say that the following basic principles should never be overlooked if we really want to form priests of the Catholic Church.

The Protagonists

We have just compared the work of forming priests with building a building. The last chapter has given us the plan and the materials, now we have to ask ourselves who can and should do the building. Many can help but there are three principle and indispensable protagonists: *the Holy Spirit, the candidate and the formator.* Each one has his specific role. *Priestly formation takes all three working together, in a full, harmonious way.*

THE HOLY SPIRIT

Preparation for the priesthood, the identification of a man with Christ the Priest, is a task that goes beyond human ability and talent. Were it not for God and the action of his sanctifying Spirit, our work would remain incomplete.

To his first priests Jesus promised the Holy Spirit who would teach them everything and remind them of all that He had said (cf. Jn 14:26); and when He conferred on them the priestly power to forgive sins He imparted to them the Holy Spirit (Jn 20:22-23). Before his ascension into heaven He assured them that they would receive the power of the Paraclete so that they could be his witnesses to the ends of the earth (cf. Acts 1:8). Indeed a short time later, the powerful eruption of the Spirit on the feast of Pentecost definitively marked them and spurred them on in an astonishing way to fulfill their mission as prophets of the Kingdom of God (cf. Ac 2:1,ff). St. Paul also realized the absolute necessity of the work of the Holy Spirit in the life of Christians. He knew that "God's love has been poured into our hearts through the Holy Spirit who has been given to us" (Rm 5:5). Further still, he affirmed roundly that "no one can say 'Jesus is Lord!' except by the Holy Spirit" (1 Cor 12:3).

The Church's liturgical hymns to the Holy Spirit, such as "Veni Sancte Spiritus" or "Veni Creator Spiritus" very eloquently relate what He is for souls. He is called the light of the heart, the consoler, the sweet guest, welcome repose from our daily labor, joy in the midst of weeping, the gift of God, a living fountain of love, etc.

He is the guide and the author of the soul's sanctification. It is the Spirit who brings as his entourage the virtues and supernatural gifts through the action of his grace. He transforms the person to the extent that his or her soul lends itself to Him.

The young seminarian is first and foremost a Christian. The most essential element in his preparation for the priesthood is his personal sanctification through his efforts to identify himself with Christ the Priest. It will have to be then the Sanctifying Spirit who enlightens the candidate's conscience to see the path along which he will acquire his priestly identity.

We know that formation is a slow, laborious process with its times of light and of darkness, its moments of joy and affliction. No one can better support and encourage from within the efforts of both seminarian and formator than the Holy Spirit.

The Holy Spirit is, then, the first protagonist in the work of priestly formation. This may seem obvious but it is not superfluous to recall and emphasize it; the candidate, the formator and the educational programs should bear this in mind. No need to remind the Holy Spirit. He committed himself to both the candidate and the formator from the moment He called the one to the priesthood and, by means of the Church, asked the other for his cooperation.

We should also keep in mind that although God could sanctify us against our will, the mysterious action of the Divine Spirit lovingly respects the liberty with which He created us. He asks for our cooperation, not only in passive availability to allow Him to do his sanctifying work, but in conscious and constant effort, a dynamic response given in the exercise of the virtues which prepare and accompany the reception of his gifts.

Formation will not take place then, without the responsible cooperation of the other two protagonists, the candidate and the formator.

CANDIDATE

Right from the start the candidate has to be acutely aware that he is also a *protagonist in his own formation.* Further still, he is the first person involved and the one most responsible for his formation. He is the one called to the priesthood by God and the one who responded freely to that call. He is the one who will be anointed a priest, and who will bear fruit in proportion to his formation and his union with God.

To try to form a person in any field without his willing and active participation is an illusion. At best, we will get the individual to take some courses and obey regulations but there will be no true formation from within.

A seminarian must realize from the start that nobody will "form him" nor "make" him from without. There is no room for passivity, indifference or simply going with the flow in an established system of formation. The young man who aspires to the priesthood enters the seminary not "to be formed" but "to form himself." The principle of self-formation which we will comment upon later is the practical consequence of this decision.

Naturally, since the first protagonist of priestly formation is the Holy Spirit, the candidate must understand his personal work as working together with Him. He must allow the Holy Spirit to work without impeding or distorting his action. He should be like a piece of soft wax for the Holy Spirit to stamp the figure of Jesus Christ the Priest on him. This means that prayer, interior silence, attention to his inspirations, and the candidate's sincere, docile response to them are principal and integral elements of his effort to form himself as a priest.

It also means that, since God has wished to make use of human collaborators, the candidate's attentiveness to the Holy Spirit logically has to be translated into attentiveness to the formators who will help him to know the goals, tasks, the when and where.

FORMATORS

St. Paul addressed the Galatians as: "My sons and daughters, with whom I am again in travail until Christ is formed in you" (Gal 4:19). He felt personally responsible for the growth of the Christians in the churches he founded. Ever since the Incarnation of the Word, we have proof that God wants to act, not from the heights of an ivory tower, but by being in the midst of men: He is "Immanuel." Moreover, his insistence in sending prophets to his people and having his Son elect co-workers clearly manifest that his salvific and sanctifying plan includes the participation of men. God would hardly change his tactics in the formation and sanctification of those He has called to the priesthood.

Formation in any field depends on the cooperation of someone who can show the way; an experienced counsellor, a guide, a help and even a model. The formator should be all these.

As the third protagonist in the formation triangle, he should consider himself fully responsible for this formation and grasp the importance of his mission for the Church and for society. His work is destined to leave a profound impression on the lives of his candidates. This awareness should fill him with responsible enthusiasm and make him put into play all his spiritual and human qualities, all his time and his effort, with a healthy spirit of self-sacrifice and generosity, availing of all the means within his reach.

But he would be mistaken were he to think himself *the only* or principal one responsible. He must remember that he is a *cooperator,* a helper, and should act accordingly.

First of all he is a co-worker of the Holy Spirit, the great Master and Teacher. The formator is the instrument and the channel through which the grace of God passes. Naturally, the better the instrument, the broader and cleaner the channel, the better will God's grace flow. This divine action must reach the candidate through him, through his advice, his firmness and motivations.

Therefore, his first concern is to be close to God and open to his Spirit. He is a man of intimate and deep prayer who is not afraid to ask God for light, and he is docile to his inspirations even if they go against his natural likes and desires. He demands of the candidates what he believes before God he should, even though his feelings are otherwise inclined. He knows how to follow God's tempo in the formation of each individual. He constantly intercedes before God for those who have been entrusted to him and he sacrifices himself for them.

Objectively, the formator has to admit his own limitations and the enormous disproportion that exists between his possibilities and human resources, and the transcendent mission which he has received. In this way he recognizes that all progress in the formation of the seminarians comes from God and is the product of his sanctifying action. He cannot attribute to himself the fruits that God matured, nor consider his own intelligence or popularity, nor even his own closeness to God, as the reason for the growth of Christ in the candidates. Success in his work is not an occasion for personal vanity. Instead it should inspire him to admiration and genuine gratitude to God, and to acknowledge the candidate's effort and generosity.

He realizes he is a cooperator of the candidate. The term "formator" must not deceive us. Clay pots are formed from the outside, a person is formed from within. The formator doesn't "form" but "helps the candidate to form himself." This means that he must not demand without motivating, nor guide without enlightening, nor blindly design a mold and impose it unthinkingly on everyone. Yet it also means that he cannot simply wash his hands of the matter and allow "whatever happens" to happen. He has an active, indispensable role. Only that his role is above all to make sure that the candidate fully assumes his own part: the desire to form himself and work personally and responsibly towards his goal. The success of the formator's work lies in arousing the candidate's conscious and free initiative in such a way that he takes the reins of his formation into his own hands, open to the Holy Spirit and the orientations of his formator.

OTHER PARTICIPANTS

The Holy Spirit, the candidate and the formator make an effective formation team when they work together in harmony, each one playing his own part respecting and seconding the role of the others.

Nevertheless they are not the *only protagonists in the formation of priests*. The entire people of God must feel itself responsible for the preparation of its priests.

Naturally at the head of the community is the *bishop*. He is the shepherd of his future priests. He establishes or approves the formation programs of his seminary. He carefully chooses the formators of his students. He directs their educational work and if necessary he corrects it. He personally participates in the formation of the students by his encouraging and motivating presence and through his conferences and sermons, his dialogue with the seminarians (and even giving classes if it were necessary and possible). He is the one who has the last word in the delicate task of approving the candidates for Holy Orders. Finally, by laying his hands on them, he remains forever linked to them by a profound and sacred bond of paternity. It is important that the formators and above all the seminarians see in him a close, interested and available father. And it is important that he, aware of his responsibility born of a divine mission, place himself always in God's hands, "Come Holy Spirit."

The priests of the diocese, regardless of their particular apostolate, cannot be indifferent toward the progress of the seminary and the formation of their future brothers in the priesthood. From the moment the candidates enter the seminary the priests should treat these young men as brothers and lend a hand whenever they can as circumstances allow. Each priest has to find a way that is compatible with his own responsibilities, yet the opportunities are endless: from giving class to inviting the young men to cooperate in his work, and, of course, the encouragement of his genuine and clear priestly testimony and personal prayer.

Finally, all faithful Christians should see the seminary as their own. They cannot be indifferent to it. Our effort should be to get them involved. It is not enough that they give a donation every year. They should know the seminary, its programs, its achievements and needs. They should also know the seminarians and how many and which ones will be ordained each year. They should pray for them. In a word, they should see the seminarians as a part of their own Christian life. It is up to the bishop, the directors of the seminary, the priests of the diocese and the seminarians themselves, to achieve this involvement of the faithful.

Formation as Self-Formation

As we said earlier, the candidate is the one principally responsible for his own formation. Doubtless he needs the help and guidance of the formators and the support of an atmosphere conducive to this, but we must affirm that *the formation process is above all a process of self-formation,*[1] and further, that there is no real formation without self-formation. That is to say, if we do not succeed in having the candidate work personally for his own formation, moved by deep convictions and with a clear attitude of sincerity, then there is no formation.

---

[1] Obviously the degree in which we apply the concept of self-formation depends partly on the level of the candidate's maturity. An adolescent, for example, in a high school seminary needs more external elements of formation than does a well-tried young man close to ordination. Even so, the efficacy of the formative system in a high school seminary resides in its ability to help the adolescent gradually assume the responsibility for his own preparation out of personal convictions.

Perhaps few of us would disagree with this in principle. Yet though it is usually taken for granted, perhaps we do not reflect enough on its importance or draw the proper practical consequences. Nonetheless, its impact on the overall outcome of the formation process is such that we can consider it a fundamental principle.

If we neglect it we could be courting outright disaster. There might seem to be no special problems in the seminary: the seminarians regularly follow the schedule, they take notes in class... This is wonderful and may certainly be a sign that things are going well, but it is not enough. We must ask ourselves if beneath the veneer of outward appearances, these seminarians who fulfill their duties, attend Mass and study are really forming themselves. Do they believe in what they are doing or is it because "Big Brother is watching"? Are they really giving it all they can or are they simply getting by? Only when we are sure that our seminarians live everything the seminary requires of them because they want to form themselves and sincerely strive to do their best in spite of their shortcomings, can we be sure that our formation work is fulfilling its objectives.

To neglect the principle of self-formation is to undermine seriously the future perseverance of the candidates for the priesthood. Without it the seminary becomes a wasteland, or, if there is a healthy environment, it becomes an incubator where formation is no more than a fictitious atmosphere in which the seminarian lives according to the discipline; he studies, works, prays, and even does apostolate, going with the general flow of things following a routine. Once outside the incubator, since he lacks true lived convictions, he runs the serious risk of wilting at the first summer sun or the first winter chill.

CONVICTION

Self-formation implies *conviction.* The seminarian has to want to form himself. He must *want* to be a man of God, holy and virtuous. This means that deep inside he has to want to pray, live the life of grace and overcome his selfishness. We have to develop in him as well a firm desire to be a well-educated priest. This will motivate him to study, master all the subjects and broaden his culture. He must long to be a true apostle, and thus make good use of all that favors his pastoral formation. He must also be convinced that he has to shape his human personality with his priestly mission in mind.

The roots of conviction are to be found in a firm *fundamental option*. The candidate's option is first of all for Christ, but it is also a fundamental decision to follow the call to the priesthood.

Some seminarians spend many years without clearly defining their option for Christ and for their vocation. They drag it around like a bothersome burden which keeps them from fulfilling their secret aspirations. You cannot do any constructive work with a person in such an interior situation.

Logically, there is an initial period of questioning and searching before God to discern one's vocation with certainty. And vocational stability is one of the principle fruits of the candidate's years of formation. Yet the more decided he is at the beginning, the greater his desire to form himself will be. On the contrary, to live all his formation years in indecision is a grave risk for persevering in his vocation and blocks effective progress in his formation.

Therefore one of our priorities is to clarify this point for the seminarians, and help them love their priestly vocation deeply and value it as a marvelous gift of the love of Jesus Christ. That is, we should help them become enthusiastic with their calling and the idea of a life given to God and to people everywhere as priests of the Catholic Church. It is important to use retreats, conferences, homilies, and personal counseling. We must never tire of revealing to them the beauty of their vocation and encouraging them to respond conscientiously and responsibly to their divine call.

By deepening the loving acceptance of his priestly vocation the seminarian acquires the necessary *vocational stability.* Nevertheless, stability has to be constantly defended and fortified. We all know cases of young men who, having made a vocational decision and having grown sincerely enthusiastic about it, reconsider it again and again. A brooding or unstable temperament, or perhaps a lack of generosity in the face of difficulties, etc., makes some seminarians rethink the vocation every time a problem arises in any area at all, whether it be obedience, human relationships, chastity, studies...

We should help the candidate understand "that the gifts and the call of God are irrevocable" (Rm 11:29), and that therefore for him the question of his vocation must become non-negotiable. When any type of problem arises we must help him tell the difference between a difficulty and the absence of a vocation. He must also understand that problems in chastity, study, prayer life, faith, etc., do not automatically mean that God is not calling him to the priesthood. Most of the time they are normal obstacles to be overcome with generous and patient effort, and which can even help him to grow stronger in his love for Christ and for his vocation.

KNOWLEDGE OF SELF

The candidate for the priesthood who truly wants to form himself will see the need to know himself well.

You cannot start in a flurry of blind action. You need to know the goal and the foundation you will be building on. The identity of the Catholic priesthood is our goal, but our starting point and the foundation we have to build the priestly personality on are proper to each individual and require his conscientious introspection if we are to get to know it. This involves the first two points of the well-known aphorism, *"Know yourself, accept yourself, better yourself."*

"Know yourself" means thorough knowledge of one's temperament, qualities and defects, spiritual sensitivity, intellectual capacity, virtues and vices... A profound knowledge of self is not the fruit of a day's labor, but the prized acquisition that follows years of formation and even a lifetime. Yet it is necessary to teach the candidate, from the moment he enters the seminary, to begin this work of self-analysis. Continual reflection on his own actions, reactions and general behavior; his daily examination of conscience; his preparation for the sacrament of penance; his personal dialogue (either formal or spontaneous) with his formator, etc., should all help him gradually gain clear insight into his inner self.

Acceptance of self should go hand in hand with this knowledge. As the candidate comes to recognize objectively his positive and negative facets, he must always remember that God knows him and loves him as he is. His call to the priesthood was not a miscalculation on God's part. He knows the material He has chosen to reproduce the figure of Christ the priest. This is the basis for an attitude of realism and optimism, of profound humility and holy pride.

SELF-FORMATION

Acceptance of self is neither defeatist resignation nor egoistic self-complacency. The seminarian who really wants to form himself finds a strong and constant incentive in the knowledge of his limits and possibilities. He is ready for the third recommendation: *better yourself.*

This desire is expressed in a clear sense of *responsibility,* which permeates the candidate's entire life and activity. He does not wait until "they" tell him to study. He does not avoid what may hurt his vocation because "they" prohibit him, but rather because he feels responsible for it. He does not fulfill his duty because "they" are watching him but because he wishes to respond to the One who always watches him with an eternal love. *Sincerity* is closely related to responsibility and makes a person noble, loyal and consistent. The young man who wants to form himself acts the same alone as with companions, in the street as in the seminary, before his own conscience as before his formators.

His conviction also helps him to acquire a positive attitude of *enthusiasm and self-conquest.* He wants to conquer himself for Christ. He wants to overcome his defects. He wants to prepare himself as well as possible. With the knowledge he has of himself and what he needs, and his spirit of self-conquest he can realistically set goals for himself and work effectively to attain them.

SELF-FORMATION IS NOT SELF-GUIDANCE

But the term "self-formation" could seem to some to convey a mistaken idea of formation, as if all depended on the candidate and on him alone. If we say that he is the first one responsible and that nothing can be done without his personal and sincere effort, we do not mean he does not need support and direction in his work of self-formation. This has been touched on when we spoke of the Holy Spirit and the formator.

If a seminarian were to understand his formation as a path of absolute independence, isolation or being closed off, he would show he hasn't understood the meaning of self-formation. The sense of responsibility we speak about should bring him rather to place himself in the hands of those whom God, through the Church, has appointed to assist and guide him in his preparation to receive the priesthood.

Love, the Fundamental Motivation of Priestly Formation

Our reflection on the principle of self-formation has shown us that the success of formation ultimately depends on the desire the candidate has to form himself and the force with which he makes his own the ideal his vocation presents to him.

Man is always moved by *motives.* As we saw in chapter one, the impulse to act comes from needs seeking to be satisfied and from values we seek to possess, in other words from a motivational dynamism. In this, everyone is the same. Every act of our will has a content and tends to a goal (either in itself or as means to another). The dynamism of grace also enters this human psychological structure, enriching it and giving it greater potential.

Without deep, serious motivation, no one would endure the effort and sacrifices of formation. Many things can motivate. For some it will be money, for others fame, for others pleasure. But what can sufficiently motivate a candidate to the priesthood to give himself completely and decidedly to his own formation?

The path of the priesthood is arduous. Like other careers it requires dedication, constancy and discipline. But it also entails renouncing many good and proper things which life can offer: the close company of a wife, the formation of a family, the practice of a profession that might attract us, etc. Priestly life — and therefore formation for it — thrives in a different environment, and consequently has different motivations and values that have nothing to do with the world and its attractions.

Egoistic self-realization could possibly be a motivation, even in the renunciation of other goods. But the call to the priesthood is, in essence, a call to a mission of service which will demand forgetfulness of self and one's own interests. More importantly, progress in formation, principally in the spiritual life, is intrinsically linked to an ascetic effort that counters selfish tendencies to self-satisfaction.

Ordinarily, the initial discovery of the vocation carries with it a rather strong emotional motivating charge. The young man who attends a vocational get-together or visits a seminary for a time does so moved by an interior attraction, by an impulse which will eventually make him capable of breaking with his past life and embracing a new lifestyle. This initial emotional force may or may not endure with the passing of time. It is helpful for every priest to recall often the moment in which he first perceived the voice of God, and rediscover the force of that attraction. But this force by itself cannot be the central and permanent motivation of an entire life. Sentiments come and go, even those which accompany profound natural and spiritual convictions.

Interest in an integral formation in order to help the Church in its needs, the aspiration to serve others in sincere self-giving, and the healthy search for personal sanctity are all legitimate motives and can be particularly helpful to some candidates. But they will never be sufficient, in themselves, to focus an entire life and give it lasting meaning.

The only definitive force is love. It gives us our "weight." Augustine said, "Amor meus, pondus meum, eo feror quocumquefero." "My weight is my love and it carries me wherever I go."[2] Love makes a person capable of difficult sacrifices, of otherwise unexplainable privations, of great accomplishments and of the total and selfless gift of self. The human person has a deep need to love and to be loved. *Man cannot live without love. He remains a being incomprehensible to himself and his life lacks meaning if love is not shown to him, if he does not find love, if he does not experience it and make it his own, if he does not actively participate in it.*[3] In love we find the meaning of our existence. It directs all our desires, activity and behavior.

The young man called to the priesthood is still human. His vocation has not changed the laws of human nature. He also needs love. Moreover, he has been called to love: to love more, to love more people, to love better. If he does not feel the enthusiasm that comes from love in his heart, we can never hope to have him respond valiantly to the arduous task of formation.

But in the life of a priest not just any love will do. The only love that is capable of truly polarizing his life in his priestly vocation, is *love of Jesus Christ, his Lord.* The essence of his vocation is his loving and vital identification with Christ the priest. Jesus Christ has called him out of love and to ask for his love. To all his priests He repeats the intimate invitation which he made to the first priests at the Last Supper: "Remain in my love" (Jn 15:9). He wants a total and exclusive love: He has chosen them to be with Him (cf. Mk 3:14), and He clarifies right from the beginning that

---

[2] St. Augustine, *Confessions,* XIII [IX], 10.
[3] John Paul II, Encyclical letter *Redemptor Hominis,* n. 10.

whoever is not capable of loving Him more than father, mother and even his own life, cannot be his disciple (cf. Lk 14:26).

This call to love Christ also implies the call to love all people, and to love them not just in any way whatsoever but as the Lord has loved them (cf. Jn 13:34).

And so if the young seminarian has been called to love Christ and identify himself with Him in order to partake of his priesthood for the benefit of people, is there any other motivation that could genuinely and vigorously move him to transform himself into Christ and form himself to be a priest of his Lord? Naturally there can be many other motivations that back up the strength of this love for Christ, in the various circumstances the seminarian goes through. Wisely and tactfully a good formator takes advantage of these, but they can never be the foundation of formation. Only love for Christ and for humanity can give meaning to the renunciation, the effort, the asceticism and the discipline which priestly formation entails. It alone can make the candidate to the priesthood responsibly and actively take charge of his own formation.

Without this love, formation becomes an uphill battle, celibacy grows intolerable and obedience loses all sense. Without this love, a seminarian might put up with the program and passively tolerate the advice of his formators but he will not seek to make them his own. This tendency to dispersion will bring him to avoid any effort, to merely go through the motions of prayer, to evade study, or perhaps to study as an evasion. We said it before: formation for the priesthood is not easy. Without this love, desertion will always be a lurking possibility. The temptations to opt for an easier life, to conform himself more to the world and to his passions are constantly there.

We have to remember that to take the decisive step to the priesthood is to make an irreversible choice. A priest is forever. Any man who takes this step must *be resolved... to discharge without fail the office of priesthood tending the Lord's flock.*[4] For this he has to have found for certain in his love for Christ the meaning of his life, and he has to be as sure as humanly possible that he can persevere and continue on without failing. He has to have discovered already the lasting motivation that will satisfy all his desires for life. To go into the priesthood without having achieved

---

[4] Rite of Ordination, 1978.

this love leaves him open to spending his later years in dissatisfaction and doubt, searching for compensations outside of the priestly state and substitutes to fill the emptiness of a life consecrated to love but lived without love. Ruinous failures in priests' lives occur when they are not built on a sincere, loyal and lasting love for Christ.

It is obvious that the love for Christ and for humanity is a *goal* of priestly formation. We cannot hope that a young man who enters the seminary has already fully developed it. On the contrary, that is why he has come to the seminary! Thus it is the objective of formation, but it is also its starting point and fundamental motivation. This means that the system of formation and the formators should consider love for Christ to be the motor and power with which it itself and all the primary and secondary goals of formation will be achieved.

Along this line we could say that not only spirituality but the whole of priestly formation must be *Christ-centered.* The program of activities, the directives of the formators, and even the atmosphere of the seminary will be a complete success if they have Christ as their center, model and standard. In the formation of priests, anything that is not related to Christ is senseless and useless, and we should have no qualms about excluding it from our programs.

Formation as Transformation

Let us grant that our seminarian has made his fundamental option, and that he sincerely wishes to form himself principally out of love for Christ — even though it is a love that still has to mature. It is not enough. We must ask ourselves if our system of formation is really helping the candidate develop his personality as a future priest, to the extent that what he learns, experiences and practices, becomes an intimate part of his life. Otherwise his time in the seminary is just water off a duck's back.

God's intention on calling a man to the priesthood is not just for him to acquire some knowledge, do a "course of studies" and then "exercise" the priestly ministry. He wants each priest *to be* a priest; that is, to identify with the person of Christ the Priest, until he reaches the point where he is sincerely able to echo St. Paul, "It is no longer I who live, but Christ who lives in me" (Gal 2:20). He does not want him to be a mere functionary of religious services but rather an apostle who radiates what he carries within and personally lives.

Only the real priestly configuration of his own being can give the priest the profound satisfaction of living what he professes. Otherwise he will feel the priesthood as a false shell which does not configure him internally — the priesthood will be incarnated in a personality which is not prepared harmonically for it, and so he will not experience human fulfillment in it. A formation which does not change the seminarian's way of being and living, gives meager guarantees of perseverance and priestly fruits.

Therefore *formation* is *transformation*. This is a general principle of formation in any field. "To form" is not simply "to inform" or to give a few ideas. It is rather to help the person acquire a new form. When a person at the outset does not possess the form that he seeks after, then he will have to be *"transformed."*

Priestly formation is designed for the effective transformation of the seminarians. First of all, it must be a transformation into Christ the Priest: "Until Christ is formed in you" (cf. Gal 4:19). It must be a transformation of the entire personality of the candidate: his way of thinking, feeling, loving, reacting, acting, and relating to others. Everything in him must be configured according to the high ideal of the Catholic priesthood. The role of formators is to see that seminarians are assimilating, making their own, and living from within, all that is proposed to them during their period of formation.

To form, we must bear in mind the dynamic process of personal transformation. If we want the seminarian to make the contents of formation his very own, we must help him first of all value them in such a way that they become his motives for action. However, since he is a free and intelligent being we can hope for no fruit until first we help him to know and understand these contents. Intelligent and free, a seminarian needs to value the elements of his formation if he is to identify with them. In light of this, the best thing we can do as formators is to help him know what his formation consists in and help him understand the reasons behind it.

We must therefore help the seminarians *know*. Man is guided by ideas. Feelings evaporate as easily as they appear. External pressures influence only as long as they are present. It is of prime importance to think of formation as *enlightening* the candidate's intelligence. We must help him deepen his knowledge of Christ, the Church, the priesthood and the meaning of his own vocation. We must explain to him the reasons behind things such as rules and regulations, religious traditions or lifestyles. We should never take for granted that the seminarians already understand the meaning of everything proposed to them as part of their formation. Much less should we impose some practice or formative activity without giving them any opportunity to ask questions or clear up doubts.

As a classic and timely example, they should understand the reasons for priestly celibacy in the Catholic Church. This means to know the natural tendencies of every human being, and consequently to understand the meaning of certain norms, customs or dispositions that are there to aid them in the total donation of their celibate heart to Christ for the sake of the Kingdom of heaven.

We must give abundant explanation of the notions and ideas that shed light on priestly life and formation, in conferences, group meetings, homilies, classes, personal dialogue, etc. We should not hesitate to insist on the more important ideas as often as necessary so that our seminarians incorporate them into their own vision and understanding.

This is the only way they can come to *value* for themselves what is given to them. No matter what he does, a person acts for a value... although it might not always appear that way. Take the case in which we know that a certain student hasn't yet recognized the importance of his studies for his priestly formation. But he studies all the same! It would be wrong to think that he is not moved by any value. Some value (whether it is correct or misguided is another question) drives him to study. It could be a sense of duty, a fear of failing his exams, a desire to please his formators, love for God, whatever. It's not enough to see that he does what he's supposed to do, we have to know what values move him. Only then will we be in a position to help him find the genuine values that his formation is grounded on.

We cannot value something without first grasping its internal worth, but at the same time its not enough to understand that something has a value — the value must be understood as a "value for me." Therefore the formator must help each candidate discover the value of things for himself, to help him value them — (going back to the example above — to value the total gift of his heart to Christ and the dedication of his whole life for the service of his brothers in living celibacy, and consequently to value all the elements that contribute to form and protect the consecration of his heart to God). In this effort, the most efficacious means at the formator's disposition is, without a doubt, his own example. We understand a truth when our mind grasps it as such. We appreciate a value when we understand its worth, and many times we understand something has value for us when we see that others value it and live it.

Once the seminarian has understood and appreciated a value, we must help him *to live it.* To repeat a premise, it is not enough for him to understand and value. If a person has an inactive temperament or if living by a certain value entails sacrifices and difficulties, he runs the risk of never getting beyond theory, and of the value loosing its attraction. In this instance he wouldn't be transformed. He has to be encouraged to act on what he has understood and valued. He needs support and guidance to live by the values he discovers. We must channel his effort and, occasionally, demand it.[5] To continue with our example — we should help the seminarian to live and act according to the norms and decisions that will help him form his celibate heart, putting into practice the means that will help him preserve it.

The practice of what we have truly understood and valued is of itself stable. But we know that by nature human beings tend to be inconstant. We need constant help in order to persevere in the practice of our interiorized values. External props are useful but, above all, we need the support which comes from within. In this vein the formation of *habits* becomes indispensable. The constant repetition of an action creates in us a second nature which makes subsequent acts easier and favors stability. It is extremely important that our seminarians finish their years with a solid store of habits in conformity with their priestly vocation: the habit of profound and personal prayer, the habit of making good use of their time, the habit of study, the habit of watching over their heart and senses... It is especially important that they finish the seminary convinced that as priests they must maintain and cultivate these habits using also external means such as frequent sacramental confession, spiritual direction, keeping to a schedule, and so on.

---

[5]   In chapter five we will see how discipline of community life can be a guide and obligation which the seminarian should interiorize.

Finally, it is interesting to note that all the components of the dynamics of transformation that we have summarized overlap and mutually influence one another. When a person values a reality deeply he understands it more clearly; when he puts it into practice the appreciation of its value is reinforced and is better understood. On the contrary, when one stops living a reality his esteem for it is easily weakened, he might even cease to understand what once he saw so clearly. We will have to work, then to strengthen all the elements of that dynamism.

Dialogue with the spiritual director, examen of conscience, retreats and spiritual exercises, programs of personal formation, etc., must always keep this objective clear: vital transformation. Without transformation there is no formation.

Community and Personalized Formation

The formation we have been speaking about refers to the transformation of a person, of each individual in particular. Nevertheless we frequently allude to the "seminary" or the "formation center" in a sense that is more than just the building that houses the aspirants. It is much more. Above all, it is an ecclesial *community* which lives united by the ideal of priestly formation, as service to the Church and to the world. It is an important community for the effectiveness of the future priest's formation. There are exceptional cases of seminarians who must be formed under the guidance of a priest without the possibility of attending a specific formation center.[6] But generally speaking, the vocation should mature in a climate of openness and dialogue with other people who share the same ideal.

COMMUNITY FORMATION

All Christian life is steeped in the sense of community. In the Old Testament the salvific action of God is almost always directed to his

---

[6] These cases do not enter our reflection here, but they are certainly frequent in some countries. We only note that in these cases as well, fundamental principles of priestly formation are valid because the essence of the priestly figure and mission is always the same, and because the conditions of the human person called to the priesthood are also fundamentally equal naturally, such cares require an ample margin of adaptation.

people: from the vocation of Abraham (cf. Gn 12:2) to the last renewal of the covenant in the prophets (cf. Zc 8:8). Jesus Himself, sent as the salvation of all people (cf. Mt 1:21), gathered a group of followers in order to form them in common. When the New Testament speaks to us of the group of "twelve" (cf. Mk 3:14; Jn 6:70-71; Jn 20:24; 1 Cor 15:5; Ac 6:2), it is clear that it signifies something more than the mere sum of twelve people. It is a true, living community gathered around the Master.

Moreover, the priesthood only has meaning within the Church inasmuch as it is the people of God, the community of believers. Whoever prepares himself to receive and live the priesthood must be profoundly imbued with the sense of "communion," which is not simply a theological category but a lived reality. As shepherd, the priest will have to be guide and leaven of a community, such as a parish, for example. It will be very difficult for him to transmit the meaning of community to the faithful if he has not personally experienced it first. This experience is also vital for those priests who, following what Vatican II recommended, seek to share some form of common life with fellow priests.[7]

Community life also offers excellent opportunities for the formation of the true priest, called to serve and not to be served. It prompts him to dialogue and openness with others. It helps him to know and understand their needs. It teaches him to divide and share material and spiritual goods. It invites him to broaden his horizons, to serve and to give himself freely. And finally, the support of a healthy atmosphere, the witness of classmates and the encouragement of his formators can be decisive for persevering along the road he has taken, and for sustaining his personal effort to form himself.

Priestly formation as community formation involves drawing up some global educational plans which establish community activities that enhance the formation of each one of the seminarians as an individual and as a member of a community.[8] It also implies an effort to create a community atmosphere which helps and stimulates each one in his effort to form himself. There must be a harmonious environment, common

---

[7]   Cf. CD 30; PO 8. See *I Have Called You Friends* by Carlo Bertola (New York: Alba House, 1989).

[8]   We will go into depth on this subject when we speak of the formative environment in chapter five.

ideals, openness, happiness and responsibility. To achieve this the formators have to see that all the candidates fully integrate themselves into the group or community. If someone feels isolated and lives his life on the side, not only does he not benefit from the contributions of the community, he also negatively affects the community by diminishing its cohesion and harmony.

PERSONALIZED FORMATION

Community formation is not formation "en masse." On the contrary, formation must be *personalized* if we hope to overcome the perils of "mass formation," depersonalization, sameness and anonymity. There has to be a certain unity in the formation of priests, and a certain style among the priests formed in the same seminary will be evident, but it does not mean that we should apply only one educational mold to all the candidates.

If on the one hand, God loves and saves his people as a whole; on the other, He chooses specific individuals as cooperators and not massive groups. In the Old Testament, God called each one by name, as He did with Moses (cf. Ex 3:4; 33:12-17). Jesus personally chose his apostles and personally invited each one: "Follow me" (Jn 1:43). It is true that He gathered them together as a group but He treated each one of them in a personal and specific way. It is remarkable to see the wide range of temperaments present in the group of apostles and the way Christ knew how to adapt perfectly to each one of them. He chose three of them to be with him in special moments (cf. Mt 17:1; 26:37). He treated Simon, the impulsive man who sincerely loved him, differently from the way He treated Philip or John. He had a different and very personal plan for each one. When Peter asked about John's destiny, the Master replied: "If it is my will that he remain until I come, what is that to you? Follow me!" (Jn 21:20-22).

A vocation proceeds from the absolutely free love of God and is totally gratuitous, but it is also given with a view to the mission which God will entrust to that person. Thus the mission is strictly personal and nontransferable in continuity with the vocation. A man's answer has to be just as free and personal, and the path to fulfill it will also be personal.

Consequently, priestly formation has to take into account each person in particular. Each man as an individual is unique and unrepeatable. Each one of the young men who enters the seminary is singular in his psychology, his qualities and defects, his formation, his personal history, and in his family and social background. A formator must always keep these differences in mind. He cannot apply the same standard to all. Pedagogical experience teaches us that personal attention stimulates and tangibly improves any effort towards self-betterment, and that, on the contrary, a person will easily give up when he feels that he is being treated like an anonymous number lost in a large mass of people.

Above all, personalized formation means that the formators, from the rector to the professors and including the spiritual director, must strive to *know* each one of the seminarians personally. Long gone are the days when the rector barely got to know his students' names. Fortunately, the relationship between formators and candidates in general has become closer and more cordial. It is the only way. And even then, knowing each seminarian is not enough. A good formator is also personally *interested* in each one, in his needs and problems, in his likes and projects. Thirdly, this interest brings with it the desire to *follow him closely,* to analyze attentively his situation and real progress in the diverse aspects of formation, and to allow him to feel the close and available companionship of his formators. Finally, it is necessary to *adapt* the principles and general directives of formation to the nature and situation of each person. Global programs are necessary but one must be careful not to turn them into absolutes. If a young man can go beyond the programs in a given area — for example studies — it is not only proper for him to do so, it is his obligation. In the same way, we should be ready to adapt the spiritual and apostolic formation we offer to diverse temperaments, to different levels of maturity, and to the present situation of each one. This adaptation demands a good dose of flexibility and prudence on the part of the formator in order to keep the essential while permitting, if necessary, changes in the accidental. He must always seek the good of the candidate.[9]

---

[9] Personalized formation obviously implies sufficient seminary staff. It is easy to affirm this principle but not always easy to make it a reality especially in certain countries or regions. Having a sufficient number of competent formators is always a priority.

If the concepts of community *and* personalized formation seem mutually exclusive, maybe we haven't understood either of them. An in-depth analysis reveals that there is no true development or personal fulfillment if there is not openness to dialogue and cordial living together with others. By the same token, a genuine community does not exist if each one of the members is not reaching his potential as a person.

Integral Formation

The above principles referred especially to the internal dynamics of formation. Now we focus our attention on the target of this dynamism, on what our formative efforts seek to achieve. And the answer is simple and absolute, the candidate's integral formation. We spoke before about formation as transformation. Here we will round out this idea saying it is the transformation of the *entire man,* the formation of an integral man who will later be an integral priest of Christ.

As we noted in the introductory chapter, every human being is unitary, even in his complexity. So when God calls a man to fulfill a mission, He chooses the whole man. He wants him to be consecrated to his service and to the service of others in his entirety. He is to be totally stamped by the priestly character. Every aspect of his character should be identified with Christ — the perfect man, the eternal priest. It is not a question of resembling Christ in one of his facets but identifying with Him in the entirety of one's own personality, even with one's many imperfections.

By its very nature, the priestly ministry demands this integral formation. The priest, like St. Paul, is "for everyone" (1 Cor 9:20-22). In his ministry he will have to offer counsel to scientists, artists, athletes, workers, politicians, etc. His daily pastoral activity is varied and demanding (preaching, offering advice, administering the sacraments, etc.). For other professionals it might be enough to rely on certain talents while neglecting the rest, not so for the priest.

If a priest develops some facets of his person unilaterally or partially, the human fulfillment that God also wants for him as part of his vocation will be at risk. In that case he would have less guarantees of persevering. Every point of his personality that is not formed — especially if it is important — is like a breach in a city's walls, a weak point. What will happen, for example, to a priest who, during formation, develops his compassion for others but who ends his seminary years with a decrepit will?

HARMONIOUS FORMATION OF ALL ONE'S FACULTIES

Before all, integral formation means the *harmonious development of all the faculties* and abilities of the seminarian. Naturally, each one has his own particular talents and particular defects. We are not trying to make them all perfect in everything but rather to attain sufficient maturity in every facet of their human personality. This involves, on the one hand, the development of their various facets, and, on the other, establishing a harmony or hierarchy among the various aspects that make up a complete person.

The members of a rowing team have to be strong and fit. But they also have to row together. Above all there must be a hierarchy, they have to follow the lead of the coxswain who directs their efforts and steers the boat. In order to be an integral priest, the seminarian must form his soul, his mind, his will, his sensitivity, his affections, his body... and he must also achieve the harmony of a structured hierarchy among all these elements.

HARMONIOUS FORMATION IN ALL AREAS

Integral formation also means comprehensive, and refers to a priest being sufficiently prepared in all the fields which pertain to his identity and mission. Certainly, everyone has his own capacities, likes and tendencies. Not everyone can be a great intellectual or a great organizer. But neither can we resign ourselves to letting the seminarians confine their formation to a single field limiting in this way, from the outset, their future contribution to the needs of the diocese. Later, the bishop with pastoral prudence will send each priest to the position where he can best carry out his work in accord with his gifts and his preparation. Before this however, the formators in the seminary can help him equip himself, as best he can, with all the elements which can enrich his personality and give greater potential to his future ministry.

If this principle is not respected, one can easily fall into partialities that become deformations. Thus *academism* occurs when we give the priest undoubtedly an intellectual formation but fail to form him spiritually, humanly or apostolically. Another pitfall is *pastoral technicism:* we form experts in group dynamics, in apostolic methodology, in human relations... but offer a poor philosophical or theological formation, or a mediocre preparation in the human virtues. They will be inclined to frenetic activity in the apostolate that, sooner or later, dampens the spirit. Even today we are tempted with *spiritualism,* normally considered a thing of the past, in which piety is made the only standard of judgment as regards the preparation of a candidate for the priesthood, even though he may lack an academic preparation, and his human qualities and his apostolic methods leave much to be desired. Lastly, the secularization of today's world continues to present the temptation to reduce the priestly mission to the perspective of a horizontal humanism which ignores or relegates its supernatural dimension.

The next chapter, on the *areas of formation,* is rooted in this fundamental principle of priestly formation. Comprehensive formation can be divided into spiritual, human, intellectual and apostolic formation. We will obtain it when the general programs, the community activities and personal guidance of the seminary take into account these four areas and their specific components.

An Eminently Pastoral Formation

One of the aspects of integral formation is preparation for the apostolate. We know that all priestly formation is aimed at preparing the candidate for his mission, so we understand that pastoral formation cannot be considered a specific area of formation but is rather the focus of the entire formation, its leitmotif. It therefore ranks among the fundamental principles.

As seen in the first chapter, the vocation of the priest revolves around a mission: he is a shepherd to the souls which the Church has entrusted to him in the name of the Good Shepherd. Priests, by *exercising the office of*

Christ, Shepherd and Head, within the limits of the authority which is theirs, assemble the family of God as a brotherhood... and through Christ in the Spirit they lead it to God the Father.[10] We can say without hesitation that *the fundamental trait of the priestly personality, according to Vatican II, is that of the shepherd of souls.*[11]

Hence, the formation of priests, if it is to respond to the demands of the priestly mission, must be *eminently pastoral.* This was one of the fundamental points, if not the principal one, that the Council stressed concerning priestly formation. And quite rightly, since to neglect the preparation of the priest for his specific mission in the Church would be to annul in a certain sense the other aspects of his education.

Vatican II's document on priestly formation, speaking about major seminaries, brings out this principle when it affirms that "the whole training of the students should have as its object to make them true shepherds of souls after the example of Our Lord Jesus Christ, teacher, priest and shepherd."[12] The paragraph dedicated to pastoral formation as such affirms its central place in the formation of the seminarian and begins: "Pastoral formation... should characterize every feature of the students' training."[13] The Congregation of Catholic Education's *Directives concerning education in priestly celibacy* explains that "by pastoral formation one understands not only one aspect or an educational sector among the rest, but rather the characteristic proper to the preparation of priests, which must penetrate all the aspects of the formation of the aspirants. The personality of the priest-shepherd is the goal which seminarian education must try to reach in full harmony. This means that all the constitutive elements of the structure and function of the seminary must be thought out and planned with a view to obtaining the indicated purpose. The teachers must have the pastoral formation of the seminarians as a goal of their specialized work."[14]

---

[10] LG 28.

[11] Congregation for Catholic Education, *Directives for education in priestly celibacy,* April 11, 1974, n. 29.

[12] OT 4.

[13] OT 19. The Code of Canon Law also underlines the importance of pastoral formation in number 255: "Although the whole formation of students in the seminary has a pastoral purpose, a specifically pastoral formation is also to be provided..."

[14] *Directives...,* n. 29.

In the first place, *spiritual formation* has to be geared towards and *strictly united to pastoral formation.*[15] The heart of this formation is zeal for souls and pastoral charity. This rather than pastoral techniques, methodology or theory, is the first and essential element of pastoral formation. If the seminarian has Christ as the motivation and meaning of his priesthood he will necessarily love what Christ loves, he will not be indifferent to the good of the sheep which Christ entrusted to him in the Church. The aspirant to the priesthood has to finish seminary with his heart filled with this pastoral love, the natural overflow of his love for Christ.

A spiritual formation based on sentimental or romantic piety, divorced from apostolic commitment and resulting in spiritual narcissism, is therefore not acceptable. A true relationship with the Holy Trinity opens man to the mystery of God who is love and Christ the Redeemer. This openness imbues him with God's love for all people and his desire to save them.

Furthermore, an attempted "pastoral" formation which is not united to a solid spiritual formation is a deception destined to fail.

If the essence of pastoral activity is to communicate to others what we have contemplated before in prayer, it is necessary to unite contemplation and action very closely. Pastoral action imbued with supernatural spirit and laden with supernatural effectiveness is a natural fruit of prayer. When a young man who is preparing himself for the pastoral ministry nurtures his zeal in an intense and rich interior life, on a deep friendship with Jesus Christ, he is setting his future apostolate in the right direction. All his preaching, evangelization and self-giving to the faithful will have the effective support of his union with God.

Academic formation must also be directed towards pastoral formation. An intellectual preparation that is unrelated to the apostolic mission leads to scholarism and not to the true formation of the priest.

The pastoral focus of academic formation has two dimensions. The first is its "intentionality," by which he prepares himself in study for an effective apostolic mission, and offers up for love of souls the sacrifices that a serious philosophical and theological preparation ask of him. By teaching the seminarian to give an apostolic meaning to his studies we help him understand that his whole life has this meaning.

---

[15] OT 8.

The second dimension consists in pointing out the intrinsic relationship between his studies and his priestly mission. A formation in which professor and students strive to see the connection between the course content and both pastoral activity and the specifically priestly mission is very different from a cold and purely scientific teaching of these subjects. At the same time we should be careful not to alter the method or content that is proper to each subject.

Along these same lines, Vatican II's decree on priestly formation recommends that philosophy students be shown the relationship that exists between this field and the true problems of life. It also invites professors to explain the connection that exists between philosophical themes and the mysteries of salvation.[16] In like manner, the study of theology must be undertaken in such a way that the students can proclaim, explain and defend in their priestly ministry[17] what they have assimilated. The teaching of theology in seminaries is principally aimed at forming priests for the pastoral ministry.[18]

Likewise, their *human formation* must be infused with a profound pastoral orientation that adds *new elements* and *new perspectives* to this formation. It adds *new elements* since there are qualities a priest must acquire due to his mission that in other walks of life are not as necessary. Here we are dealing with the formation of the one who has to be a guide to his brothers and sisters, a spiritual leader and a herald of the message of salvation. It adds *new perspectives,* because we deal with human virtues as related to the mission. The rich array of human virtues which the priest must possess does not have the finality of forming a perfect man, full of his own perfection and locked into his own self-contemplation. He seeks his human perfection in order to fulfill better his pastoral mission. The better the quality of the man, the better will be the quality of the shepherd.

All the areas of the integral formation of the priest must be at the service of the priestly mission, explicitly and continuously. But at the same time we have to offer our seminarians a *specifically pastoral prepara-*

---

[16] OT 15.

[17] OT 16.

[18] Congregation for Catholic Education, *Directives concerning the study of theology in seminaries,* February 22, 1976, n. III,II,5,1; cf. RFIS 94.

tion.[19] We will discuss this in depth in chapter three when speaking of the elements and resources to effect this formation.

Lastly, it is extraordinarily important to form in the future priest the awareness that he will be a *shepherd in the Church, for the Church and of the Church.* When Christ chose him to be a shepherd, He called him to be a minister of the community founded by Him, of the Church which He has built on the rock of Peter (cf. Mt 16:18) to whom He entrusted the care of his sheep (cf. Jn 21:15-17). Therefore love for the Church forms a part of the seminarian's correct pastoral formation and is also a specific element of his spiritual life. The young man who is preparing for his future apostolate must comprehend that outside of the Church his mission loses its meaning. The content of his evangelization, the methods of his ministry, the style of his sacramental activity need to be steeped in a profound "sensus Ecclesiae." Naturally, his pastoral activity should be carried out in harmony with the Supreme and Universal Pastor, with his bishop, the pastor of his particular Church, and with his brothers in the priesthood.

Realistic View of Man, Realistic Pedagogy

Returning to the comparison with a building in construction, we could say that in priestly formation the "building materials" are also a primary consideration. Quarry stone, concrete and palm branches certainly don't give the same results. A *realistic pedagogy* founded on a *realistic view of man* is a fundamental and elementary principle of priestly formation.

As a principle this might seem too obvious and even superfluous to merit our consideration. But looking at some of the debacles in formation and knowing the practices that have emptied some seminaries, it would not seem unwarranted to reflect on it... When we leave a young aspirant to the priesthood to his own devices in his formation, without channeling his efforts, without initiating him into a life of prayer, without teaching him how to live a virtuous life or requiring him to study; when, knowing the difficulties that come with embracing celibacy, we allow him, or even

---

[19] Cf. CIC 255.

encourage him, to have every sort of experience... what kind of concept of man do we have? Or, at the other extreme, if we enclose him in a system which controls and determines his every step, or we impose virtue on him or impede the development and channeling of his affectivity... what kind of concept of man do we have?

Naturally, we must have a clear knowledge of the specific individual who is being formed with all his particular personal traits. Yet the knowledge of each person is based on an anthropological concept, a knowledge of the human being as he is. Our present reflection goes in this direction.

Every pedagogy operates on a specific view of the human being. Rousseau builds on the theory of the naturally good man, the *noble savage*. The Marxist theory of education builds on the idea that man is a social being immersed in a necessary process of dialectical materialism. Christian pedagogy springs from the concept of man as a wounded image of God who is restored by Christ. We already gave a summary of the fundamental elements of this anthropology in the first chapter. Now we will simply try to specify their application to pedagogy.

RECOGNIZING THE FUNDAMENTAL GOODNESS OF MAN

First and foremost, man is a created being and an image of God. He has a dignity and a nobility which place him above every other creature in this world.[20] Philosophy and psychology both tell us that he is a spirit in some way open to the infinite and that in him there is a profound dynamism towards transcendency. Fundamentally man is good, very good (cf. Gn 1:31).

This basic goodness unfolds in a series of faculties, qualities or "talents" as Christ calls them in the Gospel (cf. Mt 25:15): from his physical condition to his higher, spiritual dimension. There is a fundamental goodness and positiveness about his body, emotions, affections, sentiments, intelligence, will, conscience and freedom.

---

[20] In the *Pastoral Constitution of the Church in the Modern World,* the Second Vatican Council has wished to highlight this truth of the greatness of man and his superiority above other created beings: *Man is not deceived when he regards himself as superior to bodily things and as more than just a speck in nature or a nameless unit in the city of man* (GS 14).

We cannot ignore this radical goodness of the human being. A realistic formator recognizes the marvels that creation has worked in each candidate. His fundamental appraisal of each young man is positive, though he has no illusions about the fragile human material which he must educate. To start off on any other footing would be to deny the work of God and to found the process of formation on an erroneous base.

The task of the educator is to help the innate goodness of each one of his seminarians flourish and reach its highest development. He has to be able to discover in the candidate the image of God which, though hidden at times behind a wall of defects, is not any less real because of that.

KNOWING THE LIMITS AND POSSIBILITIES OF MAN

Nevertheless it would be a grave error to dismiss the limits and even the miseries that this young man who is preparing for the priesthood brings with him. He is a finite being, conditioned by the parameters of his corporeity and historicity and jostled about by his conscious or subconscious psychological influences. Above all he is a man whose nature has been touched by sin. The goodness of the divine image has waned in him. By turning our glance inward, each one of us can verify the effects of this wound: our inclination to evil, our proud self-preference over the plans of the Creator, and our frightening capacity to barricade ourselves in selfishness.

A good formator can never forget this reality and must work accordingly, in the first place by recognizing the wound and detecting its practical consequences, secondly by looking ahead and thirdly by healing.

Recognizing the wound and its side-effects is a sign of a realistic pedagogy. The candidate for the priesthood will fall many times; he will have built-in physical, psychological or moral imperfections. His intelligence may not always adhere to the truth, sometimes because it falls short, others because of culpable error. His will might pursue the first apparent good that comes along. His conscience might be obscured by false arguments or silenced by passions. He may abuse his liberty and reject the right use of it within his acceptance of the plan of God. If we accept the fact that human nature bears a painful scar we will spare ourselves unpleasant surprises and unnecessary heartache in our work.

Looking ahead for possible disorientations in the candidate means shoring up his defenses, promoting an eminently positive program, strengthening his soul with continuous motivations and taking into account occasions or situations harmful to the candidate. To foresee is also to watch out for each candidate's needs and meet them at the best moment. It means to smooth the way and avoid him unnecessary or counterproductive mistakes. It is to point out the dangers and the rough spots along the road just as any experienced mountain guide would do for the novice to lead him on a sure path.

Healing and curing the passions, tendencies, possible mistakes and bad habits might seem to be negative action, but it is not. First of all it seeks a positive end: the restoration of the integral dignity of our human nature. Secondly, on many occasions the cure consists not in repression but in the positive channeling of a person's inborn forces which perhaps are not correctly oriented. The grace of God cures one radically. Nevertheless, even with the help of grace, there remains in the soul what the Council of Trent called *concupiscentia* or *fomex peccati* which has been permitted by God for man to wrestle with *(ad agonem)*. Properly speaking it is not sin but rather proceeds from sin and inclines toward it.[21] These *reliquia peccati* are corrected through a long process of formation which implies time, patience and the repetition of virtuous acts contrary to our negative tendencies.

RECOGNIZING THE EFFICACY OF DIVINE GRACE IN MAN

Fortunately, the history of salvation continues beyond the first sin and in spite of all sin. In Christ, the "imago Dei" has been restored. In the new era begun at the consummation of the Paschal mystery all men and women are called to "reproduce the image of the Son... first-born among many brothers" (Rm 8:29). This is the new era of grace that carries within it man's inclination towards glory. In this perspective, an earthly anthropology gives way to a heavenly one: "Just as we have borne the image of the man of dust, we shall also bear the image of the man of heaven" (1 Cor 15:49).

---

[21] *Decree on original sin*, n. 5, DS 1515.

If we disregard the power of grace and the call to glory we risk confusing realism with the pessimism typical of a horizontal humanism. *Christian* realism takes into account all the dimensions of the mystery of man, a mystery which only becomes clear in the light of the mystery of the Incarnation (Gs. 22) and the Paschal mystery. It is the supernatural realism of the man of God, of the man who firmly believes in the continued action of the Holy Spirit in souls, who relies on the power of God, who knows that the wisdom of God acts through the paradox of the cross (cf. 1 Cor 1:23).

The formator of priests recognizes the presence and the action of grace in the soul of his seminarians. He is able to discern the work of the Spirit in their hearts and contemplate the greatness of their dignity and supernatural destiny. By counting on the action of grace we give a new dimension to the whole educational process. Seemingly lost cases appear in a different light when we are aware that grace can work in unexpected ways, along paths known only to divine wisdom. This fundamentally optimistic realism puts a seal of confidence and serenity on the entire work of formation.

ANTHROPOLOGICAL AND PEDAGOGICAL REALISM OF CHRIST THE MASTER

This is the material with which we have to work. It is not perfect but we can do a lot with it if we know how. This is the challenge for the formator of priests.

In his difficult task he can find encouragement and inspiration by contemplating the figure of Christ, the realistic formator *par excellence.* The Gospel presents Christ to us as one who knows the human heart in depth (cf. Jn 2:25). This knowledge comes from a passion for man whom He loved deeply and for whom He went to the extreme of giving his life (cf. Jn 13:1). Jesus is capable of discovering the sincerity of a true Israelite like Nathanael (cf. Jn 1:47) and the false hypocrisy of the Pharisees (cf. Mt 23:13-32). Christ recognizes the divine seed present in the soul of the human being; He is not unaware of Peter's passionate nobility and John's fidelity. But He also knows them well. He knows their innermost being. He knows that "the spirit is willing, but the flesh is weak" (Mk 14:38); He knows that in spite of Peter's claim to love Him (cf. Mk 14:28), when the hour of truth arrives he will deny even knowing Him (cf. Mk 14:66-72).

He trusts in man, but He has no foolish illusions about him. He knows that man is capable of heroic and noble deeds and generous self-offering and, at the same time, capable of treason, denial, abandonment, cowardice and ingratitude. But what surprises us most is that in spite of knowing man's weakness perfectly well, He calls him and gives him a mission far beyond his own capability so there will be no doubt that sanctification and evangelization are a work of grace (cf. 2 Cor 12:9-10).

It is worth our while in passing to bring up another application of this realistic view of man: the formator is a man as well. We should never forget it. I, as a formator, am also a mixture of greatness and misery, with a tendency to transcendence and to selfishness, influenced by impulses, passions and psychological conditioning. I too, am a fallen and redeemed image of God. When I carry out my formation work of directing, demanding, correcting and supporting, I must be attentive to see if my conduct responds to what the candidate needs from me, or rather to my own needs; if what I say and do is born of divine inspiration or born of my own human, perhaps too human, impulses.

EXCURSUS: SPECIFIC TRAITS OF MODERN MAN

Up to here our considerations have dealt with man as he is seen from the point of view of a general anthropology. Yet the formator has to work with young men who have specific personal histories locked into a very definite time and place. He must also know the cultural, religious and social influences prevalent in the *social context that candidates come from.* In a way, they are children of their civilization. They were born in it. They have assimilated its customs, its perception of reality, its values and its characteristic handicaps.

All these factors figure in a realistic pedagogy. If we overlook or refuse to accept this reality as formators, our efforts to form the aspirants for the priesthood could be negated. Either we will never make the solid contact with them necessary to transmit our message because we are unfamiliar with their context, or we will be unable to provide solutions to their specific problems in life, or the candidates will simply feel we do not understand them.

On a general level, we recognize that in our civilization there is a *profound crisis of faith.* The pluralism of society, the frequent neglect of religious teaching, the confusion and dissent regarding dogma and morality, etc., make it quite possible for a young man entering the seminary to arrive without a sufficient knowledge of his faith and how to live it. On the other hand, almost as a response to all this, we can see among today's youth the birth of a new search which is made evident in the appearance and growth of lay movements and in their greater apostolic awareness.

The *mass media* undoubtedly have a decisive influence on our young people. Frequently they are used to create needs or attitudes in order to push the sale of products, and to promote opinions and human behavior which favor the interests of whoever is in control, without the slightest regard for human, moral or religious values.

Due in great part to this influence, today's youth are often driven to an avid *pursuit of sense experiences.* In contemporary culture we have a blatant (and therefore culturally endorsed) promotion of the quest for sense pleasure. It has reached the point that we can speak of a cult of immediate gratification. At every turn we are flooded by images, spectacles, situations and behavior which invite us to reduce life to this sense dimension. Candidates for the priesthood, to a greater or lesser degree, all bear the mark of this tendency.

Extroversion of the senses affects the *formation of the intelligence,* and in particular the formation of the habit of reflection. Our society of visual images and immediate results, along with certain educational systems in vogue today, do not foster reflection, concentration, a healthy critical sense, nor the capacity to analyze, synthesize and relate concepts. We commonly detect in our young people a strong bent towards mental dispersion, superficiality, distraction and digression. The *formation of the will* is also affected. A society based on easy and immediate consumption promotes and exacerbates the human tendency to comfort and the abandonment of all effort and sacrifice.

An alarming *lack of a cultural and artistic sensibility* is spreading, although in some places more than in others. Young people dedicate their time and attention to studying the sciences and their technical applications, and they forego the study of other subjects which would give them a greater knowledge of man, a more profound understanding of the values and ideals more proper to him, and the opportunity for a better formation of their human sensitivity.

Another aspect of the cultural poverty affecting our youth is the *incapacity to reflect about their own lives*. That is to say, they lack a healthy sense of self-criticism as regards their own behavior, tastes, customs, and the habits they are acquiring.

This is why so many young people easily find themselves at the mercy of their *feelings, likes and whims of the moment*. They regulate their life by the sway of their emotions, the current fashion and the pressure of the environment in which they live. If it is true that youth in every age are restless and inconstant because their personality is still maturing, perhaps it applies more than ever to today's youth.

The moral consequences are inevitable. It is not difficult to discover that their *consciences have been minimally or poorly informed,* or worse still, *they have not been formed.* The relativism of pluralistic society, its endemic hedonism, diminishing religious education... all easily lead to the deformation of moral conscience.

The effect that all of these negative factors have on the formation of a young man who is aspiring to the priesthood can be readily understood. The development of his interior life, the strenuous conquest of virtue and his intellectual preparation run into serious obstacles because of these shortcomings. The formator must be aware that his work will often have to begin at an elemental level: formation of the will, intelligence, moral conscience and, therefore, formation of the use of liberty, a sense of responsibility, the capacity for sacrifice and self-donation, the explanation of the basic elements and demands of Christian living, etc. We should not be surprised if progress in their spiritual life and in their overall formation is slower and more laborious since we are working with a human base which is not well prepared.

But it would be an outright mistake to overlook the *positive traits* that also characterize the young people of our time, and which also contribute positively to the process of their priestly formation.

For example most young people share a healthy spirit of *spontaneity*. This candid approach in their relationship with companions and elders, when present in a seminarian, favors his frankness, his openness to others and his sincere spirit of understanding with his formators. If we use this quality well it can be decisive in obtaining a good formation. The media and the widespread means of transportation have favored an enormous increase in our young people's knowledge of the world, and the necessities and problems of the people who live on the other side of the globe. This has heightened the natural *spirit of solidarity* that exists among youth across the world and their desire to help their counterparts. So too, the greater spirit of *"protagonism"* and *participation* which modern culture has promoted among them becomes a positive force in the formation of active priests, sensitive to the needs of their neighbor, desirous of contributing to the good of the whole people of God and society at large.

The list goes on and on. The objective of our reflection in this section was to remind the formator that he should know and respond to all the positive and negative traits which today's young men bring into the seminary with them. This consideration, together with the anthropology viewed in the first chapter and summarized here, are key factors for the true effectiveness of the formator's work.

Gradual and Ongoing Formation

Our "realistic pedagogy" helps introduce the final fundamental principle. It is a principle that uncovers two latent temptations on the path of formation. It is not unusual for a young man aspiring to the priesthood to make readily evident progress after only a short time in the seminary or center for formation. He is like a good piece of wood. After only a few strokes of the sculptor, the silhouette of a new form starts to appear. Both he and his formators might hastily conclude that practically everything is done. Thus, he slackens in his efforts and the process of formation grinds to a stop. On the other hand, some people want to see more profound changes or obtain immediate results. The slowness of the formation process disheartens them, they slacken in their effort, and the process of formation comes to a stop. These extremes have a common denominator. Both temptations come from forgetting that formation has to be *progressive.* It is necessary to understand that formation is not a goal but a journey on which we can always take another step.

GRADUAL FORMATION

The tendency to continual growth is natural in man, even when his body has begun to decline. In this natural dynamism the divine call comes through, "You must be perfect as your heavenly Father is perfect" (Mt 5:48). This invitation of the Lord is directed to every Christian, but *priests are bound by a special reason to acquire this perfection. They are consecrated to God in a new way in their ordination and are made the living instruments of Christ the eternal priest.*[22]

At the same time, the human person (essentially finite and temporal) never obtains absolute perfection. He must pass through stages of growth and maturing. The call to perfection is an invitation to progressive growth, in pursuit of a goal that will always be ahead of us.

Progressive formation implies the concept of *gradualism.* Formation is a fruit which matures little by little, through daily effort. It is not reached suddenly or by leaps and bounds, but rather step by step, just as one ascends the steps of the altar. Normally, spectacular progress does not occur, though the grace of God can always work miracles. The education of an aspirant to the priesthood has to abide by this gradualism when setting personal goals. It would be an illusion to think that the young man who is beginning his formation could immediately reach full maturity in his spiritual life or in his intellectual preparation. The habit of prayer, for example, is only obtained after years of effort and work. There is a very strong temptation for both the candidate and the formator to dash along. Yet it is necessary to respect the gradual nature of each person's growth and follow the rhythm that God sets for each individual.

Progressive formation also means *continuity.* Gradual progress over a limited span of time is not enough, it must continue. We must be persevering in the work of formation. Continuity also requires an ongoing dialogue among the various formators in such a way that each one builds on the work of the other. Intercommunication is especially necessary when, for whatever reason, there is a change of formators. By no means should each new formator have to begin from scratch, without knowing what the previous ones have done, and without knowing how the candidate is and what formation he has received. But communication between formators is always to be carried out with absolute respect for each person and his conscience.

We should strive for a perfect progressive continuity among the

---

[22] PO 12.

various stages of formation.[23] Both the programs and their practical application by the formators must be set up so that one step builds upon the base of the previous one and prepares for the next.

Continuity is not simply a directly ascending linear graph. In the general history of humanity and in the small histories of each individual there are moments of retreat, there are falls and delays. This is part of the finite condition of the human being, and it is also a consequence of sin and its effects. There is a real need for a *fighting spirit,* a constant search for self-betterment, and a struggle against selfishness, discouragement and routine. This is the lot of all men and women: "Has not man a hard service upon earth?" (Jb 7:1). There is a parallel need for *humility and patience,* and the permanent disposition to lift ourselves up after falling and keep moving on.

Constancy in formation also demands order. Wild action will not give effective results; to obtain results in any field of human activity we need a program. Why should we try to do without one in priestly formation? This does not exclusively refer to the general programs established by the directors of the seminary. We are also speaking about the *planning* that a seminarian can do for his personal formation: a program for his spiritual life (with specific goals and means) that motivates and guides him in his effort to eliminate his defects and acquire the virtues which he personally needs most; a program for his intellectual formation drawn up according to his abilities, needs and specific interests, etc.

ONGOING PERMANENT FORMATION

All of these elements will help the seminarian in his progressive preparation for the priesthood. Yet it would be a grave error to think that he has reached the goal on the day of his ordination. Evangelical perfection and complete identification with Christ stand always before and above us as the ideal we strive for. On the day the candidate receives the sacrament of Orders, God invites him to set out on the path once again. Modern pedagogy calls this *ongoing formation.* It means to be up-to-date in the complete living of his priestly vocation, continual growth in his friendship

---

[23] Cf. Chapter six.

with Christ, his love for the Church, his pastoral zeal, and his attitude of generous self-giving to others. It means persevering in his fervor. It means continuously increasing his academic competence.

The demand to keep up with the latest advances is particularly felt in the sphere of secular professions because of our rapidly changing society and the constant progress of science and technology. A professional who is not up-to-date loses prestige and competence in his own field. It is no different for a priest. Theology and philosophy have continued to evolve since his last exams in the seminary; society, culture, and the men and women to whom he offers his service also keep changing at a dizzying pace. He himself also continues to mature both physically and spiritually. He has to stay "up-to-date" by means of periodicals, seminars, etc. This permanent formation is so important that we consider it one of the "steps of formation" — the last and longest one.

There are no dogmas in pedagogy. Our intention has been to reflect carefully upon several elements worthy of consideration as we fulfill our task as formators of priests. Doubtless, many of these elements are found, either explicitly or implicitly, in other writings on the same topic and in existing programs of priestly formation. Yet, as we said at the beginning, it is always good to have a clear map which marks our path, even if it is somewhat general. In the art of forming priests the most important thing is constant self-giving with love and prudence in the tangible reality of everyday life. If we want to work methodically and effectively, it is always useful to have before our eyes these fundamental principles of priestly formation.

CHAPTER THREE

FOUR DIMENSIONS
OF PRIESTLY FORMATION

In the first two chapters we sketched the essential outline of the identity and formation of the priest. One of the fundamental principles we mentioned was "integral formation." Now we intend to examine its multiple components with an in-depth look at the different dimensions of priestly formation.

We are all well aware that a human being is a complex unity. He cannot be taken apart as if he were an assembly of separate pieces, and therefore we cannot mathematically divide his formation into hermetic compartments. We can, however, distinguish diverse aspects of this unified and complex reality, and focus our attention on each individual aspect for the good of the formation of the whole person. An experienced teacher covers his ground methodically with clear objectives, each well defined by its distinction from the others. He knows how to distinguish without separating.

Following the classical order of our present topic, we will talk about the *spiritual, human, intellectual and pastoral* formation of the future priest.

SPIRITUAL FORMATION

The most important and decisive aspect of formation for the aspirant to the priesthood is the spiritual dimension. This is his characteristic; he forms himself as a man of God, identifies himself with Christ the priest, and is united to Him as to the Vine that gives life. The "transformation" we spoke of as a fundamental principle has to be, above all, a priestly transformation. Our last principle reminded us that the invitation of Christ: "Be perfect..." must resound in a special way in the man chosen to be the prolongation of the only Mediator between God and men.

This formation is based more on experience than on learning. It is the experience of love: it begins with love for God and for humanity, and ends in this very same love, strengthened and perfected. It is to begin loving in order to end loving more.

This living experience has its vital center in Christ and its principal source in the Gospel. The age-old Church tradition passed on to us by masters of the spiritual life constitutes an important aid and serves as an example. In essence, Christian spirituality is one; the Gospel is one and the same for all. Yet we can speak about "priestly spirituality" as we do about "lay spirituality" or the spirituality of an institute of consecrated life. The elements we analyze here are common to all, but they also have some special peculiarities proper to the priest's spiritual personality.

The Priest, a Man of God

Men and women seek a friend in the priest, someone in whom they can trust and find understanding and a warm welcome. They expect him to be a prudent and well-prepared man, capable of offering them sound advice in their personal struggles and in the dark moments of their faith. But more than anything, they want the priest to be a *man of God*. The priest, "appointed to act on behalf of men in relation to God" (Heb 5:1) and thus a mediator between both, the prolongation of the only Mediator, has to be a man of God in the depth of his being, his sentiments, his thoughts, his intentions and his actions.

The man of God has allowed himself to be possessed by God: "You have seduced me, Yahweh, and I have let myself be seduced; you have overpowered me: you were the stronger" (Jr 20:7). In virtue of this possession he approaches human realities imbued with divine thoughts and desires. Those who listen to him and see him act sense the presence of God who speaks and works through him. As an authentic prophet and pastor, he clearly shows men and women the path to the Father, teaches and reminds them what God expects from them, and what He is rightly due. He is an authentic light for their consciences and a teacher of prayer. He arouses and nourishes in their hearts the longing for God and he shows them that their definitive citizenship is in heaven.

For a seminarian, becoming a man of God implies a gradual and dynamic process in which God, little by little, penetrates all of his faculties, sentiments and behavior. God elevates them by grace in proportion to the soul's generosity and collaboration with the divine action. His surest route is prayer, understood as contact with God that rejuvenates the soul and bears fruit. Prayer solicits and at the same time nourishes a generous response through the practice of the virtues, through positive and loving asceticism which is necessary to purify a person from sin and its effects, and through docility to the inspirations of the Holy Spirit.

Faith, Hope and Charity

Like a reliable thermometer, the measure in which we live and grow in the theological virtues indicates the degree to which God is taking possession of us, and the degree in which we are being turned into men of God. There is no better sign of spiritual well-being and of God's work than to see that one is growing in these virtues whose object is God. They are virtues that purify and beautify the soul and are the foundation of every spiritual life.

FAITH

Faith is the window through which the soul beholds spiritual realities. It is the foundation of all Christian life and also the priest's Christian life. But for a priest, faith is even more necessary.

First of all, his entire existence revolves around the mysteries of our faith. Every day he offers the sacrifice of the Son of God and takes his body in his hands; in the name of Christ he forgives sins, which only God can do (cf. Mk. 2:5); he represents Christ the head before the people of God.[1] Can a priest live dedicated for life to "the things of God" (Heb 5:1) if he does not live in faith and by faith?

---

[1] Cf. LG 28.

Secondly, the priest has been called to be a prophet of the Kingdom of God, a teacher of the faith: *If this virtue is necessary for all, it is especially so for the priest, who has the mission of communicating the faith to others by the proclamation of the Word. This man cannot efficaciously preach the Gospel if he has not profoundly assimilated its message... Every priest has to be a beacon of the faith...*[2]

How can he be a beacon and teacher of the faith, if he is not deeply steeped in it?

Finally, the cross and difficulties often line the life of a priest. There are moments in which faith is everything and without it, nothing can subsist.

It is therefore vital that the spiritual formation of the seminarian be centered on bringing his faith to maturity.

Faith is a theological virtue which is not limited to a mere sentiment of the presence of God in one's life or a more or less erudite knowledge of God and of revealed truths. Believing is much more than knowing or feeling. It is to see God in every person and in every event. It is to direct constantly our every action and activity to Him. It is to trust in God and his promises, accepting his word, always trusting in spite of the surprises, scares, falls, fears and the thousand difficulties of life.

Faith is a divine gift. We must ask for it humbly every day, and be thankful for it. We should show our thanks by our cooperation, that is, by broadening and deepening our knowledge of it as much as possible, by keeping it free and detached, and for this we purify our heart and curb our tendencies to rationalism and self-sufficiency.

There are moments and activities in seminary life which can especially help to vivify, enlighten and strengthen the candidates' faith. But a good formator is a teacher and a witness of the faith to them in every moment and circumstance. In his viewpoints and judgments, in his remarks, in the testimony of his prayer life... in spiritual direction, in confession, in an informal conversation... everything provides an occasion to transmit a live and fresh faith to the souls of his seminarians.

---

[2] John Paul II, *Angelus,* December 17, 1989.

Luminous and operative faith engenders true Christian hope with its two complimentary aspects: hope which becomes confidence in God, and hope which heralds the growth and definitive possession of the Kingdom of Christ.

He who believes in God, trusts in Him. And he trusts completely because trust is either total or not at all. Hope assures us that God will give the strength and the courage we need to finish the race, and that in Him we will find the fullness and happiness created things cannot offer. A person with hope is convinced that God profoundly loves humanity, despite the numerous obstacles the evil and weakness of men and women create for the establishment of God's Kingdom. Hope knows that the Holy Spirit will continue in the Church the work of salvation which Jesus Christ brought to us. When we live with hope we trust in the coming of the Kingdom of God and we desire the future happiness that only God can give.

Here, as with faith, the young man who is preparing himself for the priesthood must acknowledge that his hope is not only for himself.

> The priest is the man of hope... To form a priest means to form a man with the mission of being a witness of Christian hope and strengthening it in others. The world is thirsting for hope... The priest, man of hope,... has to, above all, build the hope which does not fail (cf. Rm 5:5).[3]

Nevertheless hope is often the forgotten virtue. We take it for granted or simply overlook it. But a formator of priests cannot ignore it. For example, when a seminarian is going through times of darkness and difficulty, a formator certainly has to use human means to encourage him, but more importantly he must help him to raise his eyes to God and find in Him hope and strength. In this way, a negative circumstance becomes an opportunity for the young man to strengthen his Christian resolve and better prepare himself to be a witness of hope.

---

[3] John Paul II, *Angelus,* December 24, 1989.

God is love (cf. 1 Jn 4:8). This New Testament truth is the definitive feature of the progressive, mysterious and surprising revelation of the Face of God. God created man and woman in his image and likeness (cf. Gn 1:27), capable of loving, made to love. Christ was clear in making love the distinguishing characteristic of his disciples (cf. Jn 13:34-35). The Christian's principal task is to resemble God through the diligent exercise of the love which has been poured into every heart through the Holy Spirit who dwells in all the baptized (cf. Rm 5:5). Charity is the summary and fullness of the Law (cf. Mt 22:40; Rm 13:10), the queen of virtues (cf. 1 Cor 13:4), and the greatest of the supernatural virtues (cf. 1 Cor 13:13).

Therefore it cannot be absent from the heart and life of the priest. He has been chosen to prolong the presence of Jesus Christ and make his love present among all people. He has been appointed as a mediator between God and men. Hence the double aspect of his priestly charity: love God as all men must love Him, and *love all people* as they are loved by God.

Love God Above All Things

The best way to help the seminarian to love God is to help him to know Him. The more he knows and discovers God the more will he find pleasure in Him. His heart will love Him as the only One who can be totally loved, and his free will be able to choose Him as the only One who satisfies all his yearnings and longings. A seminarian comes to know God in prayer, in the exercise of faith that recognizes Him as always present, and in listening attentively to the inspirations of the Holy Spirit.

Nothing moves us to love more than knowing we are loved. This human experience is also valid for theological charity. Someone who has been chosen by God from among others for a mission as lofty as the priesthood has many cogent reasons to feel loved by his Creator and Redeemer. How easy, yet how important it is to remind the seminarian and help him evaluate this truth: God loves you! It is as true in the moments of fervor and enthusiasm as it is in the moments of dryness and discouragement.

Like the other theological virtues, charity is a gift of God. We should use all available human means to obtain it, but above all we must ask for it, wait for it, and welcome it humbly and openly.

Love of God inspires works of charity. Forming the seminarian in theological charity also means teaching him to live always with an attitude of authentic donation of self to God's will. We should remind him that whoever loves God fulfills his commandments (cf. Jn 14:15), helping him to understand that God's will is made manifest above all within his conscience,[4] but that it is also expressed through those who legitimately represent Him: from the Supreme Magisterium of the Church down to the formator closest to him. It is necessary to show him that the love of God must move him to strive sincerely to avoid sin as the negation of love. Further still, we should strive to create in him the ardent desire that everywhere, among his companions and friends, in family and in society, love will always reign over sin. The love of God will thus radically influence the meaning and essential objective of his future apostolate. His love for the Father will make him go out to meet his brothers and sisters.

Love Your Neighbor as Yourself

The second dimension of a priest's charity is to love all men and women as they are loved by God. His Master requested it when He mystically identified Himself with every human being: "As you did it to the least of these my brethren, you did it to me" (Mt 25:40). John's forceful words are also directed to him: "If anyone says, "I love God," and hates his brother, he is a liar" (1 Jn 4:20).

It is necessary to form the seminarians in the authentic spirit of Christian love for all people. We may have "pious," educated, dependable seminarians, but if they do not live the charity of Christ they will never truly be "other Christs." Rather they will be priests who live outside the Gospel.

This virtue has many aspects and nuances. Paul reminds us of some of them: "Love is patient and kind; love is not jealous or boastful; it is not arrogant or rude. Love does not insist on its own way; it is not irritable or resentful; it does not rejoice at wrong, but rejoices in the right" (1 Cor 13:4-6). Although a reflection on each of these characteristics would be too lengthy, we can mention a few to illustrate the point.

---

[4] Cf. GS 16.

Love resides in the heart of a person. We can then speak of some aspects of *"internal charity."* It is *goodness of heart,* which brings us to accept benevolently any and every person. Goodness begets the habit of *thinking well* of others. Jesus warned us: "Do not judge and you will not be judged, do not condemn and you will not be condemned" (Lk 6:37), so we have to help our future priests to overcome the all too human tendency to think the worst about others always. They should strive to replace it with the more Christ-like and just attitude, "believe every good thing you hear and only the bad things you see." And if there is an evil impossible to ignore, we must know how to pardon it. We have to learn to distinguish between the sin and the sinner, and be able always to *forgive* sincerely, "Forgive and you will be forgiven." It is vitally important to form these dispositions from the very beginning since they make the priestly heart.

From a priest's heart come the attitudes and actions that express his *"external charity."* First of all, he must *speak well of others.* Unfortunately we are too accustomed to criticism and defamation. We can even get the impression that some consider that a life of piety, daily Mass, and even religious consecration are perfectly compatible with criticism, gossip, and ridicule of their neighbor. It's as if we had lost a few pages from our New Testament: "Do not speak evil against one another, brethren. Whoever speaks evil against a brother or judges his brother, speaks evil against the law and judges the law" (Jm 4:11). The priest cannot allow himself a similar inconsistency. The formator should remind the seminarians of this and help them in their daily life, above all by his own example, teaching them not to criticize their companions, formators, bishop, other priests, or anyone else. If they feel they must comment about another person for his own good or for a greater good, they should always have the possibility of expressing their observations to whomever has the ability to remedy or improve the situation.

But to speak well of others is not simply to avoid speaking badly. Besides not bringing out the faults and defects of others, sincere love engenders the desire to speak well of them. One word of praise or a fleeting positive comment is enough to make a good name for our neighbor and build up esteem for him. We should be ready, when necessary, to come nobly to the defense of a companion or any person who has been unjustly criticized. Few gestures of genuine charity are more impressive. A community in which everyone counts on the support of the rest, in which there is no talking behind another's back, in which *everybody speaks well of one another...* is it too idealistic? It is the Christian ideal.

The members of the primitive Christian community "were of one heart and one soul" (Ac 4:32). Seminary and priestly communities also aspire to be a family united in brotherly love and in *mutual relationships of cordiality, respect and readiness to serve.* Thus, external charity is not limited to speaking well of others. It must be expressed in specific acts of selfless *service,* generous collaboration and mutual help. Seminary life offers untold opportunities for a man to forget about himself and serve others. Community life if we so desire is a true workout for charity.

Lastly, love of neighbor engenders a sincere interest for *justice.* A priest has to be a just man and a promoter of justice. First of all, he should be just in his relations with those who work with him. He should promote justice through his preaching, his pastoral relationships with those who commit injustice and his support for those who suffer it. From the outset of his journey to the priesthood we have to make each seminarian more sensitive to the needs of others and to the demands of human and Christian justice, and help him form himself to work for justice. We should make sure he understands on the one hand that this is part of his priesthood insofar as it is service to the whole human person, and on the other that a priest should always remember the spiritual dimension of his mission and never reduce himself to being a civil rights advocate. He should also realize that there is no true promotion of justice outside of authentic Christian charity, which implies love, pardon and understanding towards all, without preferences, universally.[5]

The practical suggestions of this section could be multiplied end-lessly. In any event, the best method of formation in this virtue is the witness of simple and constant charity on the part of the formator. Thus his everyday life becomes a lesson on charity. His best preaching will be his personal example, which never goes unnoticed. For instance, he will foresee and respond to the needs of the seminarians, evaluate all his colleagues and each of the candidates positively, be understanding and draw attention to the positive points of every person and event... His

---

[5] We will come back to this point in chapter IV when we speak about pastoral formation.

encouragement and his accurate guidance are also necessary so that each candidate will appreciate and exercise this virtue.

Christ, Model and Center of Priestly Life

Christian holiness consists above all in union with Christ. The Father "chose us in him before the foundation of the world, that we should be holy and blameless before him. He destined us in love to be his sons through Jesus Christ" (Ep 1:4-5). In the priest, this truth acquires a special strength. The first chapter reminded us that the essence of the priesthood is identification with Christ the priest. We observed that a merely "sacramental" or functional assimilation is not enough. The priest has been chosen to *be* another Christ in his personal life and even in his disposition. The young man called to the priesthood must strive enthusiastically to make Christ the *model* and the *center* of his personal life and his future pastoral ministry, and hence the chief task of his years of formation is his own *transformation into Christ.*

We spoke of "formation as transformation" in the sense of a dynamic process in which one climbs from the knowledge of a reality to the interior appraisal and acceptance of its value, and finally, to the personal living of this value. Transformation into Christ follows the same development: it is a process which goes from *knowledge* to *love,* and from *love* to *imitation.* Finally, a man who knows and loves Christ will experience the ardent desire to *communicate Him* to others; and the best means to do so is through the witness he gives in his own imitation of the Master.

EXPERIENTIAL KNOWLEDGE OF JESUS CHRIST

The first thing is to *know Jesus Christ*... but not only the Christ of theology. A seminarian who is satisfied with a deep study of the object of Christology has stayed in the realm of pure theory. And no one loves or gives his life for a theory. It might be enough for a scholar, but never for a good priest (and not even for a good theologian). Rather, we are talking about the knowledge that two living people have of each other. Through the experience of faith, we must bring each seminarian to a personal experience of the living and real Christ, who draws near to him through the

Gospel, is present in the Eucharist, and who wants to converse with him in personal prayer.[6] The seminarian should be familiar with Christ's standards, his way of thinking, and of evaluating people, circumstances and events. He should know Our Lord, the depth of his love and his sensitivity. He should know his way of acting, his reactions and attitudes. But above all, he has to experience the Lord's personal relationship with him when they meet in the intimacy of prayer, in the embrace of the Eucharist, or when they are heart to heart in the sacrament of pardon.

A young man will more easily grow enthusiastic for Christ if the formators know how to present an attractive Christ, that is to say, the authentic Christ of the Gospel, who wins over anyone who does not resist beauty, truth and love. Some people are afraid to present some of the less "agreeable" facets of the Christ of the Gospel, such as his conscious and loving adherence to the cross and self-denial in order to fulfill the will of the Father (cf. Jn 10:17-18). They think that a softened Christ is more acceptable to the young candidates. They think He is more appealing, more in accord with human standards. Yet only when a man knows and loves the real Christ in his human and divine nature, in the mystery of his death and resurrection, does he find in Him the challenge that satisfies his most profound yearnings for transcendence and donation.

PERSONAL, REAL, PASSIONATE AND ALL-ABSORBING LOVE

Personal knowledge is the door to *love*. Our effort is to shape a deep love for Christ in the candidate's heart. Usually, the first profound experience of knowledge and intimate contact with Christ causes a torrent of affection to burst forth in the new seminarian. Attention! This is genuine and noble affection, but we should not assume that he has reached the mature love which brings real self-giving. Formators should always explain that love is much more than an emotion or the vague appreciation of a person.

We could summarize in a few epithets the principal characteristics of the love for Christ. It is a *personal, real, passionate* and *all-absorbing* love.

---

[6] Cf. OT 8.

It is personal because it affects us as persons in the most intimate part of our being, and is directed to Christ as a living person and not merely as an object of veneration. A priest's love for Jesus Christ goes out towards a person who is both God and man, and its force is born and nurtured through divine grace. It cannot be an ethereal love, purely "spiritual," separated from real life. When Christ calls a young man to surrender himself to his love He does not want him to be any less a man. On the contrary, He wants him to fulfill completely his potential for love and wants him to love with all his heart.

Real love is the opposite of a theoretical, sentimental or simply false love, based on externals or poetic phrases. Real love is "carried out." It permeates and directs everyday life. It makes us imitate and abandon ourselves to the one we love. It is expressed in effective deeds.

True love for Christ is also passionate. Certainly there are degrees of love, and we do not all love in the same way nor with the same intensity. It depends on a person's temperament, his formation, and the absolutely free gift of the Lord who is the source of love. Yet love for the person of Christ, our Creator and Redeemer, the Friend who gave his life for his friends (cf. Jn 15:13), cannot be conceived of as anything short of a true passion of love. It is love which penetrates the depths of our being, and which is resilient and enthusiastic, strong as death (cf. Sg 8:6). It is a love capable of self-giving in difficult moments, a love that can even bring us to heroism.

Although love for Christ is an all-absorbing love it does not mean that a seminarian cannot love anyone else. On the contrary, love for Christ makes a person capable of loving more. Love for Christ gives strength to our love for Mary, for the Church, for the Pope, for all people. It is all-absorbing insofar as it should be the center of a priest's heart and life. His love for others (family, friends, and all the people entrusted to his ministry) finds its fulcrum and standard in his love for his Lord. This is the unmistakable meaning of Christ's demand that for his sake his followers leave father, mother, etc.

Thus, it is necessary to teach every seminarian, from his very first steps towards the priesthood, to live his daily life in a climate of intimate and profound friendship with Jesus Christ, discovering more and more each day the privileged love He offers him. It is a love from which no one will be able to separate him (cf. Rm 8:39). God forbid that a candidate should reach the day of his priestly consecration and find that he lives distant from Christ and his friendship! Because only for Christ can we live and give meaning to a life which demands so many renunciations. Only for Christ and his Kingdom can we joyfully live the consecration of our heart in the promise of chastity. Only for Him can we love the spirit of poverty, characteristic of the priesthood, that gives us a sense of security far beyond what money or power can give. Only for Him can we live our promise of obedience even in little things. And only for Christ and for his Kingdom can we be faithful until death, for fidelity is made of constancy and perseverance and effort.

The aspirant to the priesthood who longs for this intimate friendship with Jesus Christ, must be aware that it is a gift of God, and that all his personal effort will be in vain if God does not bless it and make it fruitful. We should invite him to pray insistently and to leave himself open to grace, in the firm conviction that God, more than anyone, desires to give him this gift.

IMITATION OF CHRIST, THE PERFECT MODEL

A person in love thinks of, tries to be with and wants to be like the one he loves. Anyone who truly loves Christ is carried along by love's dynamism and takes the next step: *imitation.*

Jesus Christ called his apostles to be with Him and to accompany Him in his apostolic work, and later He sent them out to preach (cf. Mk. 3:14). While they were with the Lord, they knew where He lived (cf. Jn 1:39), what He did during the day, and above all, they came to know Him intimately: his way of thinking, feeling, wanting, acting and reacting... On various occasions they heard from his lips the invitation to imitate Him in the practice of the virtues (cf. Mt 11:29; Jn 13:15) or the command to act in a specific way in certain situations (cf. Mt 10:5-10). This is how they gradually learned that the invitation to follow Him included not only a physical following but also a spiritual one: to be like Him. The "sequela Christi" was also the "*imitatio* Christi."

The imitation of Christ cannot be reduced to mere external or accidental resemblance. Rather it entails, as it did for the apostles, true interior transformation. The candidate for the priesthood has to aspire, humbly but tenaciously, to think like Christ, to feel, love and act like Him.

Thus the figure of Jesus Christ just as the Gospels present Him to us, with all the details of his personality, with every one of his attitudes, is the point of reference that enlightens and guides the priest's spiritual work. In the Gospel, the seminarian discovers many facets of Christ that serve as models for his future priestly ministry. But he discovers, above all, Christ's radical attitude of self-giving to the Father, to his mission, and to others, an attitude which defines the fundamental disposition of the true priest. Christ came to the world to glorify the Father (cf. Jn 17:4) and to save humanity by his free and loving sacrifice on the cross. He knew that He was sent by God to mankind (cf. Jn 16:28) and found the meaning of his life and its definite direction in the fulfillment of this mission. He lived in continual contact with his Father (cf. Jn 14:10). He had clear knowledge of his origin and destiny (cf. Jn 8:42), and this intimate conviction in every moment determined his conduct in his relationship with his Father and with those around Him. He was the man of God, the God-Man.

It is not difficult to teach the seminarian to look to Christ always as his model. It is enough to make a reference to Him, just as the Gospels present Him to us, when we want to illustrate a virtue, or when we invite the candidate to correct some error in his judgment or conduct, etc. Publicly and privately, we must counsel our seminarians: "Look to Him," and remind them of the words of his Father: "Listen to Him" (Mt 17:5).

COMMUNICATE THE LOVE OF CHRIST TO OTHERS

Love engenders love. True love is never self-centered, just for ourselves. The ardent desire to make Christ known is the most genuine fruit and the greatest proof that a seminarian has matured in his love for the Master. Whoever has discovered the breadth, the length, the height and the depth of the love of Christ for all people (cf. Ep 3:17) and has been captivated by Him, responding with generosity, cannot help wanting to make this love known to the greatest number of people possible. Apostolic zeal comes from love.

Moreover, when we work for a cause, our interior appreciation for it increases. Any activity that draws the seminarian out of himself, prompts his self-giving to others and permits him to communicate his knowledge and love of Christ, will strengthen his love for Him.

From among the many difficulties that can arise as we grow in love for Christ, let us briefly comment on two of them. The first one derives from the fact that we only see Christ through faith. He is not physically before us. So, to some, our love for Him might appear make-believe or insubstantial, something that doesn't fill their desire to love, to be loved, to feel affection, and to feel accompanied and consoled. This is a very real difficulty. At the beginning, faith has to support this incipient love. Later, the experience of Christ's friendship will also help to overcome this difficulty.

To know and love Christ means to conform one's life to his commandments: "If you love me, you will keep my commandments" (Jn 14:15); "by this may we be sure that we know Him, if we keep his commandments" (1 Jn 2:3); "he who says that he abides in Him ought to walk in the same way in which He walked" (1 Jn 2:6). Herein lies the second difficulty, which Saint John masterfully describes: "Every one who does evil hates the light, and does not come into the light, lest his deeds should be exposed" (Jn 3:20). When we have an attachment to sin, to its consequences and its roots, love and growth in love is a real struggle. Therefore, when a young man finds it difficult or even impossible to love Christ, we should ask ourselves if he has been generous enough to leave the darkness and its works behind and to come into the light. He may have to start from there.

The Priest, Man of the Church

Love for Christ leads us to the Church. *How is it going to be possible to love Christ without loving the Church, since the most beautiful testimony given concerning Christ is that of Saint Paul: "He loved the Church and gave himself up for her (Ep 5:25)"?*[7] A priest loves the Church because Christ loved her and as Christ loved her.She is mother and teacher of his Christian faith, the continuation of the Lord's mission, and the beginning of his Kingdom on earth. His Christian and priestly vocation

---

[7] Paul VI, Encyclical letter *Evangelii nuntiandi,* n. 16.

was born in the Church and is nourished by her. He is aware that he has been chosen by Christ as a priest of the Church and for the Church, and that she has confirmed this choice and has consecrated him in the name of God.

A formation center for future priests is a true ecclesial community. One of its principal functions is to forge the seminarians as true *men of the Church*. Not functionaries of the Church, but rather Christians who sincerely love this "Ecclesia" which Christ founded and loved. The formator should help the candidates mature in a *profound love for the Church*. It must be real love which watches over, suffers for, prays for, fights for, excuses, praises and understands intimately our Mother. Like all true loves, it is both *affective and effective*. It is love that contemplates the Church in faith, accepts her in obedience, *makes her grow* in the apostolate, and *sanctifies her* in one's life.

AFFECTIVE LOVE

To form an affective love of the Church, it is essential to instill a profound *knowledge* of the Church. It has to be a sound theological knowledge as well as a heartfelt knowledge of her living and present reality. With a little imagination it is easy to find ways to keep the seminarians abreast of church events: news boards, magazines, conferences, seminars... This not only applies to the universal Church but also to the seminarians' own local church. Activities can be organized to bring the seminarians into contact with the various institutions of the diocese, and to work in its pastoral programs in order to familiarize themselves with its reality from within. We cannot love what we do not know.

Since the Church is not solely a human organization it is necessary to foster *faith* in her supernatural reality, and this is the only way for a future priest to acquire a genuine "sensus Ecclesiae." We should help the seminarians to see with faith and to *meditate in faith* on the global truth of God's Church. Without this faith they will only know the shell of the Church regardless of how many cultural and experiential notions they pick up about her.

Human and supernatural knowledge of the Church will engender affection and love for her. The seminarians will then have a lively *interest for the Church,* her successes and her problems, her doctrine and her missionary work... They will rejoice with the Christians who rejoice, and suffer with those who suffer. The Church will be their Church.

EFFECTIVE LOVE

Affection for the Church must become effective attitudes and accomplishments. Priestly formation must educate the seminarians so that they are able *to accept her in obedience.* They should accept the Church with deep faith in the divine mystery that she involves, and understand that Christ intended to found a people to be guided by shepherds. True love for the Church extends to all those who represent Christ her Head and the various institutions that are the structure of her human reality. We must never think that we are forming our future priests well if we are not helping them grow in this full, mature acceptance. Formators must look for ways to assist the seminarians to become very familiar with the Church's directives, to maturely understand their meaning, and to put their faith into practice when it is difficult to understand them or accept them. Everyone knows no person or institution is perfect. But love doesn't demand perfection. Love welcomes the other "as is" and in self-giving helps the other to become better. In this way, the priest's obedience to the universal or local Church teaching must be much more than servile observance. It is a reflection of Christ's obedience to his Father. It should be warm, active and enterprising obedience. Obedience grows more easily and deeply if it is reinforced by adherence (not only theological, but heartfelt adherence) to the Vicar of Christ and to one's own bishop.

Love of the Church makes future priests want to *see her grow by means of their apostolate:* "To build Church." Seminarians have to consider their future pastoral service as an ecclesial service. They should understand that their priestly mission only has meaning in the Church, for the Church and rooted in the Church's supernatural and human mission.

Lastly, a priest must also *sanctify the Church through his own holy life.* Mystically united in one body with the entire people of God, he knows that his personal holiness enriches her, his testimony builds her, and his service in the ministry of the word and in the administration of the sacraments vivifies her in the Spirit of God.

Mary, Mother of Priests

On Calvary when He said to his Mother: Woman, behold your
son... He established a universal motherhood... Our attention
nevertheless focuses on the election of him who was then
called to become the son of Mary. John was a priest!... Jesus
did not limit Himself to entrusting to Mary this mission with
respect to priests. He also addressed Himself to John in order
to introduce him into a filial relationship with Mary: Behold
your mother.[8]

Since Calvary, Jesus Christ has wished that his Mother and his
priests remain united forever. Every priest, following the example of John,
must welcome Mary into his home so that she can form his priestly heart
as she did her divine Son's. Since that afternoon Mary has become the great
formator of priests. From that moment she has protected them from
dangers and with motherly concern has helped them to persevere.

When we program the seminarian's spiritual formation we cannot
forget this facet of priestly spirituality. It is not a question of teaching him
"devotions." We must show him the authentic, rich, and solid devotion to
the Mother of God which the Church proposes. The Church's one devotion
to Mary has different aspects. It is profound *veneration* when she medi-
tates on the unique dignity of the Blessed Virgin who became the mother
of Christ through the work of the Holy Spirit. It is *ardent love* when she
considers Mary's spiritual motherhood of all the members of the Mystical
Body. It takes the form of *trusting invocation* when she seeks Mary's
intercession as advocate and helper. Devotion becomes *loving service*
when the Church discovers the example of the humble handmaid of the
Lord who has become the Queen of Mercy. It materializes as *practical
imitation* when she contemplates the holiness and the virtues of Mary, full
of grace. It becomes deep *admiration* when the Church, though still a
pilgrim on earth, sees in Mary as in a most pure reflection all that she longs
and hopes for. This devotion is also *attentive study,* for the Church sees in
the Co-redemptrix the prophetic fulfillment of her own future.

---

[8] John Paul II, *Angelus,* February 11, 1990.

Therefore, an aspirant to the priesthood cannot limit his devotion to Mary to a greater or lesser number of devotions and prayers, nor to a detached study of Mariology. He must go further, to the imitation of her virtues;[9] above all her faith, hope and charity, her obedience, her humility and her unconditional cooperation in the mystery of redemption.[10] She is the most complete model of the new creature born of the redeeming power of Christ and the most eloquent witness to the newness of life brought forth by the resurrection of the Lord.

Those in charge of formation have to take pains to provide simple and practical means for each seminarian to develop a cordial, filial relationship with his heavenly Mother. For example, they can set aside a specific time in the daily schedule for praying the rosary, give special importance to the Marian liturgical feasts, etc.

In this way, as the seminarian draws closer to ordination he will grow in the habit of speaking with his heavenly Mother. It is a habit he will maintain during all of his priestly life, placing in her hands his own fidelity, perseverance and the success of all his apostolic endeavors.

Some Priestly Virtues

Imitation of Christ the Priest becomes reality by practicing virtue. Besides the three theological virtues, there are many others which enrich and embellish the life of a Christian. Priestly spirituality, as we said earlier, is Christian spirituality in which certain traits proper to the ministerial service are emphasized. In this sense, we can speak of "priestly virtues," i.e., Christian virtues which especially configure the life and mission of a minister of Jesus Christ.

CHASTITY FOR THE SAKE OF THE KINGDOM OF HEAVEN

By the promise of celibacy formally pronounced on the day of his diaconate ordination, the future priest totally, definitively and exclusively consecrates himself to the one supreme love of Christ. In this way he preserves his complete affective and practical availability for the service

---

[9] Cf. LG 67.
[10] Cf. PO 18; OT 8.

of the Kingdom of Heaven (cf. Mt 19:12), and his life becomes an invitation for all people to contemplate and hope for the future goods.

The promise of celibacy is not a mere juridical formality. On the contrary, it is a profound gift of self, born of a heart in love. Celibacy is not improvised on the day of ordination. It is important for the seminarian to form his heart from the beginning of his priestly formation and orient it towards the exclusive love of Jesus Christ.

As formators we must explain to the seminarians the deep meaning of celibacy, which the western Church asks of the Catholic priest, making them understand its reason, its value, its beauty and its demands.

We should also help them to acquire a correct and balanced view of the human body. They should appreciate it for its true value within the framework of the dignity of the human person: the body is the work of God and the temple of the Holy Spirit (cf. 1 Cor 6:19). One should respect it in Christian modesty, neither scorning it as sinful nor making it an idol by substituting worship of God with cult of the body. Along these lines, it is also important to give the seminarians, in the right moment and in the correct way, a balanced, serene, clear and appropriate sexual education.[11]

The renunciation of marriage in celibacy for the Kingdom in no way implies fear, repression or contempt of it. On the contrary, it will only be a pleasing gift to Christ if the candidate to the priesthood recognizes the value of marriage, and if he freely, nobly and generously renounces for Him what he holds to be a great good.[12] Formation in the seminary must present a correct view of woman which stresses her personal dignity and the specific values of her femininity as a richness desired by God for the Church and for the world.

To teach them chastity is also to teach them to *channel,* not to *repress,* their natural tendencies and passions, according to their vocation. Repression impedes maturing. As we said, God does not want the priest to

---

[11] Cf. RFIS 48.

[12] "Do we, perhaps, wish to undervalue marriage and the vocation to family life? Or have we accepted the Manichaean disdain for the body and its functions? Do we, perhaps, wish to scorn love which brings man and wife together in marriage so that they form 'one flesh' (cf. Gn 2:24; Mt 19:6) How can we think in this way if we know, believe and proclaim, together with St. Paul, that marriage is a 'great mystery' as referred to Christ and the Church?" (John Paul II, *Letter Novo Incipiente,* n. 8; cf. FC 16; *Wednesday audience,* April 21, 1982; April 28, 1983; May 5, 1983; June 30, 1983).

be any less a man. He wants him to be an integral man with all his potential in tune with the vocation for which he has been created. We should teach the seminarian to employ all the rich stock of his passions positively and enthusiastically in the service of his vocation and priestly mission.

The candidate's true *affective maturity* consists in *the harmonious integration of his capacity to love and his need to be loved with his own state in life.* Not limited to the correct integration of his sexuality in his personality, it encompasses his entire capacity for interpersonal relationships. It implies the orientation of all his affections and, as far as possible, all his sentiments, towards the ideal he has chosen for himself. This is one of the keys for developing a firm identity. A divided person suffers an internal tug-of-war between what he claims to be and what his uncontrolled affections impose on him.

Ordinarily, the experience of *total and exclusive love* becomes the best catalyst for affective maturity. For many people, preparation for marriage and married life itself are the natural occasions to achieve this maturity. Affectivity matures under the warming rays of true personal love. The affectivity of a man called to live only for God will mature if it grows in the light of a total and exclusive love for God. And this is the fruitful source of his universal self-giving to others.

Once we don't lose sight of this, the affective maturing of the seminarians is not as complicated as some people make it out to be. Everything that encourages this integration of the natural affective and sexual tendencies with the ideal of consecration to God and the celibate state of the priest, works positively towards this maturing. Everything which in some way makes this integration difficult is negative and should be avoided.

For an accurate appraisal of the positive and negative factors we should keep in mind the principle of a *realistic view of man/realistic pedagogy* which we mentioned in the previous chapter. Tendencies and passions that a seminarian, like any other human being, carries with him, are natural impulses which the Creator wants him to have. Yet sin has created a situation of *disorder* in us, and affected our ability to direct these impulses with our reason and will. We should not assume that a conscious and free choice, as profound as it may be, is in itself sufficient to correctly channel these passions. They are instinctive and blind, and always seek their own objectives, no matter how far the subject has travelled along the path of interior purification. Lives of numerous saints and Christian mystics abundantly illustrate the point. The presence of an external stimulus which corresponds to an internal tendency will cause a specific reaction in the direction of the stimulus. If the direction is contrary to the priest's definitive option of consecration to Christ, it provokes disorder and interior tension. It turns into a serious difficulty for the harmonious integration of the whole person in accord with the ideal he has chosen.

A seminarian who reads anything and everything, who indiscriminately watches movies, shows or other forms of entertainment from the endless selection our permissive society offers, will easily run into strong stimuli that incite his natural tendencies against his vocation to priestly chastity. Certain types of relationships with women arouse sentiments of affection and, eventually, love in a man. If a seminarian permits himself such a relationship he is bound to fall prey to those sentiments. They would be a serious threat to his affective maturation, for his vocation demands the total surrender of his heart and life to Christ and his Kingdom.

Nature has its own laws. We cannot play with them. The formators must be very *realistic and sensible* in this field. But not only that: they must also be *just*. By what right can we expose our seminarians — or permit that they expose themselves —to experiences that endanger the chastity that forms part of the vocation to which they have been called by God, and not by us? What right have we to allow or make them foster, during their formation years, a type of relationship that later they will have to renounce by their promise of celibacy?

Good sense is not narrow-mindedness. To educate the seminarian for affective maturity is not to isolate him from the world. It is equally erroneous to expect that the tendencies proper to every human being are not present in him. Education for chastity consists in helping him to *channel,* not *repress* his tendencies. It must be an eminently positive, open, joyful task, with the joy of a person who offers all his renunciations out of love.

Acquiring this maturity ordinarily requires an ample period of time since it is intimately linked to the individual's physical and psychological development. Both the formator and the candidate must keep in mind that, because of diverse circumstances (physiological, psychological, etc.) one can have periods of greater or lesser difficulty, of stronger or weaker affections, of greater or lesser temptations. All of us should proceed prudently, serenely and tenaciously in applying the means which the Church, after long experience and with profound knowledge of man, advises for the acquisition and safeguard of priestly chastity.

"BEING RICH, HE MADE HIMSELF POOR."

In Christ's life we admire his total and constant *liberty of spirit.* Christ was a free man because He had only one Master, the Father, and because He did not attach his heart to any created thing. He wished to strip Himself of his divine splendor in order to make Himself like us (cf. Ph 2:7), "Being rich, he became poor" (cf. 2 Cor 8:9). He did not attach his heart to the goods of this world. Yet He never scorned the things of the earth and, when the occasion arose, He used them with that same liberty of spirit with which on other occasions He did without them. The concept of *priestly poverty* finds its origin in this reflection.

The future priest, whose portion and inheritance is the Lord (cf. Nm 18:20), has to seek to imitate this example of Christ, gratefully receiving the material goods which Providence allots to him, using them moderately, responsibly and disinterestedly. He should detach his heart from the desire to possess anything that is unnecessary, superfluous or improper for a person who wants to follow his Lord more closely. His poor heart will open his eyes to discover Christ in the most needy, and make them the privileged focus of his pastoral charity.

The formator must encourage this *filial and complete confidence in the Providence of God* (Mt 6:25-34), in order to prevent the seminarian's personal security from resting on material things alone. Little by little, avarice can make its way into a priestly heart, especially in certain environments. A priest possessed by this vice is a sad scandal for the faithful and greatly limits his apostolic action. But it doesn't always take a surplus of goods for the human heart to grow attached. Greed affects the rich and poor alike, either by possessing riches, comforts and privileges, or simply by desiring to possess them.

In order to love spiritual poverty the aspirant to the priesthood must cultivate it by detaching his heart from the things he uses, avoiding vain ostentation, and living as a pilgrim on the path to the eternal possession of God. Both the seminary environment and the formator should inspire the candidate to appreciate this virtue. He has to experience how unpretentious evangelical poverty keeps the soul open to God and to others, and creates a spiritual climate of interior docility, prayer, dialogue and collaboration. Gospel poverty nourishes hope, engenders justice and mercy, increases love, and grants serenity, peace and liberty of spirit. When he has tasted these fruits, poverty will become for his soul a precious good, a coveted treasure.

Yet the spirit of priestly poverty and freedom from attachments is not the same as misery, nor is it in principle opposed to the use of material goods in one's apostolic work. Christ lamented that the sons of darkness are more astute than the sons of light (cf. Lk 16:8). He knew that they make use of all the means within their reach to achieve their goals. Also the priest, even during his years of formation, has to be diligent in the use of anything that can promote the cause of Christ and better serve the Church and her faithful. Not to do so under the pretext of evangelical poverty is a misinterpretation of poverty's true spirit and a defense for either false human prudence or our laziness in fulfilling our mission.

Because of the poverty he lives the priest is also subject to the law of work, and therefore he has to make the best use of his time, keeping in mind, certainly, the words of Christ, "The worker is worth his wages" (Mt 10:10), but also the words of Saint Paul to the Thessalonians, "If anyone will not work, let him not eat" (2 Th 3:10). There is nothing less edifying to Christians than a lazy priest who does not make good use of his time.

HE HUMBLED HIMSELF BECOMING OBEDIENT UP TO DEATH

We have recalled that priestly holiness consists, more than anything else, in identification with Christ the Priest. One of the most outstanding characteristics of the priestly figure of Jesus is his *obedience* to the Father. This was the greatest expression of his love. According to Paul, the obedience of Christ is what justifies mankind (cf. Rm 5:19). Thus he invites the Christians to have "this mind among yourselves, which was in Christ Jesus, who... humbled Himself and became obedient unto death, even death on a cross" (Ph 2:5,8). This is the path of Redemption: "Although he was a Son, he learned obedience through what he suffered; and being made perfect he became the source of eternal salvation to all who obey him" (Heb 5:8-9).

A priest, called to be "another Christ," has also been called to practice this virtue, which can be considered the virtue *par excellence* since it requires the loving surrender of the greatest gift man has received: his freedom. Freedom is the gift from God that we love most after the gift of life and it is the hardest to give up. If we do so, it is only out of love and as a gift in imitation of Christ. Obedience is the most difficult virtue to exercise since it is the most radical expression of the free and constant, total giving of our whole selves.

Like their Master, priests have also been called to *consecrate their free will to the service of God and their fellow Christians, accepting and carrying out in a spirit of faith the commands and suggestions of the Pope, their bishop and other superiors.*[13]

The key to this virtue (which from the day of one's priestly ordination becomes a promise to one's bishop) is found in the daily practice both of a principle of faith given to us through Revelation, "He who hears you, hears me" (Lk 10:16), and of the dynamism of love which longs to identify its own free will with the will of the beloved, "Because I do not seek my own will, but the will of Him who sent me" (Jn 5:30, 6:38). As Christ said on another occasion, "If anyone loves me, he will keep my word" (Jn 14:23).

We should not forget either that Christ's obedience to his Father also became submission to those who had authority over Him (cf. Lk 2:51). This is the example and ultimate foundation of Christian obedience as Peter affirms in his first letter, "Be subject for the Lord's sake to every human institution" (1 P 2:13).

When the candidate learns to obey like this, enlightened by these truths, he will always see his superiors as the representatives of Jesus Christ. He will not compare his own wisdom, age, experience or perfection with his superior's.

It is not the obedience of a servant, but that of one who is born with the "glorious liberty of the children of God" (Rm 8:21). It is not blind obedience, but motivated. It is not only practical, but spiritual. It is not merely tolerated, but is prompt and joyful. It is not passive, but active and dynamic. When a man obeys out of love he is not satisfied with a simple mechanical execution of the command, but he uses all the strength of his

---

[13] PO 15.

intelligence and will, all his natural and spiritual gifts, to carry out the directives he has received.

Christian and priestly obedience are rooted in the love of Christ and *humility*. We are not interested so much that the seminarians submit, but rather that they obey freely.

This is why personal initiative does not go against obedience when exercised with a right intention and proper dependence. We could rather say that personal initiative is part of active obedience. Initiative in one's own assignment (pastoral work, teaching, mass media...) and in proposing new apostolic endeavors and pastoral goals to the Bishop or competent authorities. Without initiative, obedience would be servile and bear meager fruits. Without obedience, initiative becomes selfish independence and keeps us distant from God's blessing.

To achieve this ideal in the candidates, formators besides being models of this virtue[14] must help by exercising their authority in a spirit of service to the candidates, in such a way as to express the charity with which God loves them. They must govern them as children of God, respecting their dignity, listening to them with interest and attention.

Gentle and Humble of Heart

On very few occasions did Christ openly present himself as a model of a specific virtue. Nevertheless, there is one virtue which He lived in a special way and about which He said to all Christians, "Learn from me, for I am meek and humble of heart" (Mt 11:29).

Through personal experience, the formator knows human pride makes humility a difficult virtue to accept. Only Christ's example enlightens this virtue, gives it meaning and transcendence, and keeps it from being falsified. Humility is the truth and justice with which a Christian presents himself before God, before others and before his own eyes. It is therefore closely related to obedience, since humility makes obedience possible and perfects it.

An important virtue for every Christian, it is crucial for a priest, for "he himself is beset with weakness" (Heb 5:3), he carries his "treasure in earthen vessels" (2 Cor 4:7), and because, in spite of all this, he must take

---

[14] Cf. RFIS 49.

Christ's place, "to show that the transcendent power belongs to God and not to us" (2 Cor 4:7). A priest has to be humble, following the example of his Master who "came not to be served, but to serve" (Mt 20:28).

When humility is real it does not instill cowardice, timidity or negligence in fulfilling one's own priestly responsibilities, nor makes us run from personal fulfillment. Instead, humility confirms the resolve of the man who realizes that he is an instrument of God. It inspires apostolic daring because it does not weigh the dangers according to the individual's strength. It never takes the credit for success, nor is it frightened by failure, rather it refers all things to God. A humble priest is guaranteed to be a zealous priest. Apostolic fruits depend on the power of Christ, and not on our own qualities, aptitude or effort, for without Him nothing can be done in the order of grace (cf. Jn 15:5).

Both formator and candidate have to realize that all progress in the knowledge and experience of Christ, and in spiritual life in general, is tied to our humility and based on it as its foundation. The more humble a seminarian is, the more full of God will he be; he will be more just, more similar to Christ, and more open, generous and understanding of his neighbor.

We should help the seminarian to live humility by inviting him to meditate often on God, on his divine attributes and perfections and instruct him to contemplate the great examples of humility which Jesus Christ left us during his mortal life and now offers us in the Eucharist. The soul that tastes the goodness of God in prayer will never be proud.

Another necessary ingredient for progress in humility is meditation and calm reflection about ourselves, recognizing frankly the gifts received from God and our own imperfections, falls and limitations. This attitude leads to the responsibility of the faithful administrator who maturely uses his talents, recognizing his successes and thanking God for them.

Meekness, is a vital component of a priest's heart. When a person is afflicted, or a repentant sinner seeks pardon, or when someone's conscience needs enlightenment, the gentle heart of the priest who welcomes him is already transforming, opening the path to grace and fostering docility. On the contrary, harshness and insensitivity can cause serious and sometimes irreversible damage.

Meekness, which accompanies and perfects humility, is cultivated through patience and self-control, but, above all, through love and understanding. One's character or temperament may make it more difficult for some than for others, but regardless, it is an indispensable virtue in the future priest.

FOR THE GLORY OF THE FATHER

As a fruit of humility, the aspirant to the priesthood must seek in everything and above all else the glory of God and the salvation of humanity, renouncing his own glory, overcoming his vanity and pride, and never doing things so as to be seen by others (cf. Mt 6:5). This was the basic direction of all Christ's life (cf. Jn 11:4, 13:31-32, 14:13) This should be the fundamental orientation of every Christian and priestly life. Anything else is fruitless, a waste of time, and sooner or later will lead to frustration and deceit.

Right from the start, we should remind the candidate to perform all his daily acts with *purity of intention:* his personal prayer, Eucharistic celebration, academic activities, sports, his community life in the seminary, his social relationships and apostolic work... and insist that he offer all his acts to God, the source of all good and the purpose of all our labor.

There are a few simple ways that can help to develop this virtue: beginning and ending each activity of the seminary program with an offering and a thanksgiving; brief moments of reflection throughout the day to sincerely examine our intentions and motivations; the serene correction of our intention when we discover that we have gone astray, and gratitude to God when we find our intentions are proper.

"IF YOU WISH TO COME AFTER ME..."

Even though the cross is not the goal of Christian life it is nevertheless an indispensable condition in order to follow Christ who, in order to save us, humbled Himself unto death, even death on across (cf. Ph 2:8). He said, "If any man would come after me, let him deny himself and take up his cross and follow me" (Mt 16:24). Paul compares the life of a Christian with the training an athlete goes through in order to win a competition: "Every athlete exercises self-control in all things. They do it to receive a perishable wreath." (1 Cor 9:25). And he confesses that he does not flail away aimlessly, but rather controls his body and disciplines it so as not to be disqualified (cf. 1 Cor 9:27). Self-denial is not an end in itself. It is a necessary means to reach the goal of personal sanctification and apostolic fruitfulness.

Thinking of our seminarians we have to be aware that abnegation by itself has no meaning or reason for being, nor does it hold any attraction for human nature which is inclined to indulge in every possible satisfaction. Only because of the cross of Christ and through its power, does self-denial become a necessary condition for holiness and apostolic efficacy. It is the path chosen by Christ to carry out his work of salvation and to bear abundant fruit: "Unless a grain of wheat falls into the earth and dies, it remains alone; but if it dies, it bears much fruit" (Jn 12:24).

Far from conveying contempt, disgust or indifference for personal values or the positive side of worldly reality, this virtue tends to free our hearts from selfishness which is the root of all personal and social evils, and it purifies them from all the disordered tendencies which close us to the love of God and neighbor. It is also an effective way to form a firm will that can tame the whims of our sentiments and emotions. With it we control our unruly emotional reactions and we strengthen our character.

Self-denial is also necessary for the aspirant to the priesthood as a preparation for his apostolate. All his work as a minister of the Lord will require dedication, enterprise, self-giving and perseverance. These are qualities which depend on great selflessness and, for the good of others, acceptance of fatigue, opposition, difficulties, misunderstanding, partial failures...

As formators, we should give witness of self-sacrifice in our work. We should point out to the candidate the many opportunities that seminary life provides him to offer something to the Lord, from the moment he rises at a set time to when he retires after a full day of intense and love-filled work.

ZEAL FOR YOUR HOUSE CONSUMES ME

Christ's life had an essential program: fulfill the Father's will for the salvation of all men and women. This is the most profound explanation of his incarnation and his birth, his hidden life, his tireless preaching, his death and resurrection.

The priest has been called to participate in this same mission, prolonging it in history. We risk failure in our task as formators if we do not make sure that our seminarians acquire a burning apostolic zeal. It is necessary to help them to discover the love of Christ towards humanity, which is the fount and inspiration of all apostolic work. In this way they will desire to fight valiantly to announce and extend the Kingdom of Christ through fervent prayer, personal witness and intense apostolic work.

In the section on apostolic formation we will develop this theme more fully and give several suggestions to imbue the candidates' hearts with apostolic zeal.

ASSIMILATING THE FUNDAMENTAL TRUTHS

A priest, as teacher and guide, must enlighten the life of the faithful with the rays of Christian faith. He has been called to be a prophet, a herald of the true and definitive meaning of human life. And he has personally discovered the need to anchor his entire existence in this profound reality.

It is important to train our future priests to reflect in their personal prayer on the "fundamental truths" so as to make them part of their life. Among these is the truth of *creation,* which teaches us that life is an unmerited gift of God, reminds us that we are created and inspires us to humility. Another is the ultimate meaning of *life* as a pilgrimage and a mission. The undeniable reality of *death* as the necessary end of this road is also a basic truth in whose shadow *time* acquires its true value: we only live one life once and what we do not do now will remain undone forever. Lastly is the truth of *eternal life* which is the ultimate goal of our existence, the long-awaited embrace with our Creator and Redeemer.

The assimilation of these primordial truths solidifies the seminarian's spiritual life and opens the floodgates of Christian dynamism and optimism.

Some General Means for Spiritual Formation

We have outlined some of the principal elements of a seminarian's spiritual formation and mentioned some specific means for implanting certain virtues. But there are a few general and fundamental practices that are the basis for the whole process. They are means which form his personality for they put him in contact with the true sources of the spiritual life: the sacraments, prayer, and the Gospel. They draw him to God, form his heart as an apostle, continually open him to spiritual values, and sustain him in the task of his sanctification.

Far from "stealing time" from his study or the apostolate, these practices are the profound needs and the normal demands of an authentic Christian and priestly life of sanctity and fulfillment of the mission.[15] Without them a seminarian will not be a good follower of Christ, much less a good priest.

PRAYER

> In a certain way prayer is the first and last condition for conversion, spiritual progress and holiness. Perhaps in the last few years — at least in certain places — there has been too much discussion about the priesthood, the "identity" of the priest, the value of his presence in the modern world, etc., and, on the contrary, there has been too little prayer. Not enough value has been placed on living the priesthood through prayer, in order to make its authentic evangelical dynamism efficacious and confirm the priestly identity.[16]

Prayer is the source of light for the soul. In it the certainties of the faith are reinforced. Prayer generates love. In prayer our will identifies with the holy will of God. Prayer is a vigorous promoter of action: in it God fills us with zeal for his service and for our self-giving to others.

It is necessary to form the seminarian so that he wants to pray, learns to pray, and really does pray. The seminary must be a school of prayer, a place of prayer, and a community of prayer.

Therefore, the programs of a formation center should set aside certain moments exclusively for community and individual prayer. In the

---

[15] Cf. RFIS 54.
[16] John Paul II, *Letter Novo Incipiente,* n. 10.

section on liturgy, mention is made of community prayer. Here we wish to offer a few ideas on personal prayer.

More than a mental construct, prayer is a personal and intimate dialogue with God which enlightens and strengthens the decision to follow his will, in our mind, will and heart. Anyone who has lived in God's service knows by experience that he cannot live his day without dedicating an ample period of time to speaking personally and exclusively with Him. We cannot fill our day with activities, study and work... and then give the Lord the crumbs that fall from our table. Deep, meaningful prayer cannot be a hasty, rushed, careless practice, done to satisfy an obligation. Prayer needs its time so that the soul can enter into intimate contact with God, and the Holy Spirit can say what He wants.

Prayer does not have to be done exclusively at any one time or place. The time has come when true worshippers worship the Father in spirit and truth (cf. Jn 4:23). Nevertheless, it will benefit the seminarian enormously if we give his prayer life some external support. With this in mind, the schedule should mark a fixed time that everyone, in a climate of silence, devotes to prayer. Usually it is better to place it at the beginning of the day so that this encounter with God can set the spiritual and apostolic tone for the day. The candidates will understand, without the need for explanations, that prayer is not just another activity in their formation, but a very important time in the life of a priest. This also avoids the very real risk that laziness or their daily commitments induce them to put off their personal prayer "until tomorrow."

Some will prefer to pray in the chapel, before Christ in the Eucharist. Others prefer to retire to the solitude of their room. The important thing is that both the time and the place, as well as the atmosphere of the center, truly favor an encounter with God and with self.

Prayer as meditation is a difficult art which one learns through continual practice. We should therefore not expect the recently arrived young man to pray perfectly. We should rather help him from the start to get patiently and enthusiastically into this spiritual adventure.

> It is ... very important that the candidates to the priesthood form themselves in prayer. Above all, they must convince themselves that prayer is necessary for their priestly life and for their ministry. Then they must learn to pray, to pray well,

> to use all the moments of prayer in the best way, according to the method which gives them the best results. Finally, they must develop a liking for prayer, the desire and, at the same time, the will to pray.[17]

In the case of students of a high school seminary, we recommend that one of the formators, or even a gifted older seminarian, direct the meditation for them in the style of an exhortation or Gospel commentary. It should be a very practical prayer which touches their lives and teaches them to speak with God. Occasionally, brief periods of silence can be left for the students to reflect on some point already commented on, or to answer in their hearts a question which the director of the meditation has left for their consideration.

If they are young men just starting off in the major seminary, we will have to teach them the first steps of prayer. This means explaining to them at a proper pace the elements of discursive, affective, discursive-affective and contemplative prayer. They should be taught to put their whole person into their prayer: intelligence, will, affections, imagination, sentiments, problems, weaknesses, desires, etc. It also helps to start them off in guided prayer under the direction of a formator for the first few months. At the beginning the new seminarians normally find it helpful if their guide speaks during most of the prayer. Little by little, a greater margin for personal reflection can be left, until they have learned how to pray in practice and they can be loosed to pray on their own.

Given the importance of prayer in the life of a future priest, it should be a frequent topic in spiritual direction. This way the formator can assist each one to overcome the difficulties which arise with time, and encourage each in constant and joyful dedication to his daily encounter with God.

INTERIOR LIFE

The spirit of prayer is much more than the practice of prayer. A priest in search of holiness and apostolic fruit tries to live united to the Vine (cf. Jn 15:4). He is not content to fulfill his duty of morning prayer like one who pays his dues and then forgets about it. He attempts to live his entire day

---

[17] John Paul II, *Angelus*, March 11, 1990.

in the spirit of prayer; he enlivens his commitments, his work and his public life with a vigorous and fresh *interior life.*

We should show the seminarians the importance of this dimension of the spiritual life, and give them the practical advice they need to cultivate it.

Interior life is not a question, of course, of spending the entire day in the chapel or thinking only about God. It is much more simple and natural. It is the growth of the seed God deposits in each Christian's soul at baptism, grace and the supernatural virtues, according to one's particular vocation. Every priest should actively mature in his Christian and priestly vocation until he reaches the maturity of the fullness of Christ (cf. Ep 4:13), making use of every opportunity to strengthen and enrich his spiritual life.

In our personal effort to enrich our interior life there are many practices that can assist us, such as: interior and exterior silence; learning to live in simple, spontaneous and cordial dialogue with God, as with our best friend; offering Him and thanking Him for each of our activities throughout the day; cultivating openness and promptness to his inspirations; telling Him our joys, hopes, difficulties and failures; asking Him pardon for our faults and weaknesses; and uniting ourselves to Him through simple ejaculatory prayers which are genuine acts of love.

These activities hardly require any time, can be done anywhere and they maintain our union with God. In this way God's presence in our lives becomes progressively stronger, and it enlightens, strengthens and ennobles what is most human in us.

LITURGY AND SACRAMENTS

The liturgy is the summit toward which the activity of the Church is directed; it is also the fount from which all her power flows.[18] The priest is called to offer and preside over the worship of the faithful. It is one of his principal services to the community. Therefore, it is indispensable for the future priest to receive an adequate *liturgical formation* through which he understands the sacred rites and fully participates in them,[19] so that his

---

[18] SC 10.
[19] Cf. SC 17.

future liturgical and sacramental ministry truly serves to edify the faithful.

Specific theoretical and practical classes on the liturgy, its meaning and celebration can be of great help.

But certainly the most important thing is *our participation in the liturgy.* In a sense, liturgical life must be at the center of an ecclesial community such as the seminary ought to be. The schedules, the internal organization and even the physical layout of the seminary can reflect this centrality. The most effective liturgy class is a liturgical celebration that reflects its deepest meaning. Our liturgy should be dignified, full of life and active participation. And, since we are forming priests of the Catholic Church, in elementary honesty it is our duty to form them liturgically according to the guidelines of the universal and local Church. The seminary is not asked to produce great inventors of liturgical rites but good celebrants of the worship which Christ has entrusted to his Church.

The living witness of the formators in their way of celebrating and living the sacraments is decisive for the lasting liturgical formation of their students.

Sacrament of the Eucharist

The center of all liturgical life is the *celebration of the Eucharist.* As an ecclesial community the members of the seminary should gather daily to celebrate together the Lord's Supper, in his memory.

Likewise, it is appropriate to adorn the principal liturgical feasts and solemnities with a special Eucharistic celebration prepared by the students and formators with special dedication. The preparation should include a personal, prayerful reflection on the mysteries to be celebrated, special care in the decoration of the chapel, songs and Mass commentaries prepared by the students, etc.

By Eucharistic devotion we show appreciation for the gift of Himself which Christ made to us, in his desire to prove his overwhelming love for us to the end. His love must move the heart of the priest to a similar love, as well as to gratitude and respect. Perhaps someday, as priests alone in a parish or in mission territory, our young men will find their only refuge and their greatest comfort in the company of the Eucharist. It is necessary to teach them from their first years in the seminary to enjoy personal dialogue with Christ in this sacrament. As formators, we should encourage them to visit Christ often in the Eucharist. There, from the tabernacle, He reinforces good habits, forms character, nourishes virtues, consoles the afflicted, strengthens the weak, invites all those who draw near to Him to imitate Him, and fills the priest with graces to increase and sanctify the Mystical Body.

There are other possible activities that help to strengthen the Eucharistic sense of the students. Eucharistic hours can be organized periodically or on some special feastdays; adoration of the Eucharist on special occasions...

Sacrament of Reconciliation

The priest is the minister of God's forgiveness (cf. Jn 20:23). But he himself is also in need of mercy. It is hard for a priest to be a good confessor if he has not often had the profound personal experience of the sacrament of reconciliation.

A man in training for the priesthood should receive the sacrament of reconciliation often as a vital and renewing encounter with Christ and the Church. He, more than anyone else, must be aware of the need for a constant conversion of heart to accomplish God's will with perfection in his life.

When the sacrament of reconciliation is received often as recommended by the Church,[20] it favors self-knowledge, makes us grow in humility, helps us uproot bad habits, increases our delicacy of conscience, overcomes spiritual mediocrity and indolence, strengthens our will and leads our soul to more intimate identification with Jesus Christ.

To prepare better for the sacrament and to avoid falling into routine, seminarians could give a special penitential meaning to the day on which they plan to receive the sacrament of reconciliation. They can do this by making penance and conversion the theme of their personal prayer, by doing a special examination of conscience and by living the day with a greater attitude of reparation.

For the benefit of our spiritual growth, it usually helps to have the same confessor over a period of time. This is another means of assuring depth and progress in our work. But this should never limit the total liberty

---

[20] Cf. PO 18; CIC 246 § 4.

of the seminarians to go to any confessor they wish whether among the ordinary or extraordinary confessors or any other priest with the proper faculties.

Liturgy of the Hours

Another important part of the spiritual life of the future priest is the *liturgy of the hours.* Through it, the Church, the Bride of Christ, speaks to her Spouse,[21] fulfills the Lord's command to pray without ceasing, praises the Father, and intercedes for the salvation of mankind.

During his years of formation in the seminary, the future priest has to gradually learn to pray the Liturgy of the hours with attentive devotion, in private or in common. For private recitation it is good that the seminarian form the habit of taking enough time for it, praying without haste at the best time and in the right place. Although as a priest he will not always be able to pray the divine office in community, the seminarian will find this practice to be an aid to personal fervor and a means to live practically an ecclesial spirit in his prayer.

It is wise for us to include an explanation of the theological and liturgical sense of the office in our programs. As a source of piety and food for personal prayer[22] it is more fruitful if one can delve into the spirit of the psalms and readings, in order to understand better the lights that the Holy Spirit pours into his heart.

SPIRITUAL DIRECTION

One of our fundamental principles of priestly formation emphasized the importance of *self-formation.* We insisted that the candidate himself is the one who is chiefly responsible for his vocation and formation, but we also recalled that the formator's collaboration is necessary. We said that he must offer *personalized* help. A special moment for this personalized assistance is *spiritual direction.*[23]

---

[21] Cf. SC 84.

[22] Cf. SC 90.

[23] Cf. RFIS 55; CIC 246 § 4.

The name, handed down through tradition, should not mislead us as to its meaning. We could call it "spiritual dialogue," "personal formation conference," "spiritual orientation," etc. The name is secondary. What matters is that we understand it as a form of *cooperation* which a competent priest offers to a seminarian[24] in order to help him walk the path God has marked for him. The spiritual "director" is not there to "direct" the candidate as one steers a vehicle, but to help him to "find the way" and encourage him to follow it freely.

The principle, *realistic view of man/realistic pedagogy* illustrates how urgently seminarians need this assistance. All of us run the risk of falling into subjectivity and enclosing ourselves in a narrow view of things, above all, of ourselves. As the saying goes: "Nobody is a good judge of his own case." In times of trouble and darkness we are all thankful for the aid of someone who lends us a hand "from the outside" and helps us to see things better, or at least offers us his support, gives us encouragement and, why not, a word of consolation.

This is why the formator's help is necessary. Actually, the spiritual director, like every formator,[25] cooperates with the candidate in the measure in which he also cooperates with the Holy Spirit. We said his task is to help the seminarian to find the best way for his life. His place is not to point out the direction that he, as an experienced and prudent person, believes to be most opportune. It is, rather, to help the seminarian to discover what God wants in every moment. In this sense spiritual direction is a *dialogue among three people* (the candidate, the formator and the Holy Spirit) in which the first two try to listen to the voice of the third in order to understand what God's will is for the candidate.

The director must realize that if spiritual direction is to be a fruitful means for drawing a soul to God it has to be motivational, demanding and specific in its conclusions. It must not be just a way for the candidate to unburden himself. It has to be a periodic encounter to sustain the "progressive" nature of his formation. It has to go deep, because the search for the will of God commits the whole person with his intelligence, will, liberty and sentiments. It has to be cordial and friendly, characterized by acceptance, attentive listening and understanding.

[24] What is said here is also valid for spiritual direction of priests, religious and lay people.
[25] Cf. the first fundamental principle of the previous chapter.

A warm, Christian reception on our part will certainly favor the candidate's openness, which is essential to spiritual direction if it is not to be a waste of time. The director should always respect the seminarian's conscience and freedom. To try to force someone to be sincere is simply a contradiction in terms. Sincerity comes freely from within or it is not sincerity. The secret is motivation. It is necessary to motivate the seminarian to speak simply and sincerely with his director, teaching him to value these qualities, showing him that it is the only way that the director can help him and that God can make him hear his voice. And we should do our part to make things easier with a benevolent, warm and understanding attitude.

Obviously it is not enough that the candidate *open* up to the spiritual director. He has to *be receptive* to the director's observations, reflections, motivations and even his corrections. This is the best way to be open to the inspirations of the Holy Spirit.

Spiritual direction is beautiful but arduous work. It is only possible when there is a sufficient staff of good directors who selflessly devote themselves to it. On the other hand the best way to prepare good future directors is to make sure that our present seminarians experience true spiritual direction.

EXAMINATION OF CONSCIENCE

Daily examination of conscience is an effective means for the necessary conversion of heart to the Father of mercies,[26] and for charting the personal progress or setbacks that we experience in our venture to sanctify ourselves and fulfill our mission.

A serious effort in our spiritual life implies that we pause frequently to check up on ourselves, just as a business person regularly checks his books in order to plan for the future. If we are conscientious and serious about our spiritual life we will also make frequent stops to take stock of our personal situation.

When teaching the seminarian to examine his conscience, it is important to help him understand that it is not a mere act of introspection, nor an enumeration of his errors nor much less a negative and masochistic

---

[26] Cf. PO 18.

self-analysis. First and foremost, it is a moment of prayer before God and it requires an atmosphere of personal and intimate dialogue with Christ who has called him, asks for his fidelity, and is ready to pardon his faults and can sustain him in the future with his grace.

What should he examine? He should look at what matters in his life: his spiritual progress, his fidelity to the commitments he has made, his practice of virtue, his self-giving to others, etc. Some kind of personal questionnaire/outline could help in this. However, what is fundamental is his dialogue with God about his personal situation not only to spot errors but also to discover progress, the graces he has answered and to make new resolutions or reaffirm old ones.

RETREATS AND SPIRITUAL EXERCISES

To go back to the example above, we could mention the regular balances any business person has to do monthly and certainly at years-end. He checks on his business, draws up balance sheets and outlines strategies and budgets for the next year. We have to teach our seminarians to be "professionals" in their search for priestly holiness and in their dedication to the mission entrusted to them.

We all feel the need for certain times of greater recollection. We need a day or a week dedicated exclusively to prayer, meditation and being alone with God. When we live in an environment of greater spiritual intensity it is easier to hear the voice of God who perhaps was trying in vain to be heard because we were too busy. We all need times of retreat. Because of our limited and historic condition as human beings we suffer the wear and tear of time. We start to forget the principles we learned, our ideal becomes blurred, our enthusiasm wanes. All of us are like this. We need moments of *renewal.*

A seminarian needs them as well during his ascent to the priesthood. It would be unfair not to offer him these important opportunities. During the year, we can organize periodic retreats: a day or half day every month, or during a special time of the liturgical year, etc. Gatherings for group discussion on specific themes are often useful yet we must also provide some days dedicated especially to personal prayer in an atmosphere of interior and exterior silence.[27]

---

[27] Cf. RFIS 56.

The same could be said about *spiritual exercises.*[28] There is no doubt that activities like meetings, group reflections, conferences, and information panels can be very rewarding. But nothing can substitute the renewing force of a personal encounter with God which characterizes the spiritual exercises. It is an experience that has shown its effectiveness throughout the centuries. It would not seem justifiable to jettison out-of-hand this means of spiritual growth which God gave the Church through St. Ignatius of Loyola. Of course, it is necessary to continually update their content and application but we must safeguard their essential structure and elements. If we are going to change these, then we should give a new name to our invention.

It can be very good for the seminarians to have spiritual exercises annually. They should follow the dynamics proper to the Exercises. This includes: a combination of meditation, times dedicated to self-examination and reflection; a fundamental thematic structure with all the necessary adaptations; focus on conversion and renewal of our own life that should imbue all the activities; total silence to create a climate of openness to grace; complete dedication to the exercises, leaving aside all other business or concerns; a personal general confession covering the period since the last spiritual exercises (if the confessor thinks it advisable); and dialogue with a spiritual director to check our own life with his help and analyze the direction we have to take in the immediate future.

Spiritual exercises are a powerful experience. We are underestimating the ability of young people today if we think they are not able for them. It is always surprising to see so many young lay people from movements and parishes all over the world participate in spiritual exercises every year with great joy and abundant spiritual fruit.

SPIRITUAL LIFE PROGRAM

We spoke about being "professional" in our spiritual life. We cannot deny that there is an unpredictability in matters of the spirit. For God "one day is as a thousand years, and a thousand years as one day" (2 P 3:8; cf. Ps 90:4). He can give us in an instant what we have been trying to obtain for years. There is a lot of "intuition" involved in the spiritual life and it

---

[28] Cf. RFIS 56; CIC 246 § 5.

must always be very spontaneous. Yet when someone really wants to reach an objective he uses all the means at his disposal. In the field of spiritual work the principal means are prayer and confidence in God. But if He has given us reason capable of organizing our efforts, it is because He wants us to use it in all the facets of our life. Perhaps especially so in the primary task of our interior growth and transformation into Christ. Saint Paul took his "spiritual race" very seriously. He did not "run aimlessly" (1 Cor 9:26) but rather did what was necessary to win.

This is the reason for a *spiritual life program*. Its meaning is rooted in two of the fundamental principles we mentioned in chapter two. We said formation must be "transformation," gradual identification with Christ the Priest through the living of the priestly virtues. Formation is also "progressive" since transformation normally occurs step by step, conquest after conquest. These steps are what we "plan."

A program of spiritual life is not like a computer program that sets up everything to run automatically. Its purpose is to channel our work. First we have to pinpoint our personal needs. We look for our most frequent defects (these often have a "dominant passion" as their common source) which obstruct our progress in holiness. We single out the virtues we most need to counteract these deficiencies and to mature in the path to sanctity. After this we select several means which are especially helpful to us in fulfilling our resolution. These include better use of the ordinary means at our disposal or other means that respond to a more particular need.

Spiritual exercises are a privileged occasion for drawing up a plan of spiritual work. In their climate of recollection and intimacy with God, and with the inspirations of the Holy Spirit, we can establish our program for the upcoming year and review it with the help of a spiritual director.

A program of spiritual life is profitable only when it becomes part of our life. We should go back to it often. We can examine our conscience on it daily, make it a topic for spiritual direction or prepare for the sacrament of reconciliation on it.

Spiritual Reading

Lastly, it is good to introduce the seminarians to the practice of spiritual reading. Reading is an important exercise in all fields. A good book puts us in contact with the best results of research, experiences and reflections. It is a goldmine at our fingertips.

The best reading for any seminarian, as for any Christian, is what God Himself has written. We must encourage the candidates to read the Scriptures and "taste its sweetness" (Ps 119:103). Besides Scriptures it can be undoubtedly of great help to read the Fathers of the Church, the classics of spirituality handed down over the years, the principal documents of the Magisterium, as well as good modern spiritual authors.

Spiritual reading, to be true nourishment for one's spirit, should be regular and frequent. It could help to have a time on one's daily schedule for it.

This is a sketch of some elements for a priest's spiritual formation. It is easy to talk about. The task of each formator still remains to be done. He must find the particular path along which God wants to guide each candidate, and help him to follow it generously with the certainty that the climb to the summit is worthwhile.

THE PRIEST'S HUMAN FORMATION

"Chosen from among men." The new and better wine of grace, with its gifts, commitments and demands, needs new wineskins to receive it fittingly, preserve it faithfully and allow it to develop its sanctifying dynamism effectively. Supernatural grace does not suppress nature but elevates it.[29] *Spiritual formation presupposes and relies on the human formation* of the future priest.

> The seminarian's formation as a man has to be in step with his formation as a Christian and future priest, in order that his natural energies be purified and aided by prayer, grace and the sacraments... as well as by the influence of the supernatural virtues which find in the natural virtues a defense, and at the same time, an aid to their fulfillment.[30]

---

[29] St. Thomas Aquinas, *Summa Theologiae,* I, q.1, a.8 c.
[30] Paul VI, Apostolic Letter *Summi Dei Verbum,* November 4, 1963, n. 18.

Human formation does not only benefit the candidate but also profoundly influences his future ministry. His maturity, his psychological balance, and the strength of his will will greatly impinge, for good or evil, on the fruitfulness of his apostolate. A priest's human and social make-up (his way of thinking and acting, his personal presentation and manners, his way of expressing himself, etc.) opens or closes the door to dialogue, trust and friendship. Many will seek or avoid a priest because they are attracted or repulsed by the impression his personality makes on them. Thus, human formation is neither indifferent, superfluous nor just a nice touch.

Formation programs, activities in the seminary, and, above all, formators and candidates themselves have to confront this basic aspect of a priest's integral formation.

The main goal of human formation for the seminarian is *full human maturity*. This is a very rich and detailed concept which is difficult to define and circumscribe since there are so many different ways of approaching it, none of which is absolute.

We propose a descriptive route in three steps. First of all, human formation requires the *integral, harmonious and hierarchically structured development of all the facets of the human personality, in tune with what the person should be and wishes to be.*

Secondly, we think it is essential to educate the individual's moral dimension, which defines him as "good or evil" as such.[31] Above all, this entails *formation of one's conscience* according to the ethical principles of right reason based on Christian Gospel principles and according to the demands of our state in life. In like manner, it implies living the *moral virtues.*

Lastly, one has to acquire those *human and social virtues* which favor interpersonal relationships and makes one's pastoral work more effective in the social milieu in which one works.

Integral, Harmonious and Hierarchically Structured Development of the Human Faculties

To help a person acquire maturity in his personality we must firstly develop to the maximum all the different forces that make it up. Secondly,

---

[31] St. Thomas Aquinas, *Summa Theologiae,* I-II, q.34, a.4 c.

we must strive to develop them harmoniously and avoid imbalance. Thirdly, they should all fit in their own place on a scale, each fulfilling its own function without infringing on the others. The comparison we made earlier with a rowing team pulling together under the command of the coxswain validly illustrates this point.

Personalities are composed of a variety of psychosomatic elements. Instead of reviewing them one by one here, we present some of our fundamental faculties to see how they develop and where they fit into our personality as a whole.

It is clear that every seminarian has his own personality, including a unique, congenital temperamental structure, and faculties with a greater or lesser degree of perfection. Following our principle of "personalized formation" we should apply to each individual the general guidelines of this reflection.

FORMING INTELLIGENCE

Human intelligence is the ability to grasp the essence of things; it is the window of the soul. It is the coxswain of our personality. Not surprisingly, human maturity requires maturity of the intelligence in the first place.

This influences decisively a priest's pastoral ministry. He must receive solid intellectual preparation in order to deal with the problems which the faithful bring to him, to give the advice they seek. He necessarily has to make judgments regarding people and situations, and deal with men and women of our society, believers and nonbelievers alike.

Forming the intelligence means developing its four principle functions: to analyze, synthesize, relate and judge.

To analyze means to successfully divide a whole into its parts. This "whole" can be a lesson, a conference, an article, a human situation or problem, a paragraph, a phrase or even a word. A person who immediately recognizes the place of a part in the whole to which it belongs is someone who analyzes well.

To synthesize is the ability to bring together elements found in various sources to form a meaningful whole, and to quickly distinguish the essential from the accidental and peripheral. It is to say precisely and concisely what has been expressed in many pages.

To draw relations is to compare, distinguish and unify the various aspects of a single complex reality, (for example, the different chapters of a book or various books by the same author, from the same period or on the same topic; the subdivisions of a course; different historical eras or manifestations of a given era etc), to form an organic whole in one's mind.

The high point of human intellectual activity is judgment. To *judge well* means that a person grasps and objectively evaluates the truth he discovers in messages, problems, people, human situations and actions; that he is not rash in his opinions, nor a mere conformist; that he overcomes his personal biases and those of his family, environment, culture and society; that he tries to judge according to the truth of things even above his own judgment.

We have to make sure that each seminarian acquires as far as he can, the qualities which are part and parcel of a rich and strong intelligence.

For example, one important quality is depth of thought, which means reflecting carefully in order to penetrate into the essence of things. Qualities which complement depth are clarity, precision and logical rigor. A quick, intuitive, dynamic intelligence is a great boon. There are some people who have a rather passive, receptive intelligence and others who possess an active, creative mind. Some people are especially speculative while others are very practical. There are even some who have both qualities with equal ease. It is also important to be able to think objectively and independently, without allowing sentiments or emotions to overly influence one's judgment. Finally, we should work towards mental flexibility, the opposite of rigidity and stubbornness.

We should not expect all the candidates to have the same intellectual capacity. There are various levels and characteristics. The important thing is to encourage each seminarian to attain the maximum development of his intellectual qualities.

So the first step is to find out the qualities of each individual. Certainly a candidate must discover what kind of intelligence he has. But as formators we also have to know so that we can personally and effectively assist him. Aptitude tests can be of help here. Observation of a seminarian's ordinary activities, academic or otherwise, is also advisable.

Once we know what kind of intelligence a person has, we must find the best way to form it. Kierkegaard would mention here what he calls

"Socratic knowledge" that can only be taught "in action," getting the seminarian to experience it himself. The seminarian must learn how to think by thinking. The formator's principal task, therefore, is to help him think.

The regular curriculum of a priest's formation, (above all his study of philosophy and theology), is the best training in this field. Yet the degree to which formation of his mental structure as a whole benefits from these studies depends largely on whether the student studies actively or passively. The formator should invite and ask the student to reflect intelligently on what he studies, to analyze and synthesize, etc. We might even consider giving an explanation of the human intelligence, its activities and qualities, as an aid to the students' personal effort.

Yet the purpose of forming the intelligence is not limited to the development of its potentialities. As we said at the outset, it must be the faculty which steers the entire person. It is crucial to help the seminarian to form the habit of using his intelligence to dictate his personal behavior. His reason should be well formed and enlightened by faith; it, and not his sentiments and passions, should always decide his course of action.

The main challenge for a formator is to *offer clear criteria* that enlighten the candidate's mind. This external enlightening has to be strengthened by means of one's personal *reflection* which probes and fathoms the values at hand in order to assimilate them. Reflection applied to ourselves, or *introspection,* reveals to us the ingredients of our personal behavior: principles, values, impulses, sentiments... The candidate has to develop this habit to use it all the time and not just on special occasions, in order to be always on top of himself, attentive to what he must do, and to what he does and why he does it.[32]

Reflection is guided and complemented by the *search for truth*. As a fundamental attitude all seminarians must have an honest desire to enlighten their behavior with well-founded motivations, and to know and understand the why of the Gospel criteria, the demands of morality, and the characteristics of priestly life. Only this personal effort guarantees that their formation is truly a case of interior growth.

---

[32] In some cases it is necessary to avoid the opposite extreme, characteristic of scrupulous and insecure people.

As we form their intelligence we should watch out for attitudes that can warp the use of this faculty. These can also exist in people who have already developed extensively their intellectual capacity.

One of these possible deformations is an exaggerated *desire to study,* characteristic of those who prefer the company of books to the company of people. Beneath the surface, this is usually a form of self-enclosure. It is necessary to help these people to channel their interest properly without extinguishing its positive aspects, and to encourage them not to neglect the integral formation of their personality.

Another possible obstacle is *self-sufficient rationalism.* At times we meet seminarians who have a habit (almost the obsession) of measuring and weighing everything exclusively according to their reasoning and knowledge, showing their self-sufficiency and excessive attachment to their own judgment. This type of person usually has a cold and dull spiritual life, and little spiritual sensitivity. If this tendency is not recognized and corrected on time it can eventually lead to loss of their vocation and faith, since they will gradually discard all supernatural criteria.

Others suffer from a *"Cartesian complex."* They are characterized by systematic doubt: they doubt everything and anything that can be doubted, even things that can rightly by no means be doubted. They live in uncertainty and confusion. If a candidate is like this, we must help him to mature and acquire serenity and self-confidence, and arm him with correct, solid criteria which can enlighten his way of thinking and acting. We must teach him to calmly resist and dismiss the pernicious doubts that attack his mind.

FORMING THE WILL

Our will is a key element in our personality. On a strictly natural level, the value of a person depends, in great part, on the degree to which he forges his will. A person's will is where he sets the course that guides and controls his entire being. In other words, a person is free in the measure that he is *master of himself,* and in the measure in which he directs and dominates his passions, sentiments and instincts. A man is free when, in spite of external circumstances, he acts according to the criteria of his reason enlightened by faith.

Seen in its true dimensions, formation of the will is vital. It cannot be omitted from the formation of a candidate to the priesthood. Unless God assists in an extraordinary way his success in all fields (human, spiritual and apostolic) depends on his strength of will. Everything else (the benefits of grace, human qualities, etc.), faces serious threats if the will does not support it.

Therefore, a seminarian has to strive to form a strong will which is docile to his intelligence, effective and constant in wanting the good, tenacious in the face of difficulties, and capable of governing and channeling, gently yet firmly, all the dimensions of his being.

Forming the will is to *exercise it in wanting the good,* in earnestly, effectively and constantly seeking it. All the suggestions listed below are aimed at promoting this exercise.

Nowhere does formation ever consist in purely negative action. This is especially true here for we are forming the faculty that desires. The positive desire for "good" and the pursuit of an "ideal" are indispensable conditions for formation especially in this case of our will. The best element to form it will therefore be to make it *gravitate around love.* When we love something, freely desiring it is very easy, almost necessary.

The obstacles to this work come from the very nature of man. On the one hand, man suffers an interior division as a consequence of sin, as we have noted. On the other, he finds that in his limitation he cannot choose every good at once. To choose means to renounce one value in favor of another. Often we hesitate when we have to choose one good and leave others aside. Contradictory tendencies within us make it difficult or hard to desire what is good, or make it difficult to choose the good which faith and reason dictate above other inferior values.

Little surprise, then, that *formation of the will always implies renunciation.* Self-renunciation is a magnificent means to forge and educate our ability to will. It is not a negative means because what is important is not to renounce a good, but rather to opt for a greater good. On a human level we are now talking about what is traditionally called abnegation or renunciation of ourselves.

Ordinary life offers countless occasions to exercise it: renouncing our whims by responsibly choosing to fulfill our duty; renouncing our personal plans by freely choosing to live community life and embrace obedience; not letting ourselves be carried away by fatigue, pessimism or sentiments by freely choosing the path of serenity and self-control; renouncing the desire of a comfortable life by choosing austerity, etc.

While this exercise of our will makes it easier for it to choose, we also need exercise to make it *effective and constant* in what we have chosen. There are numerous ways each day to train our will: not going back easily on our resolutions; making ourselves finish what we start; paying special attention to detail; always working with order and foresight and not being carried away by the urge of the moment; doing everything with determination, never procrastinating; demanding that extra effort it takes in the small things of life such as organization and punctuality; effort in the good use of our time; dedication to study, work and prayer... Actually every human activity is an occasion to fortify our will. The opposite is also true: by doing things lazily and carelessly our will grows feeble.

FORMING PASSIONS

A passion is a tendency developed beyond the normal. This can happen to our intellectual or to our sensible tendencies.[33] In and of themselves, passions are not negative, they are simply forces of greater or lesser intensity.

It is an error to think that formation of the passions consists in repressing or suppressing them. This is actually counterproductive: the natural impetus of a passion, if suppressed, may hide itself in the subconscious and from there, unseen, wage war. On the contrary, true formation of the passions is to correctly and firmly channel their valuable potential, elevating and directing them, so that they become a stimulus and energy in our more arduous endeavors.

Sin has left man in a state of interior civil war. The disorder that it causes in his nature permits his passional forces to push him in directions contrary to those which he consciously and freely tries to follow, according to the dictates of his reason and his faith. Although passions may be positive forces in themselves, their impulse carries a *positive or negative charge,* depending on whether or not they support our goal in life. There

---

[33] Sensible passions are for example the tendency to food, rest, self-preservation, reproduction, etc.; spiritual passions are the tendencies to truth, beauty, self-affirmation, etc...

are, then, two simultaneous and complementary measures to be taken: *encourage the positive and rectify the negative.*

It is important to point out, as Thomas Aquinas does, that our influence over the passions is not "despotic" but "political."[34] Passional forces automatically tend towards their own objective. The will does not have direct control over them. We can exercise indirect or "political" action using certain means which calm, "distract" or redirect these energies.

The first and most basic means is *to be completely absorbed by our ideal.* Profound love for a personal ideal in life makes our entire personality gravitate around it. Not only our intelligence and will but also our passions will exercise their influence according to the uniting direction we have.

But it is not enough to want the ideal. The passions, given their automatic nature, can "rebel" at any moment. We need vigilance and firmness to *avoid whatever might trigger our rebel passion.* Personal experience teaches us which external or internal situations usually provoke our natural tendencies to go in the wrong direction.

Sometimes it can be very useful to *exercise the opposite passion* to the troublemaker. For example, we feel despair creeping into our hearts. It may not be easy to control it directly at the moment, but we can use our intelligence or imagination to stimulate the passion of hope to balance or even nullify the negative influence of despair.

It is also possible to *channel our passions* towards objects that suit them and which conform to our personal convictions. Instead of discharging hate against someone who has wronged us, we can direct it at sin... at the sin of hating our neighbor, for example, increasing in this way our capacity for pardon. Instead of getting carried away by sadness we can use this tendency to identify ourselves with the agony of Christ; by doing this we can come to appreciate his suffering so much that we feel the profound joy of knowing that we are so loved by Him to such an extreme.

We must also be very careful to *control the growth of our passions.* If we allow any passion to run wild, sooner or later it can take over the reins of our personality. When this happens, we are absorbed, agitated, totally obsessed with that passional impulse. Other passions, the body, and even

---

[34] Cf. *Summa Theologiae,* I, q.81, a.3 c. and ad 2; I-II, q.17, a.7; q.56, a.4 ad 3.

the intelligence and will are subject to it. The consequences can be disastrous: behavior diametrically opposed to a person's convictions and fundamental option, and even, in its extreme, the development of a pathological disorder, especially if the passionate force persists over time.

Another way to educate our passions is by *reflecting on the motives of our personal behavior.* Once in a while we should look within and ask ourselves, where does this thought, this reaction, or this resolution which I am about to make come from? Does it come from my reason and free will acting at full capacity? Am I allowing myself to be carried away by the impulses of my passions?

Lastly, when other means just aren't enough, it can be wise to have a *"cooling off period."* If we realize that a passion has caught fire within us and is blindly pushing us in an improper direction, it is wiser not to act, not to make any important decisions until calm returns.

FORMING SENTIMENTS

A sentiment is usually defined as a subjective psychological experience brought on by different causes (lasting or fleeting states of mind, unconscious reactions to one's surroundings, physical condition, events, situations, etc.) which make a positive or negative impression on a person, arousing in him various instincts and tendencies.[35]

Knowing what kinds of sentiments there are will help us to understand this aspect of our self. First we have *vital sentiments.* These are generated by the range of perceptions we have of our body, and according to their nature they give our lives a sense of well-being or uneasiness, freshness or sluggishness. Our humor is an echo of our vital sentiments and has repercussions in all the areas of our life.

A second type are *sentiments about our own individuality.* Among them we have the sentiment of personal power or worth: superiority or inferiority, sufficiency or insufficiency based upon our perception of our personal dignity, gifts and qualities. At times it is based upon our own opinion of ourselves and at other times more on the opinion of others.

---

[35] An emotion is a more intense sentimental state which brings on a typical somatic reaction which is usually simultaneous with it but can also follow or precede it. For example, with fear comes trembling; with happiness a smile; with anguish depression and with sadness tears, etc.

Another type of sentiment is a reaction to the world around us: suffering, hope, resignation, despair. There are also corporal sentiments, (hunger, thirst, tiredness, etc.) and those which touch our psyche, such as sadness which oppresses us, happiness which uplifts us, gratitude which touches us, love which softens our heart, etc.

It is obvious that among these various sentiments there has to be an order and harmony, so that chaos will not reign in the life of our spirit and in our life in general. If we allow free rein to our sentiments, we become whimsical and unpredictable. When our corporal sentiments have a monopoly, our body and its drives become the center of our personality. The same can be said about our merely psychic sentiments, for insofar as they are solely sensitive in nature they do not follow any reason or moderation. They seek only release but in that release they can take our whole life in tow.

Lastly, we have spiritual sentiments which are the most precious gift of human sensitivity — affective sympathy or empathy with goodness and virtue — and are aroused in the soul by the presence or absence of a moral good: gratitude, friendship, esteem for sincerity, etc. The whole maturing process of our psyche must collaborate in the development and strengthening of such sentiments, without in the process running roughshod over others which is also a human characteristic.

Formation of sentiments seeks to capitalize on their force, using them for the overall good of the person and for service to the mission each one has received from God. In this way sentiments enrich the candidate notably and make him capable of profound human experiences, of drawing close to God and to others. The first indispensable step is to *recognize that we always have the possibility of controlling,* directing and harmonizing our own personality with all its wealth, to make it upright, strong and master of itself.

As a second step towards forming his sentiments, the candidate has to analyze and *know his own sentiments,* principally the dominant ones, and be aware of the degree to which they influence his conduct, since *sentimentality*[36] can do extreme damage to his formation. Ordinarily these

---

[36] By sentimentality we mean a habitual state in which sentiments overpower a person, making him experience unfounded fears, illusory hopes, vain happiness, inferiority, etc. If they get to dominate the entire person they can even deprive him of the soundness of his judgment, his capacity of analysis, and also his strength and decision of will.

factors depend on one's temperament, by which one tends to happiness or sadness, optimism or pessimism, excitement or depression. The formator has to help the candidate to discover this habitual component of his temperament, its potential, its positive and negative aspects and its implications. We should help him to accept himself serenely, joyfully and thankfully, and to strive constantly and positively for balance, self-control and improvement.

We noted the principal means of formation in the previous section: *encourage what is positive and correct what is negative.* If a sentiment helps, it is welcome. If it hinders, weakens or disturbs, then the candidate needs to exercise his will to encourage the opposite sentiment or focus his attention on something else, etc. In this regard it is very important for him to educate his imagination and not allow it to wander aimlessly, for its images by their nature induce to the action they evoke, and provoke the sentiments that go with it.

This same interior mechanism can benefit a person when he allows and encourages sentiments that support his convictions: enthusiasm for his vocation, sensible fervor in his love for God and compassion for all people, etc. Thus, freely chosen principles are no longer cold and merely intellectual, but become operative convictions which encompass the whole human person. Personal sentiment adds a subjective dose of resonance to the objective attraction which a value arouses.

As a result of his effort the candidate acquires stable *equanimity* which consists in habitual preponderance of a serene state of mind, equidistant from wild joy and dejection. From an ascetic point of view, this means habituating oneself to fulfill the will of God in the various circumstances of life sustained by one's will, faith and love. Orientation towards this ideal creates an habitual attitude of healthy spiritual optimism capable of transforming any sentiment or state of mind into a positive element. Everything is grace for a heart in love with God. As Paul says: "For those who love God, everything works for good" (Rm 8:28). A man who loves his vocation and fully identifies with it will form an habitually positive state of mind.

Education of sentiments is also related to the correct formation of one's artistic sensibility. That is, one's capacity to recognize and appreciate the beauty of nature and works of art.

FORMING IMAGINATION

Imagination is a human faculty of creativity and originality. Our present age, dominated by the media (especially movies and television) has created a true "sense-image civilization." Men and women, young and old, appreciate everything that is original, inventive and tangible in a priest's preaching and writing. They will retain his message better if it is presented to them in the pleasing and varied wrapping which only a rich imagination can create.

Besides, a well-cultivated imagination is also an unending mine of initiatives in a priest's apostolic work and in his life in general.

As always, the first task in training the imagination is to develop and strengthen it. The second step is to channel it. Some people have a weak and dull imagination. They should try to sharpen it as much as possible. Exercises which develop an individual's capacity for oral and written expression can be quite helpful, and reading especially creative authors can also light a spark in those who don't have this quality.

There are others who have such a developed imagination that it becomes a problem. Once again, what interests us is to channel this force so that the imagination stops being "the madman of the house," as St. Teresa of Avila called it, and becomes a humble and efficient servant to the individual and his apostolic mission. This means that at times we simply have to put the reins on our imagination. But it means especially that we have to get it to cooperate with our intelligence and will, focusing on the object they pursue. For example, instead of allowing our imagination to wander during study or prayer time, we can put it to work, helping our mind penetrate more deeply into the concepts we are trying to learn or helping our spirit identify with the object of our meditation.

FORMING MEMORY

With the coming and going of generations and cultures, the role of memory has been at times overstressed and at others underestimated. Today our culture does not favor its formation, but not on that account has it lost value or importance.

Memory, a talent and gift from God, can become a valuable treasure of knowledge and experience. It is like a faithful secretary who instantly

comes up with the sought-after fact and neatly files away what is entrusted
to his care. It draws from its rich warehouse things both new and old, like
the scribe of the Gospel (cf. Mt 13:52).

Forming memory is arduous, slow work. It has the bitter taste of a
rookie mountain climber's first trek. It requires the discipline of concentration, an intelligent methodology and the constancy of daily effort.

It is not a question of exchanging understanding and reflection for
memory work but rather enriching the individual's intellectual baggage
and ability. Many times it is quite useful to remember some important fact
such as the exact words of certain classical philosophical or theological
definitions. It is good for a priest to be able to quote verses or passages from
the Gospel without needing to read from the book. It is an advantage to
know outright quotes from well-known authors, dates of important historical events, names of people we meet, etc. We can do it if when we come
across these facts, we pause to commit them to memory and once in a while
check to see if we have retained them.

PHYSICAL FORMATION

The pace in the seminary (spiritual life, the constant practice of
virtue, intellectual formation, etc.) is intense. Sports and recreation are
necessary to recover physically and mentally, to conserve and increase
good health, and to foster friendship. The Second Vatican Council affirms
this when speaking generally of education in our day: *Sports can help to
preserve emotional balance... and to establish fraternal relations.*[37]

These activities offer magnificent opportunities to know and form
oneself and exercise many virtues such as diligence, effort and toning
one's will, generosity, charitable openness towards others, etc.

Moreover, the majority of students aspiring to the priesthood are
young men who need sports for their healthy physical growth and
psychological balance. This does not mean that all necessarily have to be
athletes, but a certain amount of physical exercise does everyone good,
such as playing in a community game, walking, or outings to the country-
side or mountains. Normally a young man does not shy from exercise and

---

[37] GS 61.

physical effort, or work which supposes sweat and fatigue. If he does, it could mean he is lazy, has a psychological block, or is withdrawn.

Therefore, there must be time, space and the necessary activities to develop this facet of priestly formation. The seminary program must take it into account.

Physical exercise, especially sports, is an excellent means of self-knowledge, openness, self-giving and formation.

Physical formation is not limited exclusively to sports. It includes the need to exercise oneself now and again in *manual labor* that takes physical effort.

Work is a facet of Christ's life that we should imitate. It helps to form character, strengthens the will, forms the habit of hard work. We discover new talents, gain firsthand experience of the conditions, labor and fatigue of many people and get to understand them better. It helps us overcome our inclination to comfort and live a more authentic spirit of poverty.

Both sports and physical work bring all the members of the community together and identify them with the formation center. They give the community an authentic family atmosphere and make everyone think of the seminary as their own home.

MORAL FORMATION

A man who knows many things is a wise man. A man who has developed his will is a vigorous and firm man. When we find a man who does good and avoids evil, we call him a "good man." Human formation necessarily includes education of the *moral dimension* which makes a human being "good" as such.

At the core of this dimension is our *moral conscience.* For someone who wants to be a "man of God" it is going to be of prime importance to form *man's most secret core, and his sanctuary. There he is alone with God whose voice echoes in his depths.*[38] Thus to form one's conscience is to prepare oneself to encounter God, to hear his voice.

Our conscience is a light for our path: "The eye is the lamp of the body. So, if your eye is sound, your whole body will be full of light; but if your eye is not sound, your whole body will be full of darkness. If then the light in you is darkness, how great is the darkness!" (Mt 6:22-23). A

---

[38] GS 16.

formed conscience is a guarantee against insincerity and hypocrisy, whereas a deformed conscience is a source of darkness and anxiety.

Besides, *a priest's conscience is at the service of others.* He has been called to teach the faith and guide others along the path that leads to God. He must educate the moral conscience of the faithful entrusted to him. A good part of his daily ministry consists in enlightening consciences and counseling the men and women he meets in confession, spiritual direction, meetings and conferences, and even chance encounters. On these occasions his theoretical knowledge of moral theology is obviously helpful, but the accuracy and discretion of his judgment about the lives of others remains strongly determined by the formation of his own conscience and his own deep moral convictions.

Formation of conscience will be influenced by our idea of man and by our idea and perception of good and evil; that is, it depends on our concept of morality. Our base here is the personalistic conception of man which we have developed from the beginning of this book.

To form one's conscience it is important to achieve a healthy *balance* between the *objective and subjective dimensions of morality.* A series of objective moral values exists (proceeding essentially from the natural moral law and Revelation) which one's conscience has to recognize and make its own. On the other hand, the "moral" character (the moral goodness or evil) of human acts ultimately comes from the subject and his responsible and free adherence to "bonum" or to "malum." Thus we have an objective moral norm (related to objective values) and a subjective moral norm (the conscience's judgment). We must educate the seminarian to consider not only the objectivity of an act, but also the subjective factors (intentionality, conditioning, etc.). In this way he can avoid, in his own life, both exaggerated and unfounded feelings of guilt and remorse, and, at the opposite extreme, easy justifications which smack of subjectivism and relativism. Later on, when in his pastoral service he has to direct others, he will be able to help them to discover and live moral truth without undue anguish.

It is also important to strike a balance when distinguishing the moral factors that depend on the "nature" of the human person, from those that depend on his "historical dimension." This is the only way to avoid the two erroneous extremes of taking something to be universal and permanent when it is only historical-cultural, or reducing everything to the historical-cultural.

We can divide the functions of conscience into three complementary acts: to *perceive* good and bad as something to be done or to be avoided (step previous to action), to *impel* one to do good and avoid evil (the force which brings one to action), and to *judge* the goodness or evil of what has been done (step subsequent to action). Forming one's conscience means strengthening these three acts because conscience deformations can occur in any one or in a combination of them.

A person can be too lax or too strict in his or her perception of the good to be done or the evil to be avoided (lax or scrupulous conscience). There are others who, after perceiving what must be avoided, do it anyway; or perceiving what should be done, do not do it; the edict of conscience is silenced by other motives (inoperative conscience). Then there are others who after having acted against their conscience smother the resulting judgment. These last have reached a dangerous point which could bring about the total deformation of their conscience.

The primary goal of conscience formation is to teach the candidate *to open up to objective values and conform to the objective moral norm.* When he does, his conscience is correctly formed.

But this is still not enough. He has to *strengthen the influence of his conscience over his will.* The strength of his conscience can be identified with the interiorized convictions which effectively govern his behavior. We could identify it with the habit of consistence, understood as constancy in acting according to what one's conscience dictates. A well-formed conscience in this sense will always help a person to act as he should.

Yet it is in the third act, *the conscience's subsequent judgment,* that formation or deformation of conscience is ultimately at stake. A man who allows himself to act against his conscience, to a greater or lesser extent enters the area of moral evil. But if he later admits that he has done wrong, and takes the proper measures for pardon and reparation, he has taken a sure step in the education of his conscience. However, if on the contrary, he stifles his conscience and disregards its protests he can damage it irreparably. Perhaps a day will come when he no longer distinguishes effectively between good and evil.

The importance of the means indicated in the section on spiritual formation is evident in this matter. Examination of conscience, the

sacrament of reconciliation and spiritual direction can all help to enlighten, vivify and purify the future priest's conscience.

The moral dimension of a person also includes living the *moral
virtues*. When St. Thomas studied fifty-four different virtues in the *Summa*
he did not intend to list them all. It is a varied and broad field in which the
seminarian can enrich his human, Christian and priestly personality. In
order not to get lost in the study of these virtues it may be good to focus
on the four *cardinal moral virtues*. All the virtues can be related in some
way to prudence, justice, fortitude and temperance. The personal situation
of each candidate will determine which ones we emphasize and how. Here
we mention only a few of those which are fundamental in the preparation
and life of a priest.

For example — *sincerity*. The urgency of this virtue in the life of a
priest is self-evident. He is called to be a living reflection of the One who
said: "I am ... the truth" (Jn 14:6) and who affirmed that for this very reason
He had come: "To bear witness to the truth" (Jn 18:37). Who will go for
advice to a priest who behaves insincerely? It is essential that every
candidate form himself to be truthful, honest and just. He might be a good
theologian and even very pious, but if duplicity and falsehood are at work
in him, he will be a disfigured priest, a semi-Christian and a divided human
being. Thus, formators should weigh the value of this virtue for the
seminarians and teach them to live it in their daily life. We cannot rest or
be at ease until they behave exactly the same when on their own as when
they are watched — for example, until they are able to take a written test
in the privacy of their own room without copying.

Gratitude is another basic virtue which, nevertheless, is often
neglected. "Father, I thank you for you have heard me" (Jn 11:41; cf. Mt
15:25). Once again Christ is our model. Gratitude is the product and sign
of a soul's grandeur, humility, respect and charity. Ingratitude shows that
the soul is petty, self-centered and spiritually coarse. Often a priest is the
recipient of innumerable favors and kind gestures. A word, a card, a small
sign of thanks — for a gift or someone's assistance in the parish catechism
program ... can be true seeds of the Kingdom of God. By the same token,
a priest can seriously disedify the faithful by giving the impression that he
feels he has the right to be served without having to say thank you. We have
to train seminarians to be sincerely and considerately grateful in ordinary
life — in their dealings with their classmates and formators, with the

people who work in the seminary and the faithful who financially support it, etc.

A human being is essentially a social being. This too enters into a priest's formation. The transformation that has to take place in a candidate must include the way he deals with others and even his external presentation and social behavior. A person's manners reflect his inner make-up.

Doubtless, these social aspects of their formation will be of great importance in their future apostolate. At times they may be decisive. Remember "the economy of the Incarnation." God could have saved humanity from his eternal abode, but instead, He wished to do so by drawing close to us and becoming one of us. From that moment, the human presence of the Savior, his way of speaking, welcoming, conversing, smiling, and even his external demeanor, became signs and instruments of salvation. People felt attracted by his personality; they enjoyed being with Him. This natural attraction quickened their approach to the Kingdom of Heaven.

In the priest too, everything (from the most internal to the most external) has to help those who come to him find the Savior. How many times a kind word or a polite gesture opens the doors of a soul! On the contrary, how many times are they closed to grace because someone treated them brusquely, or unkindly.

Of course, each priest has his own way of being, and he should act naturally. But we can always ask ourselves if there is something which could or should be changed so that the seminarian becomes more like Christ and better fulfills his mission.

Friendliness and Openness

We have to help the seminarian understand that a priest is a man who lives for others. His ministry obliges him to be in continual contact with all kinds of people. Some will be kind, pleasant and open. Others will be crass, indifferent and almost impossible to deal with. The sooner he learns to *deal with everyone, respecting and loving them as they are,* the better. The deep motive for his universal acceptance of others must be the habit of seeing every person as a member of Christ's Mystical Body, a brother or sister, a child of God destined for salvation. Only then will they be able to treat them as the Lord would treat them — seeking to win them over, not for themselves, but for the Kingdom.

Like his Master, a shepherd of souls must be gentle and humble of heart (cf. Mt 11:29). Therefore, the seminarians must strive to evince kindness and meekness so that people who deal with them will feel welcomed and accepted and not encounter coldness, indifference or harshness.

At times a priest has to be demanding. But it is one thing to demand despotically and another to demand with friendliness and understanding. Popular wisdom knows the difference: "a drop of honey attracts more than a barrel of vinegar."

A priest is a man of the word. But he must also *be able to pay attention to others.* Many times the only thing a suffering person needs is to be listened to. In their dealings with their classmates and others, the seminarians must learn how to *be sincerely interested in others,* in their concerns and in what they think and say. A priest who always monopolizes the conversation with his own concerns will keep the faithful from speaking to him about their things. He might think he has done much because he has said a lot, but the people will have gone away still burdened with their problems because they did not get a chance to explain them.

Men of dialogue. Very important. A priest who thinks he is always right about everything loses many valuable occasions to learn from others, to enrich himself, and to receive helpful insights for his apostolate. Not only this, but people will stop trying to help him, annoyed by his know-it-all attitude. Today's priest has to learn to deal with all kinds of people and mentalities. In our pluralistic and secularized society it is absolutely necessary to learn how to dialogue with everyone: agnostic, atheist and believer; with the Catholic who lives in the past, and with the Catholic so anxious to "update" that he strays from the age-old path of the Church. Naturally, to dialogue is not to be eclectic, insecure or indifferent. The dialogue of the priest-prophet with the world of today has to be based on fundamental convictions born of faith and nourished on the inexhaustible deposit of the tradition of the Church. To be solid is not to be rigid, much less to impose. The priest's mission is not to "conquer" but to "convince." There is no worse "prophet" than the "dogmatist."

We have to make sure that the candidates learn the difficult skill of dialogue above all in daily living, by listening to others, sincerely trying to understand their point of view, humbly and honestly recognizing when the other is correct, confidently explaining their own personal view of things and being ready to adapt or change it when necessary.

Distinction and Courtesy

There might be a treasure within, but the first thing people see is the exterior. It is one thing to carry our treasure in vessels of clay and another to present a vessel so crude and tasteless that nobody wants to go near it.

In today's world, above all in certain places, the question of a person's manners and even his external presentation is of special importance. Whether they are the humblest of natives or members of high society, people can feel deeply offended if a priest neglects what they consider good manners. A priest cannot afford such ignorance or lack of social education. His message is too valuable for him to throw away opportunities to preach it. This is also a form of "inculturation."

Seminarians' integral formation includes training them to be *distinguished and courteous* with others. They must acquire habits of distinction and courtesy in their way of speaking, their vocabulary, their personal rapport. They have to overcome all bashfulness, timidity and sheepishness on the one hand, and on the other, brusqueness, aggressiveness, and excessive irony which may raise a barrier between them and others. Obviously, everyone has his own style but a representative of Christ to others, a teacher and a shepherd, must strive to be firm, friendly, natural, joyful, serene and balanced.

The applications of social formation go on and on. What really matters is the principle. It is our job as formators to help the seminarians refine the many details which will shape them as priests of Christ for the people of God. We should always remember that these virtues are not acquired overnight, and that in a formation center it is not easy to perceive the importance that good training in this field has for the apostolate. We have to motivate, explain and exemplify. We have to make sure they begin working on this from the first day. The formation of their personality cannot be improvised on the day of ordination or when they receive their first assignment. By then it might be too late.

Fostering these qualities in the ordinary life of the seminary, will help greatly to create a pleasant, dignified and friendly environment in which everyone feels at home in the company of the rest. By these details we can make a reality of the psalm, "Behold, how good and pleasant it is when brothers dwell in unity" (Ps 133:1).

The task might seem overwhelming, a maze of virtues, qualities, behavior, attitudes ... But things are really much simpler than they appear. If we have a clear overall picture of formation, it will be relatively easy to detect what is needed in each candidate's personality at different times. If we truly desire to help him in his human formation we will find a way to guide and motivate him through the activities and occasions for formation at our disposal. Every personal meeting, including personal direction, can help. Classes or conferences on different topics of human formation can be useful. It all depends on the importance we give to this field of priestly formation.

THE PRIEST'S INTELLECTUAL FORMATION

The most important quality of a priest is to be a man of God. His demeanor and external appearance can also be decisive — above all in the first contact — in drawing many of our brothers and sisters to Christ and the Church. But a priest must be more. The Catholic priest, in his prophetic mission, is called to be a "teacher." The Master himself has sent him, "Teach all people" (cf. Mt 28:19). Thus we should take time to consider intellectual preparation as one of the fundamental fields of our seminarian's formation.

Today more than ever, people expect a priest to be ready to answer when asked to give reasons for his hope (cf. 1 P 3:15). Ready and able, of course. People will approach him in search of God's light for their problems. They expect clear answers based on faith and a profound knowledge of the human heart.

In a very scientific and technological society such as ours, the priest faces very complex circumstances and often hostile or indifferent environments both inside and out of the Church. He is called today to be a shepherd of men and women who are more mature, more critical, more informed, immersed in an ideologically pluralistic society where Christianity is exposed to multiple interpretations and suspicions by a culture ever more foreign to the faith.[39] It is a world with numerous intricate moral problems, awash with cults offering easy and immediate solutions to personal religious needs, confused by doctrinal aberrations. This means that today's priest has to have the breadth of knowledge and culture that will make it possible for him to reach the people of our age and effectively transmit the Gospel.

Formators and students alike have to realize that intellectual preparation cannot be substituted by anything: whether by fervor, or a big heart, or talent, or great plans for the apostolate. Ordinarily, grace acts through the quality of its instruments and does not fructify the work of an apostle who has neglected his intellectual preparation out of laziness, cowardice or irresponsibility .

Intellectual formation is not just the fulfillment of a curriculum. On top of acquiring certain data, the student has to develop and refine his *intellectual ability* and acquire those *dispositions and habits* which make him an intellectually mature person. It is only when he has acquired intellectual maturity that the *store of knowledge* he has acquired in *philosophy, theology* and general *culture* (which should be as rich as possible), will give its fruit. His *ability to communicate* to others the wealth of his learning can also be taken as part of this facet.

Forming Intellectual Abilities and Habits

In the previous section about human formation we went over carefully the education of the interior faculties of a person. It is enough to recall here that as formators we must keep in mind the interior dimension of the candidate when charting his intellectual formation. It should not be enough for us that the candidates pick up elements of knowledge in our classes or when we give them direction in their intellectual formation, etc. It is most important that they develop their ability to absorb and use well the learning that is imparted to them. The focus and style of the education

---

[39] Cf. Congregation for Catholic Education, *Theological formation of future priests,* February 22, 1976, n. I.I.3.

and study we provide for them can influence notably the maturation of their intelligence, memory, imagination, etc.

We should also be interested in helping the candidates foster dispositions and attitudes that favor their intellectual maturity. Often the young men who enter the seminary do not have serious study habits. Their intelligence, memory, imagination and all their qualities, no matter how brilliant they are, will be like the buried talent of the fearful servant if we do not succeed in creating in them a positive and responsible attitude towards their duty to form their intellect.

It is necessary, therefore, to know how always to motivate, guide, and urge them. We have to get them to really want to study, even if it doesn't come naturally. Furthermore, it is also necessary that by dint of continual effort and dedication they acquire good intellectual habits, such as: ability to concentrate quickly and stably while reading, the ability to follow a class or lecture actively, etc. These habits, besides helping them get the most out of the seminary courses, will be the best guarantee that they will continue updating themselves intellectually as part of their ongoing formation, once they have left the seminary after ordination.

Philosophical Formation

Why is the study of theology not enough for the formation of future priests? Many seminarians ask themselves this question at the beginning of their studies. We might even detect in some places a certain disparagement of philosophy. Some programs tend to reduce this area of studies or water it down with other studies as if it were a secondary aspect which has to be fulfilled to meet certain canonical requirements for ordination.

Philosophy is a privileged time in the intellectual formation of a candidate for the priesthood. Philosophical studies are a school of reflection. Thanks to them, a seminarian learns to think profoundly in terms of being, of objectivity; his critical sense is sharpened; he grows avid for the truth wherever it may be found, and he learns to detect and refute error.

By studying philosophy we receive a whole heritage of wisdom as old as humanity itself.[40] The student comes face to face systematically and

---

[40] Congregation for Catholic Education, *The Teaching of Philosophy in Seminaris,* January 20, 1972, n. III.2.

in depth with the most acute theoretical and existential problems of the human person and delves into their roots. Thus, he is introduced to ideas which have determined the course of history and which have outlined what man, "through the power of his mind," knows about himself, the world and God. Consequently it said, *philosophy has an irreplaceable cultural value; it constitutes the soul of authentic culture.*[41]

Moreover, philosophy is an invaluable aid for our faith and theology. We have to avoid at all costs any internal rupture between faith and reason. The "love of wisdom," by its fidelity to truth (and, thus, necessarily, its fidelity to the Truth) reveals a concordance between the knowledge of reason (which has to recognize its own limits) and the knowledge of faith, which elevates reason. So too, the study of philosophy proves to be a useful instrument for theology, both because of notions and principles which it lends to theological speculation, and because of the process of reflection it supplies for the correct pursuit of the discourse on God and a deeper understanding of Revelation. Therefore it is normally more helpful to study philosophy before theology, and not to study them simultaneously or mix them.

There is, finally, an apostolic motivation. Our priests must bring the Gospel to the men and women of our time, evangelize their minds and aspirations, imbue modern culture with the yeast of the Good News. Philosophy is irreplaceable for furnishing understanding, dialogue and arguments, even purely human ones; it becomes a meeting place of dialogue especially among believers and non-believers.[42]

Optatam Totius shows us the way to reach these goals. It recommends that in the study of philosophy both formators and candidates give particular importance to systematic philosophy and each one of its parts, *in such a way that students will be led to acquire a solid and coherent understanding of man, of the world, and of God, basing themselves on a philosophical heritage which is perennially valid. Students should also be conversant with contemporary philosophical investigations, especially those exercising special influence in their own country, and with recent scientific progress.*[43]

---

[41] ibid., n. II.2.

[42] ibid., n. II.3.c.

[43] OT 15; cf. RFIS 71.

This means that we must not confuse the study of philosophy with the study of the history of philosophy, which is just one subject among many others. Philosophy means learning to reflect on reality with one's own mind, supported by the contributions of those who have preceded us in history.

It also means that we should give priority to those subjects which constitute the fundamental structure of philosophy as the science which seeks the final causes of reality.[44] For example, the study of human knowledge which is the starting point of all knowledge should never be neglected. Metaphysics, since it is a reflection on being as such, gives our intelligence a very valuable means to go in depth as it analyzes any reality. It puts us in contact with the highest level of all that exists, making possible the jump to transcendent being. Philosophical reflection on God and man is crucial for men who are called to be the bridge between God and humanity.

Lastly, we should keep in mind that philosophy students in the seminary are candidates for the priesthood and that is why they are studying it. Experience teaches that it is not unusual for them to run into problems with their faith during this period of their formation. At this stage in his development the young man is establishing his capacity to judge. He is under the effect of an academic discipline that obliges him to weigh everything with his reason, and he is in necessary contact with currents of thought and authors foreign or opposed to transcendence and faith. This can all give rise to questionings or doubts of faith.

Taking this into account the professors and those in charge of studies should offer their explanations in such a way that the students understand that reason is not an absolute and definitive judge of everything that exists. It is very healthy to help them see that the human mind has its limits and it is equally enlightening to show them that there is no contradiction between what rational science discovers and understands and what is discovered and accepted in faith.

---

[44] For the overall view of philosophical subjects one should refer to the official documents of the Holy See and the *Ratio Studiorum* elaborated by local Episcopal Conferences.

Theological Formation

Theological formation is the apex of a priest's education. Here he delves into scientific and experiential knowledge of his faith and of the pastoral problems to which he will soon apply the light of Revelation, the zeal of his apostolic heart and the prudence of the good shepherd. Theology, as the *study of God,* is the science which characterizes the priest, as a *man of God.*

The curriculum must provide an overall knowledge of the totality of Catholic doctrine so that the students can study it in depth, make it nourishment for their spiritual life and, when they become priests, communicate it, explain it and defend it in their ministry.[45] Hence, our principal task is to give them a complete and organic view of the basic subjects, without neglecting the others that are less essential but are also necessary for their doctrinal and pastoral formation.[46]

To teach and study theology we have to look to the long tradition of the Church, as well as to the *legitimate renewal movements* of recent years: the role of exegesis in every subject, the rediscovery of patristics, the deep transformation in the formulation and approach to moral theology, etc. In this renewal effort we should be attentive to the contribution of the more outstanding modern authors, and to the recent guidelines of the Magisterium. The document on *the theological formation of future priests* is a very valuable point of reference. We can also add the documents of the Holy See on liturgical, ecumenical, pastoral and missionary formation, on the study of the Fathers of the Church, on the oriental Churches, on atheism and others documents which complete the picture of the entire theological formation.[47]

---

[45] Cf. OT 16; CIC 252 § 1.

[46] As regards the list of the required theological subjects, we refer to the official documents of the Church. Cf. OT 16, CIC 252 3, RFIS 78-79, etc.

[47] Congregation for Catholic Education, *Instruction on liturgical training in seminaries,* June 3, 1979.
Secretariat for the Unity of Christians, *Circular letter Concerning some aspects of ecumenical training in Catholic institutes of theology,* December 15, 1986.
Congregation for Catholic Education, *Circular letter Concerning the pastoral ministry to migrants in the formation of future priests,* January 25, 1986.
Congregation for the Evangelization of Peoples, *Circular letter Concerning the missionary formation of future priests,* May 17, 1970.
Secretariat for Non-Christians, *Note on the study of atheism and formation in dialogue,* July 10, 1970.

By its very nature, theology must lead to a personal encounter with God, moving the students to prayer and contemplation. Spirituality born of a life of faith can be said to be an internal dimension of theology. *A theology which does not deepen our faith, or bring us to pray, may be a succession of words about God; but it will never be a true discourse on God, the Living God, the God who Is, and whose Being is Love.*[48]

The student, then, should approach theology with a mind that is enlightened with a living and active faith so that the truths he studies will become the principles of his Christian life, increase his knowledge and personal relationship with Christ, help him deepen his vital insertion in the Church and make him more aware of his apostolic task.

His enrichment in theology is for others. While he is still at his desk he acquires the habit of applying God's word to temporal realities and to the changing human condition, and the habit of attempting to explain the message of salvation in the terms of contemporary sensibilities. He studies not for an intellectual and human formation for his own benefit, but for the benefit of the Gospel and of people. It is a mission. He studies now to enlighten later, he learns in order to teach, he seeks understanding in order to move hearts to God. The future priest, today a student of sacred science, must never lose sight of this. His quest for theological wisdom is in itself a true act of charity:

There are some people who want to know only so as to know. This is misguided curiosity. Others want to know in order to be known. This is misguided vanity. Others want to know in order to sell their knowledge, for example, for money or for honors. This is misguided profit. But there are others who want to know in order to build. This is charity.[49]

[48] John Paul II, *Discourse to priests,* Maynooth, Ireland, October 1, 1979.
[49] St. Bernard, *Sermo 36 in Cant.*

Broad General Culture

A priest's ministry, his preaching and pastoral service, are directed to concrete men and women of a particular time in history with its own culture. Insofar as they are *"men and women"* they share in the heritage of the universal culture of all times; insofar as they are men and women of a *particular time and culture,* they partake of the particular characteristics of the present time; insofar as they are *individual* men and women each one has his own characteristics. The priest has to know each one as an individual in order to love him and help him as he is. However, he will not be able to know each one deeply if he is not familiar with the characteristics of contemporary society and culture, or the cultural heritage of humanity.

A broad general culture is a firm base on which to build one's studies of philosophy and theology. Thanks to it, too, we can avoid the danger of overspecialization which can make of us "functional illiterates," absolute geniuses in our own specific area but almost totally ignorant of anything else.

A particularly useful area of a priest's cultural formation is the study of the Humanities.[50] They are a principal means of entering into direct contact with the universal heritage we are talking about.

History, literature, the arts, music... are reservoirs that collect the best of the passing centuries of cultures and societies. When we tap them, we tap the highest accomplishments of the human spirit through the centuries.

The "classical humanities" offer special enrichment. The study of the classical (Greek and Latin) authors who expressed in a particularly dense and pure form the most elevated human ideals, renders an almost incomparable contribution for acquiring true humanism. It is recommendable that we become acquainted with the principal contributions of the best authors throughout history, from antiquity to our present day.

Familiarity with classical languages, especially Latin, is often an integral part of humanistic formation. Unquestionably a good part of western culture has been recorded in these languages, as also the majority

---

[50] The importance of these studies has led some religious institutes to include one or two years dedicated to these studies in their academic program.

of the writings of the Church's tradition. If we recall that Latin has been and continues to be the official language of the Church we will understand the constant insistence by the Magisterium that we do not stop teaching it to those who are preparing for ministerial priesthood.[51]

It is important to remember that humanities can lend a valuable service to ecclesiastical studies. Nowadays, young men who enter the seminary often share the present-day scientific, pragmatic and technical mentality. This mentality clashes head-on with the purpose, method and mental process demanded by philosophy and theology. By reading classical authors and appreciating the aesthetic, moral and spiritual values present in the various branches of humanities, they are introduced and helped to adapt to a new way of thinking. Humanities broaden the mind's horizons towards spaces which also allow for purely speculative reflection and openness to the transcendent. According to the experts, the study of the classical languages also favors mental structure and logical rigor, which are so necessary if philosophy and theology are to be more than an exercise in intellectual digression.

The development of science and its technical applications are transforming not only the face of the earth but also, in a very deep way, culture and education. Today a high percentage of young people study almost exclusively scientific or technical subjects. A basic knowledge, at least, of *modern sciences* will help the future priest to understand people of the present generation better and to make himself understood by them.

Human sciences (psychology, pedagogy, sociology, etc...) are a useful complement to ecclesiastical studies because of their direct bearing on the understanding of the person. Other sciences will be of considerable enrichment too.

Some candidates for the priesthood enter the seminary with an already sufficient scientific background. We should make sure they keep themselves up-to-date as best they can so that they make good use of this knowledge in their future apostolate. Other candidates are less educated in the sciences and we should find a way to help them cover the basics, without detriment to their philosophy and theology.

---

[51] Cf. OT 13; RFIS 66; Congregation for Catholic Education, *Document on the theological formation of future priests*, n. IV.1.3.1; CIC 249.

General culture also includes keeping informed in fields of immediate importance to the life of men and women of our day, such as politics and economics, law, etc.

We cannot omit a reference to the seminarians' need to know some modern languages besides their own native tongue[52] for they are to work in a world which is getting smaller, thanks to the means of transportation and the mass media.

Lastly, our seminarians ought to know the particular characteristics of the culture where they will exercise their ministry.This is an essential condition for later promoting true *inculturation* of the Gospel message, especially in places where adaptation is most necessary and urgent.

Learning to Communicate the Message

When a priest's ability to communicate is developed it multiplies the dividends of a good intellectual formation, or even of an average one. If it is not developed it can almost compromise his store of theological and cultural knowledge no matter how brilliant this is. A well-read priest who is not able to communicate is like a deep well, full of fresh water, but with no bucket — the passing traveler has to go on his way parched. It is enough to hear the comments of the congregation about some homilies...

We know that not everything depends on human know-how. "For the word of God is living and active, sharper than any two-edged sword" (Heb 4:12). Divine grace can penetrate a soul without, or even despite, human intervention. But in God's plan of salvation the messenger's word is normally a link between the Gospel message and the hearts of those who listen. When a link fails, the chain is broken. "How are they to believe in Him of whom they have never heard? And how are they to hear without a preacher?" (Rm 10:14-15). How will they understand and accept it if the message has not been preached effectively?

People expect the priest to read, write and speak correctly and vibrantly. Naturally, among candidates for the priesthood some are always more gifted than others in this field. The art of oral or written expression depends largely on a person's natural qualities and his previous education.

---

[52] Cf. CIC 249.

But it is always possible to improve and polish, regardless of the natural talents we have to work with, until we get to an acceptable level.

The academic program of the seminary should therefore include activities which teach the theory and exercise the skills of communication, such as classes and exercises which develop the student's capacity to write a letter, a report, a story, or a newspaper article correctly, etc. We need Christian authors to evangelize culture and public opinion. A priest could be one of them. Classes, and more importantly the exercise of oral expression, voice projection, techniques of classical and modern oratory, and homiletics are almost indispensable. Further still, we should find a way for some, the more gifted for this, to be prepared in debating skills, group dynamics, or in radio or television communication. The priest is a man of the Word; he must skillfully use words.

Some Means for the Intellectual Formation of Seminarians

We have discussed the objectives and content of intellectual formation. It is appropriate to consider some of the principal means to achieve it in the seminary.

Naturally, one of the basic means is classes. In every branch of human knowledge, contact with persons who are well versed and experienced in their own field notably enriches students. This is especially true in the case of theoretical subjects, for it is not enough to assimilate the thought of others, it is necessary to learn how to think. A student learns to think by following the professor closely as he strives to communicate his thought to the students. Theology, by its very nature, demands a type of transmission that is live and personal:

> ...when it is a question of transmitting, not mere knowledge, but rather a tradition of faith, as in the case of Christian tradition, it is indispensable to have contact with a teacher who is a witness of the faith that has illuminated and transformed his life. Teaching is turned into a conversation by the believing and praying theologian who joins the understanding of the mystery with the intimate acceptance of the mystery in his own life.[53]

---

[53] Congregation for Catholic Education, *The theological formation of future priests,* February 22, 1976, n.IV.I.2.1.

A theology class is not a group of students who receive the teaching of a professor. It is, more profoundly, a living community of believers who, helped by a specially qualified witness, make an effort to better understand their faith.

The quality of formation, therefore, will depend to a great degree on the quality of the professors in the seminary faculty. Enlisting a good team of professors is a priority in any seminary. We have to continually assure the preparation of seminarians and priests with the necessary talents for the teaching ministry. Often it will be necessary to ask for the assistance of other priests of the diocese. At times there will be qualified lay people ready to lend a hand in certain areas.

When the seminary does not have the necessary body of professors and there is a center of ecclesial studies nearby, this could be the best option. The formators of the seminary, however, should not simply unload their responsibility for the solid formation of their men on another teaching faculty. It is not a question of just sending seminarians out to do their studies elsewhere, without being concerned for their formation. The formators should know what is being given to their seminarians, how it is given to them, and also what is not being given to them, so that they can supplement whatever is necessary in their own center.

Each professor has his own method and style, and it is important to respect these. But each one should strive to teach in a way that is systematic, ordered and complete. We cannot teach how to think with order, or form the mental structure of our students, with an education that is confused and disorderly. Our concern for explaining the core of each subject clearly should be greatest in the early years, when students are getting their first view of the field of study. Later on they will have the chance to get into accidental and particular points and "sally" into unexplored areas.

Especially in theology, teachers should achieve a balance between their ability to stimulate personal reflection and their capacity to transmit certainties of faith. Their teaching is a service to the Church. As in every ministry, professors also need *a Sensus Ecclesiae*. The exercise of their particular charism will be enriched if they blend it with the charism of those who have been called to the magisterial ministry. Finally, their personal witness as believers and priests is infinitely more valuable than a brilliant lecture.

We would have to say the same about the textbooks. We should find books that offer a complete view of the subject and that at the same time will provoke in the reader questions that call him to mature reflection and help him to broaden his horizons.

Another indispensable element of intellectual formation is *personal study*. Those who derive spontaneous pleasure from this activity are normally few in number. Hence the seminary programs and the formators themselves should promote it effectively through continual motivation, founded above all on the ultimate meaning of these studies in the vocation and mission of a future priest. Exams and other incentives can serve to reinforce. Besides motivating, it is important to create a helpful atmosphere: periods scheduled exclusively for study, a climate of silence which favors concentration... Students should also be oriented to acquire a good methodology of intellectual work. Methodology classes and practical exercises, above all at the beginning, can serve as a guide to enable them to obtain better results.

The principle of "personalized formation" has its application here, too. If we reflect on the effect a good intellectual formation has on the overall formation of the seminarian and on the effectiveness of his future pastoral service, we will understand that we cannot let him "go it alone." The formator in charge of studies should know and follow each individual closely in order to motivate him, orient him, help him in his personal difficulties... Students of more advanced courses can lend a hand as "tutors" or "auxiliaries" to younger students.

Teamwork can produce excellent results in this field: meetings in order to study a difficult problem together, exchange reflections, share material for mutual benefit, etc... The official programs of the center could offer *activities for review or group reflection* for a particular class or for the whole student body. It could be very helpful, for example, to meet under the guidance of an expert and discuss in a systematic way particularly difficult or important cases in moral, dogmatic, or pastoral theology.

Earlier we spoke about elements to enrich significantly the cultural preparation of our future priests. It is not unrealistic. With a little effort it is feasible to organize, even if only sporadically, *complementary activities,* such as conferences, day seminars, minicourses... It is also possible to supply the library with texts and periodicals which provide informative and formative material for seminarians especially interested in a particular field.

Finally, as a good long-term investment for the seminary and diocese, there is a definite advantage in seeing if certain priests and seminarians can pursue *specialization.* Their field of study depends in part on the needs of the local Church and in part on their own qualities and interests.

The time we dedicate to the good intellectual formation of candidates for priesthood and pastoral service in the Church is always time well spent, and our efforts will not be in vain.

APOSTOLIC AND PASTORAL FORMATION

The seminarian's formation in the areas analyzed up until now takes on a special meaning with respect to his pastoral mission. The principle of an "eminently pastoral formation" underlined the fact that apostolic formation must permeate the entire priestly identity in its spiritual, intellectual and human dimensions. All our efforts to form the seminarians must be aimed at this target.

Yet besides this general focus of the formation process, we need to analyze *pastoral and apostolic formation* as a specific area with its own objectives and means, because it is not a mere adornment which puts the finishing touches on a priest. Christ called twelve apostles "to be sent out to preach" (Mk. 3:14). He gave them priestly powers to be used for the mission which He entrusted to them. From the outset, they knew they were apostles and understood that their priestly nature was a part of their apostolic identity.

In the same way, the young man who has entered the seminary has been called in order to be sent as a messenger of God's Kingdom. If our seminaries only produce priests who receive a sacramental character enabling them to celebrate the divine mysteries but who do not have apostolic hearts and are not prepared to fulfill their mission effectively, we have failed as formators.

All formation for the apostolate gravitates around two fundamental objectives: *formation of an apostolic heart and preparation for pastoral work.*

Formation of an Apostolic Heart

First and foremost, we must forge in each of our seminarians the personality and heart of a zealous apostle, fully aware of his mission and its meaning. Everything else (techniques and methodology) will only help if they rest on this base, because the seminarian has been called to *be an apostle* and not simply to *do apostolate.*

Apostolic Zeal and Awareness of the Mission

The seminarian's love for Christ must lead to identity with Him, and with his ardent love for humanity. This is what sparks the urgency and passionate desire to fight tirelessly to announce and extend the Kingdom by all good, licit and possible means, until Christ reigns in the heart of all people and societies.

A priest with *apostolic zeal* is never content with the half-hearted fulfillment of his job. On the contrary, he is a man who acts as guide to his brothers and sisters; a shepherd who knows them, inspires confidence, and lays down his life for them; a man who makes use of the most effective means to bring the Gospel and salvation to all people. He is a man who speaks in order to announce Christ whenever he can: homilies, conversations, chance encounters, etc. He is an apostle who, like Christ and Paul, can speak in the field or in the city, in a church or a university, in a prison or in public places, in a boat, on a trip, or in small groups... anywhere.

To form his apostolic zeal we must make the seminarian *aware of his mission.* He must understand that his mission is identified with Christ's and that therefore his vocation and life are part of salvation history. From the moment he perceived the call of God, his personal history became sacred history.

Awareness of the apostolic mission takes shape gradually during the period of formation until it becomes an all-absorbing concern, the focal point of his whole life, the transforming yeast of his personality. In this awareness the seminarian constantly strives to better himself in his spiritual life, in his intellectual and human formation, and in his pastoral preparation. When he is engaged in the apostolate this awareness of his mission is proven in his sincere eagerness to bear concrete fruits, to be more efficient and to promote initiatives. There will be moments of tiredness, failure and discouragement but the cry of the Apostle will always resound once again in his heart: "Woe to me if I do not preach the Gospel!" (1 Cor 9:16), for he never forgets Christ's commandment: "Go into all the world and preach the Gospel to the whole of creation" (Mk 16:15).

ECCLESIAL SPIRIT

Full and genuine awareness of the priestly mission means ecclesial awareness. When He sends a priest into the world, Christ sends him to build his Church. He entrusts the assembly of the faithful to him, its maturing in the faith, its fidelity to the Gospel, and its spiritual growth through the celebration of the sacraments... As we said in the section on spiritual formation, the priest's mission only has meaning in the Church, for the Church, and stemming from the Church's spiritual and human mission.

We must form our seminarians in an ecclesial conception of their pastoral service so that in the future they will feel that their parish, school or mission territory is a part of the Lord's great vineyard. They will desire to work alongside other workers in the vineyard, give them moral support and practical assistance, and become actively involved in the pastoral plans of the diocese. If we succeed in forming this "Church spirit" in them, they will even sacrifice their own work if a superior good of the diocese or of the universal Church needs them to do so. They will be capable of offering themselves to work in the missions or help to alleviate the poverty of some particular church.[54]

The same sense of Church in the apostolate will make them want to transmit their love for the Church to the faithful. If they truly understand their mission as being ecclesial, they will preach this love for the Church in their speaking and writing, in their dealings with the faithful and when guiding the apostolic work of the lay people. They will encourage: love for

---

[54] Vatican II invites us to form this attitude in future priests when it asks that *they transcend the borders of their own diocese, nation, or rite, be accustomed to consulting the needs of the whole Church and be ready in spirit to preach the Gospel everywhere.* (OT 20, cf. CIC 257)

the universal Church; knowledge of the documents and guidelines of the Magisterium, understanding their meaning and accepting their doctrine; love for the Pope based on faith; and knowledge, love and real interest in their local church and diocesan shepherd.

PASTORAL CHARITY AND PREFERENTIAL OPTION FOR THE POOR

The priest's model and ideal is the Good Shepherd: a shepherd who takes care of the sheep, knows them by name, goes out in search of the lost one and upon finding it, rejoices and carries it home on his shoulders. He is concerned for those who still do not belong to the sheepfold and is ready to give his life for his sheep (cf. Jn 10:11-18). The good shepherd is a shepherd who sincerely loves his sheep. The apostolate is a service, not an imposition. There will be no genuine *pastoral activity* without *pastoral charity.*

Moved by this charity an apostle goes out to meet all people and shows sincere interest in their situation, their problems, their sorrows and joys. He draws near to them in order to share in their personal history.

The shepherd-priest's charity is *universal,* but like all gratuitous and self-sacrificing love it is especially dedicated to those who most need it — not to those who respond best to it, nor even to those who most "merit" it. *Although he has obligations towards all men, a priest has the poor and the lowly entrusted to him in a special way. Our Lord explicitly showed that He was united to them.*[55] In this sense, the Church speaks of a "preferential option for the poor."[56] Following Christ's example, a priest must be sensitive to the material misery in which so many human beings live, perhaps even in his own parish. The personal and structural injustices which provoke or abet this situation cannot leave him unmoved.

It is not a question of just feeling and loving. He must also act. He cannot allow charity and justice to be dormant in his heart, for he would then fail all those who come to him in hope, seeking in the priest a brother, a friend, an advocate. He would also fail in his own priestly identity, for promoting the cause of the human person is also an integral part of his priestly mission. Christ came to save *the whole person, and consequently*

---

[55] Cf. PO 6.
[56] Cf. III Conference of the Latin American Episcopate (CELAM), *Document of Puebla,* n. 1134-1165 and n. 1166-1205; LN III, 3 and VI, 5-6; LC 66-68; SRS 42.

the Church seeks the good of man in all his dimensions; in the first place as a member of the city of God and then as a member of the earthly city.[57]

Training the seminarians to have a pastoral heart includes teaching them this preferential love for the poor, as it is understood by the Church.

In the first place, it is neither the sole nor an exclusive option.[58] Christ came to save *all people*. His compassion for and dedication to the poor did not impede Him from also dealing with those who enjoyed material wealth, but were poor as regards the treasures of the Kingdom. In some way, He defined his mission by quoting Isaiah: "He has anointed me to preach good news to the poor" (Lk 4:18). Yet He was just as explicit about the meaning of his coming, when responding to the Pharisees who murmured against Him: "I have not come to call the righteous, but sinners to repentance" (Lk 5:32). The sinners to whom He referred that time were Levi and the other publicans of the city, rich men capable of offering Him "a fine reception" (ibid.).

We should help the seminarians learn to love the poor, not because they are poor but because they are people; and to know how to love the rich in the same way, not because they are rich but because they are people.

Love is the second characteristic of the true Christian option for the poor. Although certain groups try to justify attacking the rich with the excuse of love for the poor, it is a contradiction to try to love some while hating others. Class struggle is not Christian. Before it even snatches their riches from the powerful, it steals from the poor their greatest treasure: charity. To sow hatred, violence or the idea of class struggle in those who are preparing for the priesthood is to undermine the very essence of their identity as Christ's representatives. In the long run, it hurts the poor themselves.

We must look for genuine ways of helping the most needy. *Our option for the poor has to be effective.* From their years in the seminary, candidates should learn some of the necessary conditions for this effectiveness.

For example, they should understand that the best promotion of the poor is to make them *the protagonists of their own betterment,*[59] and that

---

[57] LC 63.

[58] Cf. LC 68.

[59] Cf. PP 15; LE 4; SRS 30.

we must therefore raise their cultural level and prepare them to work, to save, and to want to better themselves.

Yet if we really want their integral development, we need the *participation of those who have the reins of progress in their hands.* One thing is to favor the poor, another thing is to dedicate our pastoral activity only to them. Our option for the poor requires that we be with them, and many times among them. Yet it also demands that we be responsible enough to work with economic, cultural and social leaders, enlightening their consciences with the Gospel so that they put their leadership at the service of the most needy. Inflammatory "prophetic" preaching that begs open conflict with those who can and must help the poor is a mistake and gross irresponsibility. It only provokes a defensive attitude and abandonment of the poor to their unfortunate lot. It also at times implies a subtle moral oversimplification, for in a general, global and classist way, it denounces all those who are not "poor" as exploiters and oppressors, without taking into account the state of each individual conscience. A priest who really wants to be like the Master, whose prophetic mission he shares, has a clear example of how to deal with the wealthy in Jesus' discreet way of acting when He gets himself invited to Zacchaeus' house and works in his soul a profound conversion to justice, without outcries or condemnations (cf. Lk 19:1-10).

Seminarians, especially those we see will have to exercise their pastoral ministry among the modern Zacchaeus' of our society, should acquire a realistic and positive view of material progress and economic development.[60] In their future ministry with those in charge of production and the economy, they should help them realize that a sense of justice asks them to effectively increase production, to try to produce "more and better":[61] if there is no real increase in wealth, the only thing to share will be poverty. But they will also have to help them see that the end purpose of the effort to increase production is to increase "distribution." By multiplying job sources, increasing real output of goods and their just distribution, they will be contributing to the common good. They should understand that the universal destiny of material goods means that their property, capital and work have a deep social meaning: they are talents en-

[60] Cf. SRS 28-30.
[61] Cf. PP 48.

trusted to them to bear fruit for the benefit of everyone (cf. Mt 25:26-28). The pastoral action of the priest should promote Christian charity and solidarity to a point in which those who possess economic resources are capable of giving not only from their surplus goods, but also from what is necessary, whenever this would be needed to alleviate the misery of those who suffer.[62]

A third important element in this matter is the balance between our action towards the necessary *change in structure,* and towards a *change of hearts.* Both are necessary. The reform of the social, economic, juridical or political structures which stand in the way of progress for everyone is a necessary condition for social justice to become a reality which will effectively change unjust situations. Reforming hearts guarantees true and lasting change in these structures since these structures are fundamentally the product of the mind and will of concrete individuals who create or sustain them.[63]

Lastly, training seminarians in a true option for the poor means making them understand the *global sense of their mission,* and in that framework teaching them how to give priority to *what is essential.* The fact that Christ came to save the human person as a whole means that the mission of the Church includes the social dimension. But it also means it is not limited to it.

Our faith gives us a clear vision of our world and reveals that *sin* is the worst misery which afflicts humanity. Christ came "to call... sinners" (Lk 5:32). Even his name was chosen by God to reflect this fact, "You shall call his name Jesus, for He will save his people from their sins" (Mt 1:21). He took pity on all human misery and tried to alleviate it, but it is evident that for Him the most important thing was to rescue people from the misery of sin. Recall his cure of the paralytic as proof of his power to forgive sin, that so shocked the pharisees (cf. Mt 9:6). This is the ultimate meaning of his salvific sacrifice. He explained to the disciples at the Last Supper that his blood "is poured out for many for the forgiveness of sins" (Mt 26:28). Thus Paul would later affirm: "He was put to death for our trespasses and raised for our justification" (Rm 4:25). Jesus emphasized it before sending his disciples out into the world: "Thus it is written, that the Christ should

---

[62] Cf. SRS 31.
[63] Cf. EN 19 and 31; SRS 31-38.

suffer and on the third day rise from the dead, and that repentance and forgiveness of sins should be preached in his name to all nations, beginning from Jerusalem. You are witnesses of these things" (Lk 24:46-48).

As a witness to these things, the priest must always remember that his message is essentially a spiritual message, a message of supernatural salvation. This is the deepest desire of any man or woman, the most needy included. They expect from the priest what is specific to his priesthood. From a politician or a union leader they can only hope for bread; from the priest they expect the Bread of Life. They draw near to a man of God in order to draw near to God.

Seminarians have to realize that their work in the field of social charity is not foreign to their future priestly identity. It is a consequence of their integral mission, though it is not the only one nor the principal one. Hence, they will understand that they should never forget that the *first priority* of their priesthood is to announce the Word of God, administer the sacraments of salvation and, as pastors, take care of the people of God. The best social service they can offer is the formation of their flock through the preparation of *lay people* who will work effectively to build a better society in accord with the demands of their faith. Lastly, they should understand that since their mission is essentially ecclesial, they cannot leave aside the *"social teaching of the Church"* in their work.[64]

Formation for Pastoral Ministry

A seminarian will not become an apostle unless he has a profound understanding of his mission and tenacious zeal to fulfill it. But he will not become one either if he does not receive specific pastoral preparation. It is not enough for him to *want* to do apostolate; he also has to *know how* to do it effectively.

SOME AREAS OF PASTORAL FORMATION

The first area of pastoral formation has to do with the contents of the message. We spoke in the previous section about the pastoral dimension

---

[64] Cf. LN ch. 5; SRS 41.

of all the subjects, especially of philosophy and theology. Here it would be good to underline the importance of some subjects which some might think of as "secondary" within the overall scheme of theology, but which are necessary for a young man who is preparing for the apostolate. Such would be, for example, pastoral theology, catechetics, liturgical and sacramental practice, canon law (especially the chapters which deal with the administration of sacraments and the ordinary running of parishes), etc.

It is also good to offer courses or other means to help the future priests to prepare themselves for certain types of apostolic work which often are part of any apostolate: courses on spiritual direction, how to give spiritual exercises....

There also are many practical areas of pastoral work that, in some way, the seminarians must know before having to face them. It is clearly neither realistic nor necessary for everyone to know everything about all of them. But we can certainly single out the most urgent areas according to the necessities and pastoral plans of the diocese, the seminarians' natural qualities and inclinations and, if possible, each one's future assignment as foreseen in his final seminary years.

Parochial administration (in its pastoral, organizational, juridical and economic aspects) is an important area of formation. Other important fields are those related to youth work, marriage and family, and the pastoral care of the sick and elderly, etc.

In some places it will be necessary to pay special attention to the pastoral care of immigrants and itinerants; in others, preparation for the ecumenical ministry will have priority. In some cases we will have to train them specifically for the evangelization of the world of culture, or the work force. We can wisely prepare our more talented students to be vocational promoters. Although such a vital apostolate of the diocese requires that every dedicated priest personally try his best to foster vocations, it can also be coordinated full-time by a priest assigned to this work.

Now more than ever we should be concerned to prepare seminarians to specialize in the vast field of the media. We must first teach them as "receivers" of the media — so that they will be intelligent and critical rather than passive. Only in this way can the use of the media be of positive benefit. But we have to prepare some to use them "actively," forming them so that they will be ready to write and speak on radio and television, participate in debates and discussions, etc. Some of them should even go on to programming and direction. In this area even more than in others, they must prepare themselves with the necessary professionalism and energy to engage expertly a world as difficult and competitive as the media.

The list is almost endless, but we need not exhaust it. Let us finish by saying that we should also single out those students who could perhaps some day work as professors and formators of future seminarians.

SOME ELEMENTS OF PASTORAL PRACTICE

Regardless of each seminarian's future work, his formation should include fundamental elements of apostolic methods. We could write a whole book on this, so let us just touch on some particularly important points. Effectiveness, as a mindset and a skill, is an element that is always necessary. Effectiveness depends fundamentally on one's apostolic zeal and one's desire to bear fruit, but it can also be taught as an attitude and style of working. It is necessary to inspire in the seminarian a desire to make ambitious use of his time — to do more things, better, in less time. It is not a question of simply being occupied or extremely busy, but rather of achieving important and fruitful goals. This is the difference between "efficiency" (doing things well) and "effectiveness" (doing well what is most important).

For this, they should learn the art and skill of planning. They should know how to program for the long, medium and short terms, establishing objectives and priorities, and foreseeing the means, people and time necessary to reach these goals. There are studies done which give many suggestions and tips in this area that administrators, planners and personnel managers use widely. Seminarians can also learn all the means that the computer age offers, which if used well can greatly aid the work of a priest who must write, keep records, correspond, etc. Does a priest have any reason not to put these means at the service of the worthiest cause? Of course, the "effectiveness" that the apostle of Christ seeks does not depend so much in the last analysis on human techniques as it does on divine grace. Yet God's plan of salvation always uses man's effort.

It is not necessary here to go into the area of expression and effective communication of the message, since we have already done so when dealing with intellectual formation. The importance of a good preparation in that area for one called to be a minister of the Word goes without saying.

Another key aspect is *learning to work with others.* First of all, they should have a spirit of cooperation which will bring them to insert themselves fully into the pastoral programs of the diocese and work in coordination with the other priests. But they also need the skills of cooperation and teamwork. In the future they will have to work with other priests in a parish, in a deanery, coordinating youth apostolates... It will go badly if they are not capable of, or do not want to meet, program, or coordinate as a member of a living and effective team. Here in the seminary is the time to learn the theory and practice of teamwork.

This teamwork is not limited to his relations with other priests. It is just as important, if not more, that he be able to work with the laity. The future priest has to appreciate the specific vocation and mission of the baptized members of the People of God. The synod of bishops in 1977 expressed this when they invited priests and seminarians *to prepare themselves carefully in order to be able to promote the vocation and mission of lay people.*[65] With a spirit of faith, the priest must recognize and diligently promote the various charisms of the laity.[66] Lumen Gentium asked that priests learn to recognize and promote the dignity and responsibility of the lay members of the Church, assign duties to them in the service of the Church and encourage them to undertake tasks on their own initiative.[67] Echoing this last aspect, the decree on priestly formation asks that future priests be prepared to arouse and encourage the apostolic action of lay people.[68] The Apostolic Exhortation Christifideles laici also touches this point.[69]

---

[65] Synod of Bishops, 1977, Proposal 40 (Quoted in the Apostolic Exhortation *Christifideles laici*, n. 61).

[66] Cf. John Paul II, *Letter to priests,* 1989.

[67] Cf. LG 37.

[68] Cf. OT 20. It is not necessary to ponder here the profound theological meaning and decisive importance of this collaboration of lay people and with lay people. Fortunately it is a theme which has been fruitfully developed in the last few decades and treated thoroughly in a recent Synod of Bishops and in the apostolic exhortation *Christifideles laici.* Seminarians should be instructed in such a way that not only do they know the importance of working with lay people, but they are really convinced of it and decided to draw the practical consequences in their pastoral ministry.

[69] Cf. CL 22.

The apostolic action of lay people should never be limited to lending a hand in the sacristy. We have to assist the lay apostolate to live up to its name. Hence, we should explain the different fields and types of action proper to the laity so that seminarians will understand that the laity's specific work begins in the structures and environment of the world, that it is the work of the yeast in the dough.

Today, we have to recognize and accept the growing feature of associations and movements in the Church. Seminarians must know the profound human and ecclesial meaning of this style of life at work in the Church today. They should know what makes these groups truly a body within the Church, what their finality is, what their legitimate place is in the heart of the people of God and its institutions. Likewise, we should help them achieve a clear understanding of the various movements which work in the diocese, above all the more significant and influential ones. When they go out on their apostolate they must be able to work in coordination with these movements, without prejudice, without favoritism, and without jealousy or unjustified suspicion.

In his future work with lay people it will be helpful to the seminarian to put into practice a maxim which summarizes his role: *act, encourage others to act and allow others to act.* The priest must be the first one to work. This refers especially to the fulfillment of his specifically priestly role, what the laity cannot or should not do. *Encourage others to act* refers to the skill of prompting the cooperation of lay people in apostolic and evangelizing tasks. The effectiveness of this second step depends on the amount of time and effort a priest dedicates to the formation of his co-workers. *Allow others to act* means to know how to recognize others' charisms and not extinguish the light of the Spirit. It means not to smother initiative, but to help, motivate and contribute towards the greatest apostolic success possible. It is a mistake for a priest to want everything the laity does to start with him, go through him and be finished by him. Many times lay people only need the priest to let them act as they know how. This requires great trust on the part of the priest — trust in others, in their qualities, sincerity and possibilities. Naturally, to encourage others to act and allow others to act does not mean to abdicate. A priest continues being shepherd and guide. He must direct his lay apostles along the path of doctrinal orthodoxy and a truly Christian understanding of the apostolate. He must recall that "the wind blows where it will..." (Jn 3:8), yet he has to discern if it is truly the Spirit which blows.

Act, encourage others to act and allow others to act is a very fruitful and useful practice by which the priest can multiply himself. With this strategy the horizon of his apostolate stretches to distances he obviously could never have reached on his own.

Means for Apostolic and Pastoral Formation

What we have said will be just theory if we do not reflect on the means we can use to achieve in practice an apostolic and pastoral formation. Let us consider, then, some means which favor the growth of apostolic zeal and some others that will be directed especially towards the necessary and practical preparation for pastoral ministry.

Before all else, we should remember that priestly zeal and a sense of mission are a *divine grace,* a sharing in the love of Christ for humanity. Therefore, the first means we have is prayer. For an apostle in formation (and his formator) *prayer* is a petition for this grace. It is close contact with the Fount of love, and an expression of his love for the souls he is called to evangelize and for whom he prays from the seminary. Recall the cloistered nun, Theresa of Lisieux, who merited to be named patroness of the missions because of her prayers.

Along this line and keeping in mind the wonderful reality of the mystical Body, it is very effective to teach the seminarians to give all their activities an *apostolic intention.* This is the best way for them to learn in practice that a priest is a 24-hour-a-day apostle. Everything (study, work, prayer, rest...) that we place in God's hands can take on redemptive value.

During his personal prayer, the seminarian should frequently *contemplate the example of Christ the Apostle,* who gave Himself totally to his mission. There is no better school of apostolate, especially for the priest-apostle identified in a unique way with the Master by the sacrament of Orders. See Him as He preached in the squares and the temple, in the towns and synagogues; walking the byways of Palestine; curing the sick long into the night. He had no time to eat; He was moved by the crowds because they were like sheep without a shepherd; He was close to sinners, the poor and the sick, etc. Contemplating all this, preferably in a climate of prayer and meditation, will fill and motivate the heart of any young man who aspires to be a shepherd of souls.

Our men can also fruitfully contemplate the example of Christ who, when he saw the crowd, felt "compassion for them, because they were harassed and helpless, like sheep without a shepherd." (Mt 9:36). The seminarians' sense of mission, apostolic zeal, ecclesial spirit and pastoral charity will be reinforced if we *open their eyes to the sufferings and injustice* which numerous men and women, and even entire nations, have to endure. Put them in touch with the actual problems that afflict the Church.

It is therefore good to give them the means to follow the current events of the Church and the world. Yet we must educate their view of reality beyond a mere curiosity for news. They should read the news in the light of faith, discovering in it the living drama of the history of salvation. Like Christ, upon seeing the suffering crowd, they should "feel compassion for them." Compassion and sympathy must move them to identify with *the joys and the hopes, the griefs and the anxieties of the men of this age*.[70] Only then will Christ's concern for the needy multitudes ("the harvest is great but the laborers few") echo within them forcefully enough to make them true workers in this harvest.

All the means we have listed up to this point are easy to apply for they only require us to give a specifically apostolic focus to already existing aspects of seminary life. But when we try to implement some of the more specific activities for apostolic formation we mentioned (media training, communication skills, exercises in teamwork, etc...) we face the problems of how and when. Doubtless, the answer depends on each seminarian's circumstances. The formators' own sense of responsibility and their awareness of the need to help the candidates concretely will help them find the best means.

Some of these activities overlap with their academic formation. If the seminarians attend classes outside the seminary we have to see if the specific training we desire is already included or if it is necessary to supplement it in the seminary. Seminars, courses, conferences and the like can be organized to cover these areas. The contribution of experts from diverse fields of study is very enriching. For example, an expert in time

---

[70] GS 1.

management can be invited to give conferences, as can a priest experienced in family counseling or in youth work or a member of some lay movement, etc... Vacation time might be suitable for these activities, but we could also try to scatter them throughout the school year without detriment to the basic academic courses.

Seminarians interested in a specific area of pastoral activity (the media, for example) can form study teams in order to exchange material, reading lists, and book summaries or hold seminars on some particular aspect... It is important to arouse their personal interest so that they make use of the materials at their disposal (magazines, manuals, videos...) to form themselves better.

The best "methodology course" is actual practice, and practice is more effective than theory in some areas. Take, for example, what was said about cooperation and teamwork.

With this in mind, seminary programs should always offer the students the opportunity to contribute directly in some apostolic activity: *Seminarians need to learn the art of exercising the apostolate not only in theory but also in practice. They have to be able to pursue their assignments both on their own initiative and in concert with others. Hence, even during their course of studies, and also during holidays, they should be introduced into pastoral practice by appropriate undertakings.*[71]

Some dioceses have introduced a prolonged period of "pastoral apprenticeship" with very positive results. In a program like this, a candidate interrupts his studies at some point before ordination to dedicate himself to apostolic work in the diocese for a period of one or two years, in a parish or somewhere else. It can be a decisive time for his future ministry, not only to learn how to carry out an apostolate, but also to experience what his future life as a priest will be like. He has firsthand contact with the faithful and their needs, and discovers the true meaning of his formation, studies, his priesthood and his mission.

Whether it take place during the school year or during vacation we should never let this apostolic internship be nothing more that a simple extracurricular activity, more or less enjoyable. It is a true means of formation. As formators, we must make sure that this work is formative and that the students get the most out of it with respect to their future

[71] OT 21.

ministry, while they make a real contribution towards the various needs of the diocese.

Formators should program and coordinate in some way these pastoral internships. They should not simply "send them out" without taking an interest in the environment they will be working in, the type of apostolate they will have, the time they will dedicate to it, and so forth. They must consider the age, maturity and qualities of the students, to see what is best for each one.

If the apostolic work of the seminarians takes place during the school year, it is good for the formators to meet periodically with groups of those involved in similar apostolates so as to motivate, plan together, review results, etc. By means of personal orientation they can show their interest in the apostolate that a candidate is doing, his difficulties and achievements, the real maturing of his apostolic zeal, etc.

However, when the young men dedicate long periods of time to the apostolate, the priests who work with them should feel responsible for their formation especially in this specific area of pastoral formation.

Obviously, though, the formators at the seminary continue being the ones directly responsible for the candidates. They should strive to help them to continue forming themselves in every dimension, from the spiritual to the pastoral, even when they are "out in the field." During this period, perhaps they could continue living in the seminary although they dedicate the entire day to the apostolate, or else form teams of pastoral work under the guidance of an experienced priest.

CHAPTER FOUR

FORMATORS

When we spoke about the protagonists of formation in Chapter Two, we described the formator as a *co-worker* with the Holy Spirit and the aspirant to the priesthood. But, as has been seen up to now, he is a collaborator who plays a decisive role. The Spirit is the true craftsman of sanctity, the candidate to the priesthood is the one chiefly responsible for his own formation. But it is the formator who can and should enable the young man who enters the seminary to understand all of this, directing him so that he opens himself to the Holy Spirit and cooperates with Him. So we may affirm that *the quality of formation will be proportional to the quality of formators.*

For this reason, this book is addressed to formators. In the previous chapter, for example, we offered numerous suggestions for their work in the diverse areas of formation. However, we should also reflect on the formator as such. We will consider first the men who make up the *formation team* in a seminary. Next we will look at *the person of the formator* in relation to the young men he serves. We will then briefly consider the qualities of the *relationship between formator and candidate* if it is to be a true collaboration in the task of formation, and at the same time we will present a few suggestions for the way a *formator should operate* in the everyday task of formation.

The Team of Formators

According to what the Church has established, the basic team of directors and formators in a seminary consists of the rector, the vice-rector, spiritual directors, ordinary and extraordinary confessors.[1] If the teaching is done in the same center, the dean of studies and professors are also members. As the third paragraph of canon 239 of Canon Law states, the responsibilities of each one must be established in the statutes of the seminary, in accordance with the norms of the universal Church and the plan of priestly formation established by the local episcopal conference.[2]

It is clear that after the bishop, *the rector of the seminary* is principally responsible for formation.[3] He must certify, once the years of formation are concluded, that the candidate possesses the necessary qualities to receive sacred orders.[4] The rector does not occupy himself exclusively with the external aspects of the center, a responsibility he could delegate in large part to the *vice-rector* and the *administrator* of the seminary; rather, he participates actively in the whole formative process of each one of the seminarians.

The work of the *spiritual director* is also extremely delicate, since he guides each student "from within" in all the aspects of his priestly formation. The spiritual director, by means of his advice, closeness and firmness, teaches the path of spiritual progress, enlightens the conscience with valid criteria, dissipates doubts, encourages generous self-giving, is with the student in difficult moments, shares his successes, directs and unifies the efforts of the candidate, invites him to assimilate his formation internally and watches over its integrity. He is definitively the Holy Spirit's closest collaborator.

It is important to remember, however, that he is also a member of the team of formators. His work, and that of the other formators, will be limited and perhaps compromised if the seminarians think of him as a confidant or external counselor. Instead, they should look on their relationship with him as part of their effort to form themselves. So too, they should be frank and trusting with the other formators, beginning with the rector.

The ordinary and extraordinary *confessors* fulfill a role of transcendental importance. They also guide the spiritual progress of the students by means of their advice. They help to form their conscience in their relations with God and with others. They foster their spiritual progress,

[1] Cf. CIC 239, 240, 254.
[2] Cf. CIC 242.
[3] Cf. CIC 260.
[4] Cf. CIC 1051 § 1.

whether by sustaining them in the struggle against sin and disordered passions, or by encouraging them to ascend toward perfection. Their silent and hidden task, a privileged channel of divine grace, will mark the soul of future confessors in a particular way: the manner in which these future priests administer the sacrament of forgiveness will depend to a great extent on the way in which it is administered to them today.

A lack of good spiritual directors and confessors, or distance between them and the seminarians, would seriously endanger the success of priestly formation. There would be little difference between formation and a simple academic preparation that does not profoundly transform the person.

If we really want the formation of our seminarians to be a personal-ized formation, we must always make sure that there are a sufficient number of formators. This does not only apply to spiritual directors and confessors. We also need the closeness of a formator who is with the seminarians in their ordinary day-to-day life and who responds to their daily needs. When the center reaches a certain number of students, some experienced priests can be appointed as *assistants to the rector*. With their witness, cooperation and direction they sustain his formative work, helping him especially to follow each one of the students personally. Each assistant could, for example, be in charge of a group of twenty-five or thirty seminarians whom he would help in a special way: working closely with them, showing them particular interest, following their programs of formation in greater detail, etc. Without this help the rector might not be able to attend to everyone personally with the necessary time and continu-ity. Assistants also provide valuable help in the organization and discipline of the seminary, carrying out the directives of the rector, giving life to community activities, etc.

In the chapter on intellectual formation we mentioned briefly the role of *teachers* and some characteristics of their ecclesial service. As for the *dean of studies,* we simply note that his presence and close help is necessary and virtually indispensable, even in seminaries whose students take classes outside. It is always helpful to count on a guide for one's intellectual work. He can attend to the students personally in order to motivate, give suggestions, clear up doubts, supervise the method of study, suggest readings, etc. It is also his task to organize the complementary academic activities that we mentioned in the previous chapter.

This is the formation *team*. It is not a simple "group" of people, with each one acting on his own. The success of a seminary depends to a great extent on the close-knit spirit of our formators: teamwork, intercommunication, joint application of principles and directives, sharing of tasks and functions... This not only improves the practical organization of the seminary, but most importantly, assures the personal formation of each seminarian. Each formator can fulfill his particular mission better if he acts guided by the same criteria as the other formators. The seminarian is thus led in the same direction by all.

Further, this team spirit among the formators is a valuable witness of charity, priestly unity, dialogue and mutual support for the seminarians. This example will affect his future ministerial practice, especially his cooperation with other priests. The rector should be the first one to have and encourage team spirit. He should neither attempt to do everything, nor dissociate himself from any specific sector he has delegated to another formator. He must know and esteem the formators, motivate them and promote their active participation, be able to delegate habitual or occasional tasks and responsibilities to them, and coordinate the efforts of all in one direction. For this, he must dedicate his time and interest to listening to, supervising and guiding each of his colleagues.

Teamwork also requires that formators meet periodically, with the rector presiding, to review the progress of the seminary, examine problems that arise, find solutions and paths of action, and program the diverse aspects of seminary life.

The term "formator" in this chapter refers principally to the rector, the vice-rector, spiritual directors and priest-assistants. Some of the suggestions can also be applied to confessors.

The Person of the Formator

GOD'S REPRESENTATIVE

The first thing to keep in mind when speaking about the formator is that he is there because God wants him there. From the standpoint of faith, before being an organizer, counsellor or friend, the formator is, for the seminarians, *God's representative*. A divine call has invited the candidates to follow their vocation. And a divine plan has placed certain men along the way to help them travel it. All of this fits in the scheme of the Church, just as her Founder has wished it: a community of believers in which certain individuals serve the rest through a *ministry of authority*.[5]

Herein lies the authority of the formator. Christ's words are applied to him, "He who hears you hears me, and he who hears me hears him who sent me" (cf. Mt 10:40; Lk 10:16). If the seminary is an ecclesial community, the rector of the seminary is, in a sense, pastor of that community.[6]

He and his collaborators have to realize that their work is a *service of authority* and that their *authority is service*. This is not a mere play on words. Formators cannot renounce their role as guides, pastors, God's representatives for those who are preparing themselves for priesthood. They cannot limit themselves to the role of more or less efficient coordinators. They would cease to be what God wants them to be. But as God's representatives, they should exercise their authority as Christ did who "came not to be served but to serve" (Mt 20:28). This authority has been given them "for building up and not for tearing down" (2 Cor 13:10). To exercise this authority with a spirit of service means that they should treat candidates with the same charity with which God loves them. It means that all their actions should be guided by the sole desire of helping the seminarians to live out their vocation and in that vocation to achieve their own fulfillment. The true welfare of the young men entrusted to them should be the motive behind their decisions and conduct: when they advise, when they demand, when they grant permissions and when they deny them... always, above all, the good of the seminarian, not their own, must be paramount.

This is the most effective way of making the seminarians see their formators, through the eyes of faith, as authentic representatives of the God who called them to his service.

---

[5] Cf. LG 18ff.
[6] Cf. CIC 262.

The ultimate responsibility for the seminary and for the formation of candidates to the priesthood rests upon the bishop, the shepherd whom Christ has placed at the service of the whole diocese. Formators receive their authority from him. Therefore, they are *the Church's representatives* before the students of the seminary. As such, they act in accord with the mind of the Church, faithfully observing the ordinances and directives of the competent authorities of the universal Church, of the episcopal conference and of their own bishop. They are asked to apply all of their abilities, their gifts and their inventiveness to their mission. But they should always do so in harmony and coordination with the one who has the ultimate responsibility for the diocese.

Moreover, their task is to collaborate in forming priests of the Church and for the Church. The seminarians entrusted to our care are called to be men of the Church, closely united to Peter's Successor and the bishops in communion with him. The formator's love for the universal and local Church should be so sincere and intense that he spontaneously at all times transmits it to the candidates, creating a genuinely ecclesial atmosphere which inspires the generous dedication of all the seminary members to the cause of the Church.

FATHER AND FRIEND

A true formator represents God and the Church, not as a legal delegate, but as one who *truly takes someone else's place.* In this sense, we can say that he is for the seminarians a true *father and friend.* Someone who does his job as a functionary will never be a good formator, no matter how competent he is.

Paul's attitude towards the faithful of his churches is a lesson for a good formator: "...though we might have made demands as apostles of Christ. But we were gentle among you, like a nurse taking care of her children. So, being affectionately desirous of you, we were ready to share with you not only the Gospel of God but also our own selves, because you had become very dear to us" (1 Th 2:7-8).

The formator is a father in his authority, his experience, and his interest for the integral maturing of the seminarians. He is a friend in his closeness, in his benevolence, always accessible... As a father he advises, motivates, demands, pardons. As a friend he accompanies, collaborates, shares. This behavior, if it is sincere, naturally leads the seminarians to look up to and open up to him. When seminarians perceive understanding, magnanimity and respect in the formator, they feel called to respond in kind.

TEACHER AND GUIDE

A young man who enters the seminary comes to learn. He needs a *teacher*. It is true that there is only one Master (cf. Mt 23:8). But it is also true that Jesus sent his disciples to teach (cf. Mt 28:20). The formator of priests has therefore been called to teach the doctrine of the Master, just as He entrusted it to his Church.

But preparing for the priesthood is much more than learning a theory or values: it is learning how to live. In this sense the formator is essentially a *guide*.

He has to teach and guide the candidates in numerous different aspects and details. All are important. But his principal task is to lead them to encounter the Master.

A Formator's Relationship with Students

Human and spiritual growth depends largely on a person's relationships. In any educational program that aspires to more than relaying information, the relationship between formator and student is an extremely important aspect. It is in this relationship that the formators can form each seminarian personally in his efforts to form himself.

If we fail to establish a proper formator-seminarian relationship, if formators become just professors or administrators, if seminarians live totally outside their influence, formation can be seriously compromised.

Since the formator represents God and the Church, his relationship to seminarians is based primarily on *faith*. It is part of the divine call that both have received. And if God acts through this relationship, it cannot be reduced to a casual friendship, or even a professional teacher-student or psychologist-patient relationship. The formator has to be the first to realize this and then help seminarians to do so also.

At times dealing with the formator can be an arduous task for the seminarian. The young man's temperament, personal circumstances, his natural tendency to independence and self-affirmation... any one of these things could lead him to distance himself from authority. A formator, too, may experience difficulties with a student. Personality conflicts may arise that, on a merely human level, seem difficult to overcome. However, if this relationship is built on a spiritual basis, these difficulties will not be decisive and can be resolved.

The spiritual aspect never cancels the human element of inter-personal relationships. There is a delicate combination of human feelings and Christian goodness, natural intuition and the grace of God in the relationship between formator and seminarian. The good will and collaboration of both together will build a close, friendly relationship, characterized by *sincerity, simplicity, openness, respect and warmth.*

If a seminarian has a frank, straightforward rapport with his formators (especially his spiritual director) he is more likely to open his conscience. Then, in an atmosphere of mutual trust, he can express doubts and problems without any hesitation; he finds concrete, personal support in the formator; he receives insight and grace from his advice, and in moments of tension or distress, he can unburden himself.

THE FORMATOR'S ACTION IN THIS RELATIONSHIP

A formator should not only establish a good rapport with semi-narians, he should also work actively through this relationship to achieve the formation goals that we outlined earlier.

Prayer, sacrifice, personal witness

The first task for any formator is to pray for his seminarians. He knows that "every good endowment and every perfect gift is from above, coming down from the Father of light" (Jm 1:17). He shares Paul's sentiments towards the first Christian communities: "To this end we always pray for you, that our God may make you worthy of his call, and may fulfill every good resolve and work of faith by his power" (2 Th 1:11). He asks for the graces that seminarians might not dare to ask for them-selves. Like Christ, he prays that none of those entrusted to him be lost (cf.

Jn 17:12 ff). He prays for himself, too, so that God will enlighten his mind and heart and help him become a sound guide (1 K 3:9; Ws 6:7).

A formator uses *personal sacrifice* to expiate, intercede, and gain graces for his seminarians. "I rejoice in my sufferings for your sake..." (Col 1:24).

The most effective instrument in a formator's hands is his *personal example of priestly life.* "Verba movent, exempla trahunt." Living witness convinces more and effects more than advice, motivations and demands. When the seminarian sees the coherence and holiness of a formator, he discovers a model of what he personally aspires to. He is drawn to admiration, openness, docility and imitation. He readily accepts what his formator says because it comes from someone convincing, a man who "practices what he preaches." Adapting the words of Christ, we could say of good formators: "Do and observe all that they tell you and *imitate what they do*" (cf. Mt 23:3).

Knowing each one well

Knowing each candidate deeply will help the formator act properly and opportunely, it will enable him to help each one better, solve his difficulties and offer the motivations that mean most for each one.

This is indispensable, especially for the rector, when it comes to judging the seminarian's suitability for orders. An important decision like this cannot be based on formal interviews or a vague awareness of a seminarian's conduct. We have to take the time and trouble to get to know our seminarians well.

To know a seminarian is to know his temperament, his natural qualities and aptitudes. A formator should also be interested in his personal history and family background, particularly those things that could affect his vocation. It is useful for the formator to know the results of his previous stage of formation: exactly what progress and difficulties he experienced, his attitudes, etc. This gives a formator the chance to adapt immediately to the seminarian's current situation without having to start from zero.

We should realize, too, that our knowledge of the young men in the seminary is not something static. A formator sincerely interested in each seminarian does not stereotype him based on some momentary observation, or worse still, on negative hearsay. Rather, he must constantly strive to know each seminarian personally in his current state without any prejudices. Then he will be able to adapt his action, especially when there is a particular problem, using the necessary means, not only for the individual but for this individual here and now.

The psychological testing done at admission time and further on during the candidates' formation often helps us understand them better. The most indispensable means at our disposal, however, is personal dialogue with each one. Each human person is a mystery. Only when he chooses to open up to others can we enter into that mystery. Along with dialogue, it is important to observe their conduct. If we live alongside the seminarians day by day and if we truly want to get to know them well in order to help them, we will have numerous occasions to see exactly how they act and react.

A good teacher not only seeks to know his students, he also helps them to *know themselves*. In personal conversation, he can help the seminarian to take an objective look at himself and discover many things about his temperament, his current situation, etc. If we keep in mind the principle of self-formation, we will understand that it is one of the greatest contributions that a formator can give to someone aspiring to the priest-hood.

Teaching

As an educator, a formator is called to *teach*. A young man who enters the seminary suddenly finds himself in an unfamiliar world. He comes in contact with values, principles, norms and customs which are new to him. There are many things he doesn't understand, and might not understand their meaning and value if left on his own. But he is not a robot. He needs to know in order to understand, in order to value, to identify freely and responsibly with all that his vocation, his new way of life, implies. Moreover, each seminarian is also on his way *to becoming a teacher.* He must acquire broad knowledge of spirituality, for example, which he will later be called upon to transmit to the faithful. So he must learn the art of teaching. The best way is for him to observe his formators.

A formator has to teach many things, which vary according to the situations and needs of his seminarians. But most importantly he has to transmit fundamental principles of Christian and priestly life. We should be very clear regarding these principles. Although we need to be flexible and willing to adapt, we cannot alter or neglect the vital fibers of a priestly vocation. A major part of our teaching will be to enlighten a candidate's conscience, the first requirement of a solid formation. We have to open the doors of spiritual life to him for him to begin to live it himself. Finally, we have to explain the norms, elements of discipline, customs, etc. that guide seminary life.

Obviously it doesn't suffice to teach seminarians *what* they should do. A formator must also make sure they know *why* they do what they do, the underlying theological, pedagogical and even practical reasons that support every aspect of the seminary, from the great principles to the simple traditions.

A formator has to be prepared to explain things patiently time and time again. He should never say: "We've been over this point already — let him who has a mind to understand, understand." At times a seminarian is closed in on himself. There are things that get forgotten unwittingly or that sink so far into the recesses of his mind that they no longer influence his behavior. A formator needs to repeat things often, explain them from new angles... sowing generously at every opportunity.

Motivating

Teaching is not enough. We said that a human person is moved to act by motives, so the formator has to *motivate* as well as teach. A seminarian may understand very well what he is taught, including all the reasons behind it, and still not feel motivated to do it. True education is maturing from within, so a seminarian cannot be treated like an employee, someone expected to carry out his duties whether or not he is interested in what he is doing. He has to be led beyond a simple intellectual understanding of what is expected of him to see the value in it for his own life. Only then will the value truly motivate him to act.

To motivate, then, means to call upon values that attract and move a person. In this sense, a formator has to be able to adapt himself to each individual, touching his sensibility and interior value-system. Nevertheless, certain values in themselves are deeper and more fitting for what we are trying to motivate the candidate towards. They are the ones that must be emphasized. These are the ones that will move a person's inner being with their spiritual resonance, and withstand the test of time. In some seminarians perhaps we will find little receptivity to deep, spiritual values. Then we have to appeal to motives that he more easily accepts, even if they are a little superficial, until we can lead him to appreciate the more important and lasting ones.

As we saw in Chapter Two, the deepest and most appropriate motive in the formation of a priest is love for Christ and all humanity. A formator should know how to present this love as the main driving force in the life of a priest. When a seminarian encounters difficulties in fully accepting the consequences of his vocation, when he is going through moments of darkness or discouragement, the best thing a formator can tell him is, "Why don't you go talk it over with the Lord? Go to Him in the Eucharist, contemplate Him on the cross and ask Him for his light and strength."

The ability of a formator will allow him to make use also of all the secondary motivations, even the merely human ones, that can encourage a seminarian. Sometimes the best thing is to praise him for a job well done, at others it is best to prod his pride by showing him what he still needs. Difficult and demanding challenges are what some need, others need easily attainable goals. At times a good, strong correction is in order while moments of tension, for example, might call for an unexpected break of relaxation and entertainment...

Motivations can lose their edge with the passing of time. Values are not always understood and assimilated right from the start. Presenting a value from a new angle can make it penetrate a seminarian's consciousness with greater impact than ever before. It isn't enough to repeat things once in a while. The seasoned formator never asks a seminarian to do anything (above all, anything difficult) without motivating. Finally, it is useful to observe that motivation depends greatly on a formator's conviction and forcefulness in presenting values. To understand something, it's enough that it be explained clearly. But to recognize it as a value, it is essential that the teacher's example — the way he articulates and lives the value — demonstrate that it is indeed worthwhile.

Guiding

The "anthropological realism" we mentioned at the beginning of this book makes us well aware that seminarians, like anyone else, experience the force of passions and pride, which frequently pull them in directions contrary to their free and conscious choice. A realistic, sincere seminarian will realize that he cannot go it alone. He needs a guide.

Formators are also responsible for the seminary community. They have to provide for the organization and community life in the center for formation.

Therefore, in addition to teaching and motivating, the formator's mission includes *guiding* the candidates.

A guide is someone who leads the way for others, not by pointing it out on a map, but by walking it alongside them. A formator, then, should be a mentor, accompanying the seminarian on his road to the priesthood.

A formator is responsible for the operation of the seminary and the authentic formation of its candidates. He cannot afford to be indifferent towards what they do or don't do. He has to be *watchful,* be informed either directly or through his helpers, follow the development of community activities closely and be especially concerned for the progress of each seminarian...

It is important for a formator to trust his seminarians and let them see his confidence in them. This doesn't mean that he closes his eyes and innocently supposes that nobody could do anything wrong. In this case, "innocence" could be synonymous with irresponsibility. Sincere concern for the good of the seminarians consists not only of trust in them, but also of distrust in human frailty.

When he is watchful in this way, the formator can exercise prevention, and this is fundamental in a good system of education. A good guide looks ahead to see possible obstacles and warns those who follow him. A seminarian meets general obstacles and doubts that come from the nature of man himself. It is easy, especially when we have a little experience, to know how and where these arise. Other obstacles depend on the individual's character and temperament, or on particular circumstances and situations. They sometimes arise suddenly, but an attentive eye can often foresee them, making it possible to remove them or warn the person. We can sum up the importance of this service of the formator in the saying that it is better to foresee than to regret.

To guide, you have to *be there.* We should take the suggestion of "walking alongside" the candidates literally. The mere presence of the formator can be a genuine element of formation and a reminder that calls them to fulfill their duty.

As guide, a formator fulfills the prophetic dimension of his priesthood, in the midst of those to whom he has been sent. He has also been placed as a "sentinel" (Ezk 3:17). On occasion, his ministry of authority requires *firmness when he demands*. This isn't always easy. When it is difficult to be demanding, recall the words the Lord spoke to Ezekiel: "...if you do not speak and warn him to renounce his evil ways and so live...I will hold you responsible for his death...if you warn the upright man not to sin and he abstains from sinning...you too will have saved your life..." (Ezk 3:20-21).

It may seem a paradox, but only a *humble* formator knows how to be demanding. Humility keeps him from acting in order to impress the seminarians. Human respect greatly inhibits a formator and drives him to look for approval; he is afraid to do anything that might hurt his image of being "open-minded" or "a good guy." People like that come across as the "nice guys" and never win the trust of the young people who want to form themselves and who seek a clear and firm guide.

Deep humility is the key to keeping firmness from becoming harshness. Curtness repels. Perhaps one of the pedagogical axioms a formator should remember most is summed up in the classic maxim: *suaviter in forma, fortiter in re (be firm in what you ask for, considerate in how you do so)*. They are not opposites, both elements are the expression of the same purpose. Firmness in principles will truly educate when it goes with considerateness in the form. A formator must be completely master of himself, never letting pride, impatience or anger affect his dealings with seminarians. Profound humility and genuine interest for the good of the young men entrusted to him give him the ability to control himself in moments when it would be easier to let loose a harsh word or aggressively impose his will. By the same token, when a seminarian is blinded by passion, these attitudes will give the formator the ability to let time pass until the waters settle and dialogue is possible.

We have to keep in mind that the ordinary life of seminarians is demanding in itself. We have no right to make it even heavier by being insensitive or inconsiderate, much less disdainful. Young men are extremely sensitive to sarcasm and slighting remarks by authority figures, above all in public. We have to avoid anything that could take the form of a confrontation (especially, but not only, in public). The best way to gain the respect of seminarians is to treat them with sincere respect.

Last but not least, a guide has to *stimulate the progress* of his followers. We should not think we have to slow them down or stop them.

We have to moderate and direct, of course, but not halt them. The Church and the world need active, creative and daring priests to push their apostolates ahead. Formators have to foster a sense of initiative, enterprise and work in their seminarians.

There are many means in seminary life for formators to fulfill their educational functions. Sometimes it will be in public, in talks or meetings. In this line there could be some regular meetings with all the seminarians or by groups to further explain or review aspects of seminary life that have been neglected or not lived correctly by all. At other times personal contact with each seminarian will be the best way to get across a point that is particularly important or difficult for him to understand, or to motivate and guide him personally. This can be done in spiritual direction or confession (when dealing with matters of conscience or spiritual progress), and even in casual, friendly everyday dealings.

GENERAL ATTITUDES OF A GOOD FORMATOR

In the previous paragraph, as we mentioned the main duties of a formator, we touched on some attitudes that a good formator of priests should have. But, we can summarize some more of a general nature that vigorously determine his style of work as a formator.

The formator has to be present among the candidates: *close-by and accessible.* He will not help his seminarians much personally if he locks himself in his office and limits himself to supervising at a distance the running of the house. Closeness means living with and like the seminarians, to be with and among them, joining them at Mass, at meals, during recreation, etc. To be accessible means to be ready at any moment to listen and lend a hand.

We all appreciate it when others take *interest* in us. When a seminarian has been worried about something, the formator should be the one to ask him how things are going. If he is sick, the formator should visit him and see that he receives medical attention if it is necessary. The formator should truly be happy when his seminarians experience some success; he should know how to share their disappointments also.

Students are usually very sensitive to the *universality* of the formator in his dealings with others. Any sign of favoritism is very damaging. When seminarians sense true equality in the way a formator deals with others, they more readily give him their trust. They know that he doesn't follow his preferences, but rather a sincere desire to help everyone as much as they need. It is natural for the formator to get on more easily with some than with others. Some young men are more pleasant and open, others not so much. A formator must be equally available to everyone. Above all, a formator must never allow rejection or disdain for any seminarian to come into his heart. Nothing could ever justify that.

Equal treatment does not mean depersonalization. Being concerned for everyone involves helping *each individual* according to his personal characteristics, needs and circumstances. Some require more attention because they need greater direction and support. Candidates with difficulties require more time and effort to help them overcome their problems. This is never a waste of our time. One will have, perhaps in the future, the great satisfaction of seeing that seminarian he saved with so much effort become a holy priest. There are others that should be helped especially to develop their special spiritual, human or intellectual gifts. In every human group there are some who influence the rest. They should be identified and helped to develop their leadership for the good of the whole seminary and with an eye to their future apostolate.

A formator is not blind to a candidate's defects and limitations, yet he must *understand and accept* him as he is. It is useless, even damaging to expect him to be perfect or to measure up to some personal standard we may have set for him. After all, God is the one who called him to the priesthood just as he is. A formator should accept him and cooperate with him and the Holy Spirit, so that the man God has chosen will truly mature and transform himself into Christ, according to his eternal plan.

Often this interior transformation is a slow, imperceptible process that can have its setbacks. The grace of God, though, works in a mysterious way which defies human expectations. Ideas, motives and, above all, habits are assimilated only gradually. Seminarians experience ups and downs and can sometimes give the impression of moving backwards instead of forwards. Formators should be *patient*. They should never despair. A patient formator can wait for "God's hour" and adapt to the rhythm of his grace. He knows it is the seminarian who has to understand and freely accept the formation we offer him. Thus when a formator perceives that a seminarian is going through a difficult time and is unable to understand or accept something, he is not in a hurry and does not resort to pressure tactics. The right moment will come.

All of this requires a good measure of *prudence*. It is impossible to give foolproof rules on how to face every possible situation. The virtue of prudence helps a formator to apply general principles to particular cases.[7] Prudence demands reflection, discernment, and a careful analysis of circumstances. It isn't just a natural quality that some people are born with. It can be acquired and perfected, especially with one's daily effort to act in a prudent way in what one does. Young formators learn a great deal working side by side with experienced ones. They clear up their doubts and observe how veteran formators lead seminarians along in their formation.

Excursus: Choosing and Forming Formators

A formator's work is so important that we can say "as the formator is so will the formation be." This work calls for a wide variety of experience and skill, which are fully human and deeply Christian. We must therefore conclude that it is necessary to select very well the men who will exercise this ecclesial ministry, and prepare them in the best way possible.

Not all priests are called to be formators. It is an inspiring and committing charism that God gives to whom He will. Just as there are gifted artists who sculpt works of art from lifeless stone, a formator serves as an instrument which the Holy Spirit uses to model his priests in the image of Christ.

That is why the Council states that formators and professors *are to be chosen from among the best*[8] of our priests. It goes on to quote Pius XI: *In the first place let careful choice be made of superiors and professors... Give these sacred colleges priests of the greatest virtue, and do not hesitate to withdraw them from tasks which seem indeed to be of greater importance, but which cannot be compared with this supremely important matter, the place of which nothing else can supply.*[9]

---

[7] "... one of these virtues is prudence. It applies universal principles to practical, particular conclusions" (St. Thomas Aquinas, *Summa Theologiae* II-II, q.47, a.6).

[8] OT 5.

[9] Encyclical letter *Ad Catholici Sacerdotii,* December 20, 1935, n. 37.

In order to select formators it will be useful to have a summary of some of the fundamental qualities of a good formator, as can be deduced from what we have said about his role and action.

As a representative of God and the Church, a formator of priests must be a *man of God,* characterized by a deep interior life, and experienced in prayer. He must be a *man of the Church,* profoundly and cordially in step with the universal Church and the local bishop.

He will not be a father and a friend if he is irritable, brusque, pushy or crude. He must be patient, kind, open, near, simple and available. At the same time, in his ministry of authority he must be respectful, show dignity and command respect. This combination of kindness with firmness is not two contradictory tendencies coexisting in the same person. It is rather two sides of one and the same attitude: sincere love for the seminarian. Love wants the best for the person who is loved. The opposite is not love but indifference.

To be both kind and firm, the formator must also be *humble.* This enables him to serve God alone, unafraid to ask the candidate what he must without human respect. It will allow him to demand what he should, kindly, respectfully, not as someone who has a "right" to be obeyed, but as one who serves others with his authority.

As teacher and guide, a formator should be of *balanced temperament,* both serene and decisive. His position as director requires *prudence;* he must carefully consider the consequences for the candidate and the community of his decisions, advice and action. He needs a sense of timing to know when to speak, counsel, admonish and encourage.

A formator has to be *strong.* He must be capable of bearing his responsibilities without being overwhelmed by his own difficulties or others' problems. He must be resilient enough to carry out his duties without his personal situation and humors interfering.

The demands of the position mean that a formator has to be *a self-sacrificing and hard-working* priest... all day, every day.

He has to be *enthusiastic* and *optimistic;* he should radiate a spirit of joy and a desire to give of himself. He should have a positive attitude, not complain, or depress others with his attitudes or words, and be able to spark initiative in others, channel, purify, guide and bring it to success.

He should have a *solid intellectual preparation* to follow and support the academic formation of seminarians. At least a partial knowledge of *psychology* and *pedagogy* can be useful in his work.

Finally, a formator should have a certain amount of *pastoral experience*. This will help him direct adequately those who will soon be engaged in priestly ministry.

Here are three suggestions for the selection and preparation of formators of priests.

First, if possible, we can have specialized courses in the field of formation. They can be useful as long as they are not merely theoretical and they orient in a concrete way this work at the service of the Church.

Second, the best way to learn an art is to be the apprentice of an expert. The long-term preparation of good formators is to make sure that present formators are good. When, for example, a seminarian has had for years the experience of good spiritual direction, he learns almost by osmosis how to exercise that apostolate; the same can be said of the way to deal with candidates, of the combination of firmness and consideration... and of all we have mentioned up to now.

As a last suggestion, seminarians that show signs of possibly having the qualities for this ministry could, in some way, begin training ahead of time. Proper selection and preparation of formators is so decisive that it cannot be left for later, improvising when we face a vacancy to fill. The formators in the seminary should be attentive to take note of those seminarians who seem to have the qualities and aptitudes to become formators.

In any event, what matters is that those responsible for the selection and preparation of formators in each diocese make a sincere effort to prepare those men who will be responsible for the formation of future priests, and therefore, responsible also, in some way, for the life of the ecclesial community.

CHAPTER FIVE

FORMATIVE ENVIRONMENT

Contact between persons always leaves an impression, and if it is a special relationship, the impression can be very deep. The relationship between formator and seminarian is one of the central elements of the formative process. But we are heavily influenced by circumstances, by culture, by the social and natural environment that surround us. For an outline of any pedagogical system to be complete, it has to consider the formative environment; in our case, the seminary environment.

In general terms we can divide the factors that make up the formative environment of a seminary thus: relations with others *(interpersonal environment),* community life and activities *(institutional environment),* organization and discipline *(disciplinary environment),* and external aspects of the center *(external environment).*

But a center of formation is neither a cloistered monastery nor an incubator isolated from reality. There is, and there must be, contact with *other environments:* family, parish, diocese, the world... The seminarian's relation with these is also a part of his formative environment.

As a general context for these considerations, one aspect which profoundly characterizes the seminary should be noted: it is a community united by one common motive, the vocation; in pursuit of one common goal, formation for the priesthood. The lifestyle of its members is permeated and determined by this motive and by this goal. These also determine the other elements of the formative environment, either directly or indirectly. they are the surest standard for weighing what can and should form part of the seminary and its programs.

Interpersonal Environment

The principal theological, pastoral and pedagogical reasons which make community life an indispensable or, at least, highly recommendable part of priestly formation were listed in the "community and personalized formation" section of Chapter Two. There we mentioned how God chose for Himself a people and how Christ brought together the apostolic college in order to found the Church. We spoke of the need to form young men in a spirit of ecclesial "communion" and of the fruits of community life, such as openness, comprehension, mutual witness and support.

The following reflection takes all these observations for granted. Here we hope to single out certain characteristics of community formation and point out other more practical aspects.

To the untrained eye the seminary could seem to be, like so many other educational institutions, just another "boarding school." It is true that there are certain similarities between a seminary and a university residence, or between a high school seminary and a boarding school for young men. Some of the external characteristics are similar, as perhaps are some of the activities and pedagogical methods. But a seminary is much more. This should strike the attention even of an outside observer. He should perceive more than a mere group of students living together under the same roof. He should sense a particular "atmosphere" characteristic of a center where future priests are formed.

If our observer were to live for a time with the seminarians, he would realize that there is a common air about them, *a family atmosphere,* made up of a delicate combination of trust, friendship and respect. It is the expression of fraternal charity which derives from theological charity, communion of ideals, closeness of the formators... But without a doubt he would also discover a *priestly spirit* generated by prayer, fervor, ecclesial communion; by profound, simple and sincere joy... He would detect an environment of silence and austerity characteristic of every house where virtue and union with God are fostered.

This point comes as a real challenge for us formators. Modern man seems to have an innate fear of silence. We've managed to fill every corner of our world with sound, motion and distraction. But we need silence. It is a condition for getting in touch with ourselves, our thoughts, our direction in life... with God.

Probably few of the men who enter our seminaries have had the opportunity to experience real silence.

Silence for silence's sake can be stupidity. It can come from shyness or introversion. External silence merely out of discipline will be an occasion for internal dissipation. But if we seek and practice silence out of conviction, it becomes a source of spiritual and human progress: it helps us to use time well, it favors reflection, it contributes to interiorizing our relations with God. In short, external silence is an opportunity for internal enrichment.

This atmosphere is a gift we can offer the seminarians in their time of formation. We have to teach them the value of inner silence as attentiveness to the voice of the Spirit above the distractions, worries, doubts and desires that fill our heart. We help them by fostering silence around the house, above all in time of prayer, study, during the night... Silence in the seminary is not simply a disciplinary measure although it certainly implies some self-discipline. It is a gift that young men preparing for the priesthood will appreciate more and more as they advance in our Lord's service.

Family atmosphere and priestly spirit in the seminary are everyone's responsibility. But formators especially have to prize and safeguard them since they should be aware of their benefits, and their necessity. The means at the formators' disposition do not change: witness, orientation and advice, supervision, constant motivation. At the same time they should offer particular help to any seminarian who is experiencing greater difficulty in making himself part of the community. His distance could be a sign that something is not going well: shyness, egotism, personalism...

Almost all college or university students establish deep bonds with classmates or with the institution where they studied. We can expect it to be even more so with a seminarian who has placed all of his life at the service of the Church and the diocese, and who lives with those who will be his companions in pastoral service. From this point of view community environment in a seminary not only favors the formation process, it not only helps each seminarian, but it also benefits the whole diocese, since it helps give birth to a fraternal collaboration which will continue afterwards as they exercise their priestly ministry.

TEAMWORK AND TEAM SPIRIT

One possible way to foster community life, support formative efforts and create a favorable atmosphere for establishing closer personal bonds among seminarians is teamwork.

Each team could be composed of ten or twelve seminarians, chosen by the formators, preferably at the same level of formation (high school seminary, introductory course, philosophy, theology) so that there will be a greater homogeneity in spiritual and human maturity, in academic interests, etc., among its members. Someone to head each team should be selected from among the more integrated seminarians.

Splitting them into teams in no way supplants or harms community life since they are not exclusive groups designed to create closed environments, but rather, to create bonds of communion and collaboration. The support of a team can be a catalyst for fervor and responsibility, favoring friendship and solidarity. It helps educate our young men for candid, sincere dialogue; it teaches the art of cooperation, fosters a spirit of service and inspires witness and encouragement among them. The fruits of teamwork are especially notable in large communities where it is easier for someone to withdraw himself and participate less in community life.

Every week or two the teams could meet to reflect on a Gospel passage, propose initiatives that could help the whole seminary or the team members, plan some apostolic activity (vocational get-togethers, CCD), etc. Team projects should take into account the general programs of formation, the responsibilities of each individual, the time available, and so forth.

Formators can use this team life to organize complementary academic activities and to assign apostolates and responsibilities within the seminary. They can use the team leaders or some members of the team to give a hand to those who have particular academic difficulties, to help and encourage, etc.

There is another formative activity that the major seminary can establish if the seminarians are prepared for it. Every two weeks, team members can meet briefly to point out the deficiencies or shortcomings they have noticed in each other's conduct, doing so with charity and simplicity, with a sincere desire to help, without judging or evaluating, making reference to the norms and customs of the seminary. It can be an expression of their care that each other gets the best formation possible, a considerable help in their human and social formation and an opportunity to exercise fraternal correction in humility. "Brethren, if a man is over-taken in any fault, you... should restore him in a spirit of gentleness... Bear one another's burdens, and so fulfill the law of Christ" (Gal 6:1-2).

Institutional Environment

The interpersonal environment of a seminary is based on a life of community; it is part of it, depends and feeds on it. We have spoken of "family atmosphere," but should point out that this does not mean simply living together under the same roof. Rather it refers to community life which, by its own formative nature, entails certain institutional elements.

Community Activities

First of all, community life obviously revolves around certain *common activities.* Said more explicitly: for community life to exist, the seminary needs a global educative plan which establishes a balance between personal and community activities.

An educational center whose members follow each one his own program and schedule, independently of the others, becomes little more than a college residence, a common mailing address for the tenants. This is no seminary. The demands and benefits of formation in *community* life call for much more. But we should not go to the other extreme either for we certainly could not seek to have a monastic style of community in a seminary. The basic reason and finality of common life for religious are not the same as those for a seminary. The educational program of a seminary has to seek a just mean between the extremes above.

What "common" activities should the seminary's program estab-lish? It isn't easy to give a sweeping answer. It is possible, however, to name some activities which almost certainly should be present in any seminary's program. It's up to us to adapt them properly to the circumstances and necessities of the seminarians, to the place, and to local customs.

In a Christian community, especially one of future priests, *community prayer* is essential. As a tradition it goes back to the apostolic community and possesses a profound theological meaning. It expresses the very nature of the Church. It is a source of communion, of fervor, of virtue... The community eucharistic celebration is a privileged, indispensable moment of community prayer. Certainly, it is the central activity of the day, in which all the members, united around the altar, offer their lives together with the bread and the wine and in marvelous exchange receive Christ, who is truly present.

Throughout the rest of the day other occasions can be set for common prayer, for example: the Angelus at midday, a visit to Christ in the Eucharist after meals, the common celebration of part of the Liturgy of the hours, conscience examen at the end of the day, and so forth.

Personal prayer deserves its place alongside prayer in common. There should be time during the day for private prayer or meditation, the rosary, etc... The schedule can reserve a time for this or each individual can be left to choose the most opportune moment of the day, if that is preferable. Even though, strictly speaking, these are not community activities, we can still say that in these moments the seminary community dedicates itself to prayer with particular intensity.

In the seminary, *liturgical feasts* should have special prominence: celebrating the Eucharist with greater solemnity, praying the rosary in community, having a time of Eucharistic adoration, etc... Along with the intrinsic value of these celebrations, there is a formative function, since the future priest learns in the seminary the importance of these feasts and the proper way to celebrate them. Only in this way will he learn to live the liturgical calendar with ever greater depth and intensity.

Mealtime is another privileged opportunity for community living as in any family. Sharing the same table and meal forms deep bonds of friendship, mutual knowledge and trust.

While conversation at table offers an occasion to strengthen the community life and atmosphere, mealtime can be used in another way to further the seminarians' formation. A number of religious orders and congregations as well as some diocesan seminaries have reading in the dining room during some meals. They choose themes of common interest such as historical accounts, current events, articles about contemporary sociopolitical or economic problems, documents of the Holy See, discourses of the Holy Father, ecclesial news, testimonies from men of the Church, etc.

Ample time in the daily program has to be devoted to *academic activities.* In the previous chapter we made reference to basic academic programs and suggested a wide range of complementary activities that it would be good to offer to students. If anything was clear there, it was that there is no time to waste.

The *periods of recreation and relaxation* are important community activities, whether they are moments of conversation, team sports, or community outings. There are many reasons to include them in seminary programs. In the first place they offer physical and mental rest, not only necessary from a functional point of view (to restore the physical condition we need to carry on our normal tasks), but also to restore calm, reduce stress, and contemplate nature. There are also formative values involved: to strengthen the will in sports and the activities that require physical effort; to learn how to live with others, practice charity and self-control; to strengthen the sense of brotherhood and team spirit; to reinforce the bonds of friendship between formators and candidates...

It is easy to take the community's pulse simply by observing recreation periods. A formator will see who the loners and difficult characters are, where personality conflicts exist or on the other hand if there is self-control, honesty and deference. At times the formators themselves could participate in the games, trying always to give good example of happiness, charity and good sportsmanship.

We cannot fail to mention *vacations.* There are many things a seminarian can do during these times, especially during summer vacation. For many it will be the best moment to spend some time at home. It could also be, as we have mentioned, the occasion to engage in more extensive pastoral activity. But we could also suggest that vacations, at least a part, be spent in community. This is a tradition of some seminaries that perhaps has been practiced less in recent years. Nevertheless, it remains an excellent way to foster community spirit and it helps prevent the seminary from being reduced to a school or a university residence.

It is not possible to do everything at one time. Seminary programs and the personal needs of the seminarian have to determine the best course.

When there is a chance for vacations together as a community, the right balance must be found between relaxation, outings, sports and some formative or pastoral activities that complement the ordinary programs.

Seminarians should learn that vacation, while indeed a time for rest, is not to be an occasion to undermine their virtue or their vocation. Whether out in the country, visiting their family or working in a parish, they are still seminarians on the road to the priesthood. Vacation, from this perspective, cannot be a "break" from formation nor a chance to go to places that are not proper for a young man preparing for the priesthood.

Just as importantly, seminarians must realize that there are no vacations from spiritual life. Prayer and sacramental life continue having priority. Time for personal prayer, Eucharistic celebration, liturgy of the hours, and rosary, should all remain a part of the seminarian's daily routine on vacations. In fact, free from academic tension, with extra time and perhaps in a nature setting, our prayer should be calmer; we should be able to dedicate more time to the Lord. Vacations like this help to restore not only our body, but also our soul and thus give new impetus to our efforts.

Christmas and Easter are especially good times to be spent in community. They can be given the liturgical importance they merit. These feasts are also an occasion to strengthen the bonds of fraternal spirit among seminarians and faculty.

In the section on human formation, we mentioned the formation value of *manual work* in order to form a spirit of dedication, strengthen one's character, and to make one better acquainted with the toil people face, etc... Here, in connection with community life, it is worth noting that ordinarily work projects undertaken in common are much more easily proposed and carried out.

SCHEDULES AND PROGRAMS

After mentioning the above, it is obvious that we must have a daily schedule and an annual program of activities. The multiplicity of activities and formation goals make scheduling and planning at the seminary an important and often complex job. Both bishop and rector will surely pay special attention to this point.

Concerning observance of the schedule, two points can be brought up. The first has to do with the *seminary's own tradition.* If incoming seminarians find an atmosphere of fervor, and care and interest in keeping the program and discipline, they will also enter community life easily. On the other hand, if their first impressions are that everyone goes his own way, choosing to go or not to Mass or meals..., we can motivate, recommend and demand all we want but our success will be severely compromised.

Another way to achieve results especially with new entrants, is to *explain the meaning* and importance of different community and individual activities in the seminary, how they are done and their fruit. This is simply an application of the principle we have mentioned on several occasions: the mind must be enlightened with clear principles accompanied by effective motivation. Explanations of the meaning of seminary life could be reinforced if we choose reliable senior seminarians to give them. This may help the new arrivals accept the seminary's policies more easily and it could well be the opportunity for them to strike up new friendships.

Disciplinary Environment

Another characteristic of the seminary that would strike an outside observer would surely be the atmosphere of *discipline.*

Number 11 of *Optatam Totius* has become a point of reference when speaking of discipline in seminaries:

> The discipline of seminary life should be regarded not only as a strong protection for community life and charity, but as a necessary part of the complete system of training. Its purpose is to inculcate self-control, to promote solid maturity of personality and the formation of those other traits of character which are the most useful for the order and fruitful activity of the Church. But it should be applied in such a way as to develop in the students a readiness to accept the authority of superiors out of deep conviction — because of the dictates of their conscience, that is to say (cf. Rm 13:5) — and for supernatural reasons. Standards of discipline should be applied with due regard for the age of the students, so that while they gradually acquire self-mastery, they will at the same time form the habit of using their freedom with discretion, of acting

on their own initiative and energetically, and of working harmoniously with their confreres and with the laity.

Here we find clearly expressed the two poles of discipline: external and internal.

External discipline derives from the observance of norms for behavior, as in every educational institution. It could simply be a practical means to achieve order among those who live under one roof (for example, the schedule of group activities, the use of facilities and installations, etc.). But discipline can also be, more deeply, a formative element which sustains the maturing process of the candidate.

In the seminary, external discipline offers a guide or channel that molds the candidate by promoting conduct that is coherent with the ideals he has freely chosen and the commitments priestly life entails.

Internal discipline has two meanings. The first is the voluntary, convinced assimilation of external discipline. That is: to know, value and live freely the style of behavior that external discipline offers, for example: following a schedule, punctuality for community activities, academic earnestness, etc.

The second meaning or level of internal discipline is self-mastery. This consists of the control of our interior world: thoughts, desires, passions, feelings. Self-mastery is not purely internal, it profoundly influences our external conduct. It is an element of personal maturity.

Discipline thus understood is far from being an arbitrary authoritarian restriction of freedom and candid self-expression. It is not an insult to a person, for it is not in conflict with liberty — it is rather a path towards it.[1]

---

[1] In the *Guidelines for education to priestly celibacy* of the Congregation for Catholic Education we read: "The atmosphere of freedom, the respect for the person, and the openness to personal initiative should not be interpreted as an exoneration from discipline. A seminarian who freely has chosen his state in life has also freely chosen to accept and respect its rules. Discipline forms part of the spiritual structure of the seminarian and of the priest not only during formation but during his whole life. 'Discipline... should not be simply tolerated as an external imposition, but should be interiorized, that is, inserted into the structure of spiritual life as an indispensable component' (Paul VI, Encyclical Letter *Sacerdotalis Coelibatus,* n. 66). This does not mean that discipline is purely internal. Given that it affects 'personal and community' life (ibid), it should also be exterior." (n. 74).

Our realistic view of fallen and redeemed man, offers us a simple explanation of the need for discipline. If everything in man were perfectly ordered and followed faith and reason, discipline would come spontaneously and naturally. But reality teaches us otherwise. Man must struggle to master his behavior. Internal order is a personal conquest for which we need external support. Discipline is an aid to achieve this goal.

INTERIORIZING DISCIPLINE

Observance of external discipline does not guarantee that a seminarian has assimilated the values behind it. It doesn't even mean that he is interested in obtaining the goals that inspire disciplinary norms. External observance is a step, a stage that can be lived passively by somebody who adapts to the system and follows its rules. In this case it is the system that marks his conduct, and not his personal convictions. There might be a lot of routine, a desire not to look out of place, to go with the flow, and passively put up with it all...

The step from external to internal discipline happens when the candidate makes the values that motivate the disciplinary norms his own. This process of interiorizing has been explained in Chapter Two when we spoke of "self formation" and "formation as transformation." There is no need to repeat it here.

As the text cited from *Optatam Totius* put it, interiorization of discipline is also related to the authority which proposes and endorses it, and therefore to the ascendancy a formator or superior has over the seminarians. At first, a formator explains the disciplinary norms of the seminary, and evaluates them clearly, promoting their fulfillment if necessary. Then he will help the seminarian to acheive his gradual personal acceptance, which brings him to the deepest level of interior discipline.[2]

---

[2] "Yet, even if it is important that discipline be part of the seminary's rules, the center of the educational process lies in the educational, human and Christian relationship between the former and the seminarian. This does not mean abandoning the student to himself, nor exonerates the teacher from being present. It rather asks that he be ever closer. Indeed, the teacher... must guide the student by way of a friendly relationship..." (Congregation for Catholic Education, *Guidelines...*, April 11, 1974, n. 74).

The physical presence of the formator is an effective support for discipline in a high-school seminary. Our pedagogical system should subsequently balance the immediacy of this presence with room for self-conviction. In other words, it should bring the seminarian to act as he ought, not because the formator is near, but rather because he himself is responsible and coherent. It has to be clear that we must always respect the seminarian's liberty, since imposition is self-defeating. Conviction cannot be imposed. Since it comes from within, we can only encourage and favor it.

At each stage of formation we have to find the proper measure of external discipline required to promote interiorization. Being overly strict slows down this process for it favors passivity and may even provoke resistance. Permissiveness also makes interiorization impossible by undermining the discipline they need to assimilate, it leaves nothing to be assimilated. It's not enough to make theoretical explanations and let everyone go his own way. Man doesn't work like that. He needs the support of external discipline to some degree or another to help him to live what he is trying to make his own.

Some examples may help to understand this. The typical seminarian wants to be a sincere, trustworthy person. These virtues, however, must be developed. During the first years of high-school seminary, for instance, we would have to give exams to the students together in one classroom. The formator who acts as proctor for the exam will always be there, but he will encourage the boys to be honest out of conviction. As the years go by, this supervision will lessen. In major seminary a young man should be at the point where he can take the exam to his room, shut the door, and do it without looking at his text books and notes. If he can't be trusted in something like this, will he, later on, live his priestly identity with sincerity and integrity when he is alone?

Interiorization of discipline leads to personal responsibility, and responsibility engenders maturity. The outstanding quality of a mature person is coherence between what he wants to be, what he is, what he thinks and what he does.

The fruit of coherence is inner harmony. A coherent person overcomes the conflicts that can arise between his desires and his duty, between his personal plans and his priestly duties. Thus he achieves a harmonious, unified personality, in which he has integrated the specific obligations of his state in life as a priest. He has taken charge of his own life and freely accepts responsibility for his actions before God and his own conscience.

Internal division is the lot of a man who has not identified with the duties and conduct which his priesthood demands of him. He has never opted definitively for the lifestyle he has freely taken upon himself. This makes progress in virtue more unsure. He will live in passivity, mere outward conformity, and be as unstable as his passing sentiments. He will not be one with himself.

This division is both moral and psychological. On the one hand he sees the obligation, at least as imposed by the seminary environment, to live as he is expected to as a priest. On the other, he feels the uneasiness of not being totally in agreement, totally convinced. It can also happen that he does understand how he should behave but is at the same time effectively unable to make this behavior his own out of weakness, attachment to another way, etc. We can even say that a priest who is consciously and consistently incoherent in his life is, in fact, risking his own psychological well-being. After publicly and irrevocably committing his whole existence in one direction, he stands at the edge of an inner abyss that separates him as he is from what he says he is and what, sacramentally and ontologically, he really is. This conflict affects his inner world; discouragement, ennui and disgust follow. If psychological imbalance does not arise, there will certainly be unhappiness, dissatisfaction, compensation, escapism and progressive abandoning of his responsibilities.

Another important psychological-spiritual consequence of interiorizing the priestly identity is inner serenity. When emotions, sentiments or impulses that are not compatible with this identity present themselves, the priest will be able easily and serenely to control and order his inclinations according to his life-option. This is ultimately what interior discipline is: the internal order of a person as master of himself. External discipline has become internal discipline, out of conviction, and finally interior mastery of one's self. This is the ulimate fruit of discipline.

THE DISCIPLINE OF LOVE

As we saw in the text quoted from the Council, forming inner convictions is also intimately related to *spiritual motives*. And this in two ways at least. Firstly, they make more explicit the goodness of the value that is proposed — i.e. they make clearer its importance for a candidate to the priesthood. Secondly, they provide a support for the authority that proposes the values or the discipline. It is no longer merely imposition or human expedience, but it is divine authority.

The seminarian should learn to discover God's will for his vocation (the call to be a priest at a specific time and place) embodied in the seminary, the formators and the disciplinary norms. This view gives everything the supernatural value proper to obedience to God's will.

This is the most powerful motive we have for interiorization: to do what God wants, above and beyond our personal preferences.

We should keep in mind what was said in the section on "love as the fundamental motivation." "I will show you a way still more excellent... love" (1 Cor 12:31,13:4). Without substituting or obscuring other motives and values which mold a lifestyle, love offers the greatest, most unifying and effective motivation. It has been said that love is reason unto itself; thus, once it exists, it needs no support. Love has its own dynamism: it tends to the beloved. It is enough to know that what we do pleases the one we love.

This is how our love for Christ invigorates and facilitates the process of gaining our own personality. It is the unifying factor that not only fulfills our desire to love and be loved, but which also draws together our whole personality and gives it a unique unity and integrality possessed only by those who have truly found the reason for their existence. St. Augustine put it well: *Ama et fac quod vis* (Love and do what you will).[3]

This does not nullify any of the other human motives or supports that we have mentioned. The role of the formator and external discipline are still important. Grace does not substitute nature. This should be kept in mind, particularly in the early stages of formation, until the motives and values do their work of transformation in the seminarian.

External Environment

To complete our description of seminary environment some observations concerning the externals of the formation center are in order.

---

[3]   St. Augustine, *In epistolam Ioannis ad Parthos* (Commentary on the First Letter of John), 7, 8.

The externals are important since they have a *direct pedagogical function*. The center and the means available should all create a favorable environment for formation. As formators, we have to realize that everything in the seminary has a pedagogical value. For example, maintaining the chapel, vestments and sacred vessels in perfect condition or neglecting them makes a difference. It is not the same to have the common areas always in order or just passable. Seminarians easily pick up these details and make them their own.

Seminaries should not lack a certain austerity. A manly character and a spirit of priestly poverty are also learned from the simple living and "no-frills" ethic of seminary life.

If the multisecular wisdom of the Church were not enough, we could learn from society today that it is not always good for a person to have every comfort. This spirit of poverty should be combined with the principle of having as far as possible all the necessay means for formation (facilities, books, audiovisuals, etc.). In all of this we should keep in mind the local customs and culture, the possibilities and resources on hand, existing buildings and so forth.

Contact with Environments Outside the Seminary

There are two premises. First, the seminarian has left the world to dedicate himself to God's service, "... you are not of the world, but I chose you out of the world..." (Jn 15:19). Second, he will return to the world to live and work as an apostle. The seminary, therefore, must form men who are in the world but not of the world.

There is no difficulty in the above, the problems begin when one aspect is accentuated more than the other. Some underline "being in the world," while others prefer to emphasize "not of the world." But the proper balance lies in a realistic knowledge of human nature. Any norm which regulates a seminarian's contact with other environments should neither be naïve nor suffocating. Anyone who spends all his time in a worldly atmosphere will not be a man of God. Someone who feels boxed-in will want to escape and use his liberty. No one who completely shuns the world will be a good apostle... We must strive for balance and a prudent openness according to the age and maturity of each stage of formation.

Leaving Seminary Grounds

Attendance and participation in community activities in a seminary is a first point to consider on this subject.

From an academic point of view it would seem necessary that seminarians, just like students from any other serious institution, attend classes regularly. Yet, as we have seen, seminary life does not consist only of academic activities. Formators should also promote, and perhaps with greater insistence, that seminarians be present and participate actively in the other seminary activities such as community prayer, complementary activities etc.

We should also consider that generous time for personal study is essential. The years of formation go by quickly. There is no time to waste.

The obvious conclusion is that seminarians and formators should make sure that leaving seminary grounds does not harm or hinder personal or community formative activities.

Moreover, we have to encourage our seminarians to practice caution and clear thinking. It is necessary to remember that our world is an aggressive place and does not understand the things a priest values, it encourages a moral permissiveness that at times goes to the extreme of trying to bring down those who have decided to follow the priestly vocation.

Family Contact

In very general terms, we can distinguish three different attitudes taken by families regarding the priestly vocation of one of their members.

In the majority of cases, the family has been fertile ground for the seed of a vocation to flourish in. The parents are the first and best promoters of the young man's decision to enter the seminary. They constantly thank God for this blessing and actively support their son and the seminary as much as they can.

But there are families who, to varying degrees, oppose the idea of their son becoming a priest. Different reasons give rise to this attitude, which can last for a period of time or be quite unrelenting. Whatever the case, the young man involved should always love and respect his parents.

At the same time, he must not lose sight of the fact that God has called him. To God he owes his free, personal response.

The third group is composed of parents who, while supporting their son's vocation, find it difficult to accept his absence from the family. They want him to be nearby; they can never make enough phone calls or visits. Likewise some seminarians always want to be with their families, to the point that it affects their priestly formation, and even their human maturing.

Each of these situations must be approached with great charity, justice and prudence. Both seminarian and family must realize that following God's call does not mean renouncing his gratitude, affection and esteem for his family. On the contrary, the vocation is almost always an occasion to enrich and strengthen this bond.

At the same time, they must accept the fact that the road to the priesthood implies certain demands: a complete dedication to formation or pastoral ministry, a certain separation from home (more or less prolonged depending on the distances or circumstances). A diocesan priest in some cases has the opportunity to live near his family or perhaps even with family members. But this is not always possible and certainly it will not be possible for the seminarian during formation years. Both the family and the young man who has entered the seminary have to learn to offer this sacrifice to God. There will be opportunities for the seminarian to go home or for the family to visit the seminary.

The demands on those who follow the call to the priesthood come from Christ Himself. We read in the Gospel: "Another said, 'I will follow you, Lord; but let me first say farewell to those at my home.' Jesus said to him, 'No one who puts his hand to the plow and looks back is fit for the kingdom of God.'" (Lk 9:61-62).

The word of Christ in this passage and similar ones is clear. His followers belong to Him. They have to follow Him before all. They are totally dedicated to the service of the flock of the Lord. A seminarian understands the Lord's demand, he consciously accepted it the day he knocked on the seminary door.

The norms of each seminary regarding family contact require careful consideration by the formators. Opinions and practice vary significantly from place to place but, no matter what, the first consideration must always be what is good for the seminarians' formation, convinced that this is the best service we can give not only to the Church and the seminarians but also to their families.

When frequent visits home are not possible, seminarians should be encouraged to write home regularly. It is a thoughtful expression of proper gratitude and respect. It gives each young man the chance to make his family feel a part of the countless gifts he is receiving from God. In some instances, it is a way to console, encourage, heal wounds, to draw his loved ones back to the life of grace...

USE OF THE MEDIA

The media's impact upon contemporary society is difficult to exaggerate. No one can deny its tremendous influence on the behavior, morals, and psychology of modern men and women.

Today's image market is characterized by a flagrant disregard for the most elementary moral, ideological or religious standards. So our seminarians have to learn to use their "window on the world" correctly, to take advantage of its value as a source of information and formation without it causing them to waste time or come into contact with programs or shows that are unfitting for a young man on his way to the priesthood.

Realism should also guide us here. Complete access to television might not be a source of difficulties for some people. For others, it could prove a valuable occasion to form self-conviction. But there will always be someone for whom it is a source of distraction, temptation, even spiritual loss. Prudence and sound judgment are the best advice.

The young people of today are doubtless generous enough and have the common sense to understand that these means should be used with control and discretion.

With the above it is clear there is a need for certain norms concerning contact with environments outside the seminary. Their success or failure, whether they are accepted or rejected, depends largely on the way we present them to the seminarians (and to the families as well, when they are affected by them).

Imposing the norms does not make it easier to have them fulfilled. Today less than ever. The ideal would be for incoming groups of new seminarians to find these norms already in place as part of the seminary. They will see the others fulfilling them. They will be the "living tradition" which characterize the seminary. Then formators can present these norms as they are, with the proper explanations and with no apologies. In this way, right from the beginning, the seminarians know how they are expected to behave, and why.

In all this, we should always keep in mind what was said at the beginning of the chapter: the seminary should be a school where the seminarian learns "to be in the world without being of the world" (cf. Jn 15:19).

CHAPTER SIX

STAGES OF PRIESTLY FORMATION

Up to this point we have been reflecting on the various components of priestly formation in a non-temporal way. But as one of the fundamental principles said, formation is a *progressive* process. It does have a temporal dimension. The young man who one day enters the seminary, little by little grows and matures in his personality. He slowly transforms himself according to the priestly ideal, in gradual identification with Christ the Priest. This means that what we have said up to here has to be adapted and applied to the *temporal process.*

This process is *one and continuous,* like the uninterrupted flow of a river that grows imperceptibly as it flows down the valley. Nevertheless, for the purpose of study it is possible and good to distinguish certain blocks of time that can be identified by their particular characteristics. Thus we can speak of the different *stages* of priestly formation.

The defining lines of these stages are determined by various factors: age and stage of development of the candidate, the level and type of studies he is in, and the meaning of each stage in relation to the preparation of the future priest.

We will first of all spend some time on a step that comes before any stage of formation: *vocational discernment.* Then we will comment on some characteristics of the *high school seminary,* where some young men begin their approach to the priesthood; on the *introductory (propaedeutic)* course to the major seminary; on *philosophy and theology* without spending too much time on them since most of what we have written refers to them; and finally we will consider briefly the ongoing formation that covers the whole of a priest's life.

Discernment of the Priestly Vocation

GOD CALLS, THE CHURCH MUST DISCERN

The priesthood is a free gift of God. No one can tell Him whom to call or not. In principle, the doors of the seminary are open to all those who feel called. There is no discrimination or arbitrary selection.

But the priesthood is an ecclesial ministry; as such, it is something which the Church must "bind and loose" (cf. Mt 18:18). Not everyone who knocks on the seminary door necessarily has a vocation. We are obliged to undertake discernment.

Essentially, the whole period of formation is a period of discernment, both for those in charge of formation and for the candidate himself. This is especially true in the beginning. Before admitting a young man it is important to analyze carefully if he may have a vocation.

The importance of this initial discernment lies chiefly in the respect that every young man deserves. It is out of respect towards him that he is admitted to the seminary only if there are clear signs that he is being called. It would be unjust to take a superficial attitude towards admissions, only to have to tell a young man later that the seminary is not the place for him. Such an experience, with the delay it means in following a career as a lay person, could be very damaging.

Concern for the other candidates is another reason for discernment. A seminarian who feels out of place and is not identified with the priestly vocation could be a negative element in the seminary. A significant number of reticent, or uncertain seminarians or those who lack the necessary qualities, make a positive formative atmosphere such as we spoke about in the previous chapter almost impossible to achieve.

Serious and attentive discernment is in order. Even when it seems that vocations are scarce, we need to find young men with vocations, not young men who start without a vocation on a path they should not, because it is not just a question of simply filling vacancies in a human institution but of accepting those whom the Lord calls. The fundamental question will therefore always be, "Has this young man truly been chosen by God?"[1]

---

[1]   What has been said here is in its own way as valid for admission to a high school seminary as to a major seminary. But admitting a young man to a high school seminary does not

Guidelines for Correct Vocational Discernment

Only the Lord of the harvest knows the answer to the preceding question. There are no foolproof systems to detect infallibly the presence of a priestly vocation. For this reason, prayer is the first duty of those who have the delicate responsibility of admission to a formation center. They must ask humbly for the light of the Divine Spirit to enlighten their minds and the mind of the young man seeking to enter the seminary.

Nevertheless there are some criteria that can be kept in mind in order to discover God's will as far as humanly possible. In every individual case, according to the time and place, there will be some specific and concrete factors to keep in mind, but we can also speak about some general criteria that are derived from the very nature of the priestly mission and vocation, and from the demands that the necessary formation for this priesthood places on the candidate.

We can group these criteria around two closely related judgments we have to make: on the *suitability of the candidate* and on the *real presence of the divine call.*

Suitability of the Candidate

There is no alternative: if a person is not apt for the priesthood God could not have intended to call him. God does not contradict Himself.

- Knowledge of the Candidate

Therefore, the first thing to be done is to learn what type of person the young man is who seeks to enter the seminary. This means that the person in charge of admissions must take time to speak with him, if possible on several occasions. It is very helpful to know his family and the atmosphere he comes from. At times, these can be very revealing. Knowing the candidate means knowing his background: his upbringing and education, his spiritual and human itinerary, any past events or situations that could affect his future...

Psychology can lend a hand in this area. It would not seem excessive to require, whenever possible, a thorough psychological examination

---

imply certainty of his vocation. Nevertheless, such institutions should be only for young men who give at least some indication of a vocation.

before deciding definitively about admission. The psychologist who carries out and interprets the exam not only must be professionally competent but should also show knowledge and appreciation of the priestly vocation. If he is a priest, so much the better. In particularly doubtful or difficult cases further interviewing by the psychologist may be advisable, assuming he fills the above requisites.

Admission of any aspirant should never be rushed. Time is needed to know the candidate and for the candidate to know himself and the step he is about to take. On occasion this time extends throughout the whole period of minor seminary. For others, it has consisted in maturing the idea of a vocation under the guidance of a priest they knew or even by visiting the seminary. In some places, vocation seminars are held which prove useful in this work of discernment.

- Physical and Mental Health

The question of suitability for the priesthood involves diverse aspects of the person. In the first place, adequate physical health is required to withstand the demands of seminary life and then to collaborate later as a diligent worker in the vineyard of the Lord. There may be some particular exceptions to this, but they should truly be exceptional and for powerful reasons.

Psychological suitability is more difficult to evaluate, yet it is no less decisive. The limited scope of our present discussion prevents us from going into much detail regarding the numerous aspects involved in this field. We can be sure, though, that mental health is a prerequisite for the existence of a vocation. The priest is called to direct and guide others. In this instance, we can stretch a little the meaning of Paul's question in his first letter to Timothy: "If a man does not know how to manage his own household, how can he care for God's Church?" (1 Tm 3:5).

At times men will come whose psychological makeup, although normal, shows signs of weakness, complication or instability. It is not always possible for the admissions director to discern immediately whether or not they are suitable. Prudence, common sense, experience, and perhaps time, will give the best answer.

Pathological and borderline cases are much easier to discern. When dealing with a case of psychosis, the decision is clear: no cure is possible; to pretend otherwise would be to deceive ourselves and the candidate. If we detect only symptoms of some type of neurosis, a good deal of examination is necessary to come to the right conclusion. In either instance, there is no room for superficiality — the consequences could be grave. In case of doubt, an expert should be consulted.

- Some Fundamental Virtues

We can't expect those entering the seminary to already have the virtues and qualities of an ideal priest. If that were the case, there would be no need for seminaries. Nevertheless, priestly formation requires an adequate human and Christian foundation to build on. What matters, then, is not that the candidate have the virtues of a good priest, so much as that he have the capacity to acquire them.

Certainly there are certain virtues and qualities that a young man starting on the road to the priesthood has to have, at least to some extent, in order to follow it fruitfully up to ordination. Take sincerity, for example. An insincere or deceitful person will have trouble maturing properly. He may be capable of submitting to external norms while he is being observed, but he will never assimilate the principles of self-formation. His problem will also affect his ability to live community life and work with others. Similarly, if a young man's temperament or upbringing renders him completely incapable of living with others, of dialogue, of teamwork, it is difficult to imagine that he will successfully form himself in a community environment, and much less make himself accessible to others in order to minister to them as a priest in the future.

Along with his basic human foundation, there must be a foundation upon which the candidate's spiritual identity may be built. At least a minimum of religious knowledge and practice is indispensable, and the ability to live in grace. A priest is a man of God, a minister who draws men to divine life and brings them back to it through absolution when they have lost it. If a young man has such deeply rooted habits of sin that they seem impossible to overcome, serious thought should be given before letting him continue ahead. We should not distrust God's power, but we should not tempt Him either.

- Intellectual Capacity

Formators should also analyze the aspirant's intellectual capacity. Called to be teacher and guide, he must be thoroughly prepared in areas that require academic dedication: philosophy and theology. Although the history of the Church speaks eloquently of saintly priests with few intellectual gifts, we should not undervalue this factor. It would be unfair to admit a young man who will later feel frustrated before the difficulties of priestly studies, or be asked to leave the seminary because he is not capable of successfully completing them.

As regards studies already completed, normally a student entering major seminary should have "the same human and scientific formation which prepares peers in their region for higher studies."[2]

- Absence of Canonical Impediments

One last parameter necessary for measuring the suitability of the aspirant is attention to the perpetual or simple impediments to orders established by Canon Law.[3] It would be useless and irresponsible to admit someone to the seminary who cannot reach the goal it is directed toward.

Existence of the Divine Call

It is not enough to ascertain that the young man has the necessary qualities to enter the seminary; we must see if he has a "vocation." Here we are not referring to "vocation" as a human tendency to one or another professional occupation. We use it in the strict sense: a real and personal divine call.

This is never easy to discern. In fact, it is much more difficult than discerning the candidate's objective suitability. There we stood before the mystery of man; here we stand before the mystery of God.

- Right Intention

The first thing that must be taken into account is the intention that motivates a young man to seek entry. Does he feel called, or is there something else driving him?

His decision must be completely conscious and free. Caution is required when a would-be aspirant is under some kind of pressure, whether it be internal or external. If his petition is not voluntary, the candidate should not be allowed to take the step.

---

[2] CIC 234 § 2; cf. RFIS 16.
[3] Cf. CIC 1040-1043.

The admissions director should make sure that the aspirant knows, at least in a general way, what the vocation and priestly life mean and exactly what they entail. In addition, the director should see that he is not being pushed to enter the seminary (by a relative, for instance) or driven by other reasons such as a failed romance, desire to escape from the world, fear of life's hardships, etc.

There are also cases — less frequent today than before — of young men who enter the seminary only to receive academic benefits. Care should be taken when parents are particularly set upon their son entering the minor seminary. They may only be interested in obtaining an inexpensive, quality education. To admit him in this case would defeat the purpose of the seminary and compromise its ability to form those who are really thinking of the priesthood. It could also prove damaging as well to the young man, since he would have to live a deception, in an environment he has not been called to and cannot identify with.

- The Voice of God

The first indispensable piece of advice is to suggest to the aspiring seminarian that he intensify his prayer-life, so as to examine with him later his interests and motivations. This way we can detect possible self-suggestion, external pressures, etc. This will also help the future seminarian to deepen his life of prayer and his experience of listening to God's voice. This practice could well prove decisive for the rest of his life as a seminarian and priest. At times God allows himself to be heard interiorly, in a way that can be both intimate and direct. On other occasions he will speak through noteworthy or apparently insignificant circumstances. God's voice may also resound vigorously and insistently in the heart of the young man. More frequently it is a soft breeze, almost imperceptible (cf. 1 K 19:12b). The Spirit makes some young men experience the love of Christ as the only thing worthwhile. He makes others see that the harvest is rich and the laborers few. He simply invites others to follow the vocation for which they were created. Some young men come to the seminary enthused with their vocation, others would like to rebel against the divine will, but bend before the Almighty. Some see their vocation clearly. Some vaguely suspect that they may have been called...

We do not have to seek absolute certainties in this area or ask for proofs. The glimmer of a vocation suffices for us to say, rather obliges us to say, "Let's see." As we said before, the entire period of formation, especially in its early stages, is a time for vocational discernment. If God is not calling, but permits a generous young man to start off on this road, it must be for a reason. A young man's attempt to give his all will never be a mistake in the eyes of God.

High School Seminaries

We saw above that the response to a vocation must be conscious and free. It requires, therefore, a sufficient degree of maturity.[4] Still, this does not mean that God has to remain silent until we think it is the right time for Him to speak. It is a fact that there are adolescents and even boys who hear God's call.

Samuel was a boy. What's more, "The word of the Lord was rare in those days." When the boy woke up Eli at night, the old priest only knew that he had not called him; he sent the boy back to bed. But the third time, "Eli perceived that the Lord was calling the boy." "Eli, whose eyesight had begun to grow dim, so that he could not see," knew well how to hear the voice of the Lord and so advised the boy to say, "Speak, Lord, for your servant listens" (cf. 1 S 3:1-10).

A boy or an adolescent is, as yet, unable to understand all that is implied in the gift of self to God and others in the priesthood. Like a plant, the vocation does not come to maturity before season. But what is to prevent the Divine Sower from planting the seed in virgin soil and asking laborers of the harvest to cultivate and protect it? For this reason the Church asks us to maintain and, even more, to establish high school seminaries and similar institutions *founded to nurture the seeds of vocation.*[5]

When a boy shows some vocational interest, it is wrong to simply ignore it or label it a childish dream. Each case has to be taken individually. Sometimes we should allow time to pass to see how things develop. Other cases of vocational interest should be personally directed by a priest or

---

[4] For this reason Canon Law prescribes a minimum age for priestly ordination (c. 1031) and for the different stages of religious life (cc. 642, 643 § 1, etc.).

[5] OT 3; cf. RFIS 11-18; CIC 234 § 1.

cultivated through Catholic youth groups. In some instances the best thing is to place this seed in an environment especially adapted to help it grow.

High school seminaries should offer this healthy atmosphere, appropriate to the boy's age and development. Everything about the seminary has to foster the human and Christian personality of the students and give the seed a chance to take root.

One essential purpose of this stage of formation is precisely to discern the student's vocation. As he matures he will gradually see whether or not this is his way. The formators get to know him thoroughly to see if he is truly suited and if there is sufficient evidence to believe that he has received an authentic call to the priesthood.

Vocation discernment is objective only if a boy feels completely free to decide. Neither his formators, his classmates, his family, nor even his own ups and downs should affect his freedom of decision. There should be no hint of pressure in favor of a vocation. But at the same time, there should be no pressure against it, which is equally an impairment to his free decision. This is sometimes forgotten by those (including perhaps priests) who in the name of liberty pressure a boy to change his path. A student responds freely and responsibly to what he sees as God's will only if we spare him oppressive influences of any sort.

High school seminaries can contribute tremendously to the preparation of a possible future priest, especially his spiritual life. If a boy learns from an early stage to live by faith, he is more likely to mature spiritually and become a true teacher of the faith for his brothers and sisters.

We have to coach him along his first steps towards intimate and personal prayer with God. At this age it is appropriate to direct the boys' meditation in common in the form of lively, very visual talks. During the talk the formator can at times engage in direct conversation with God out loud, or leave brief moments for personal reflection.

The spirituality of a boy can very well take shape around a simple relationship with Christ as his best friend and a trusting filial relationship with God the Father and with Mary. This friendship and filial love are the best motivation to help an adolescent strive to improve and to live always in the state of grace.

With the onset of affective and sexual tendencies, formation in a high school seminary can be decisive in helping an adolescent acquire a deeper understanding of the meaning of chastity as channelling these feelings and tendencies. It will be the beginning of a balanced affective maturing.

Adolescents also seek to affirm their own identity and in so doing tend to set themselves against others (especially authority figures) without even realizing it. It is a very apt time to lead them to grasp the authentic meaning of personal realization and the role of authority as a necessary ministry of service, which will put them on the road to genuine self-realization. It is a good time for him to assimilate the value of sincerity as the best way to be himself before his own conscience and before others.

Formators should adapt the academic programs to the special situation of their students. On the one hand, they must fulfill state study requirements and have their studies recognized by the civil authorities. These studies will provide the normal cultural foundation for future education and at the same time they leave the student completely free to choose another way without detriment to a civil career. On the other hand, such an academic program would have to be complemented with certain courses specific to the training of future priests. These subjects will in any case offer further cultural enrichment. For instance, knowledge of basic Christian doctrine is essential, but an introduction to Latin, the study of art, history, oral and written communication skills can also be very useful.[6] High school seminary years when well used are a valuable investment for the future.

We can say the same about his initiation to the apostolate. A high school seminarian, as well as perhaps carrying within the seed of the divine vocation to the priesthood, is a Christian called by baptism to holiness and the apostolate.[7] So we can help him to start forming an apostolic heart through apostolates compatible with his age, such as teaching catechism to children, organizing activities for them, etc.

Throughout this training, formators must always realize that while these boys are free human beings they are not sufficiently mature to understand the full meaning of responsible freedom. We have to educate our youngsters not only *in* freedom but also *for* freedom. Not yet capable of conducting themselves with full and responsible autonomy, boys require a particular channel to guide them: a complete schedule, a simple

[6] Cf. RFIS 16.
[7] Cf. LG 33 and 39.

but precise rule of life. At the beginning they will usually adjust to it unconsciously without worrying about the reasons behind each element of the schedule, following it almost like a train on its tracks. That doesn't matter. It will help them to live realities whose value they do not fully appreciate. When this is accompanied by a patient explanation of the reason for them, they will gradually interiorize these values, making them a part of their interior wealth and their free behavior.

As the maturing process continues, this channel ought to open up greater space for personal action. This will challenge him to administer his time and lead his life according to the principles he has assimilated. As formators we have to be attentive to correct him when he shows signs of erring during this process. In this way we can teach him to use his freedom responsibly.

High school students, in general, need to be constantly active. There should be ample time for sports, recreation, active participation in class and general activities, contests, etc. It is advisable that formators be with them at all times. That is the best way to get to know them, help them in their practical needs, encourage them, earn their trust and to be always accessible. We have to create a spirit of joy, friendship, and Christian charity in the school. The boys should feel at home.

It is also important that students maintain contact with their families, as an important element for their maturation. They should visit home so that they can continue to experience the love and positive influence of their parents. The number and duration of these visits should be based on a prudent consideration of the need to be in contact with the family and the various objectives of the boys' formation. Throughout the school year, we should encourage their love, gratitude and affection towards their families, teach them to pray for their families and to write to them if they live far away. Finally, it is very important that families identify with the high school seminary. We should get them to visit their sons and participate in certain school feasts and activities, understand the formation their son is receiving, value and support his possible vocation to the priesthood...

If the situation of a diocese is favorable for the establishment or maintenance of a high school seminary, perhaps these reflections will be of some use. Basically, it is a question of adapting what is specific to priestly formation to the age of the students and the particular nature of this type of seminary. As we have already mentioned, there are many different, equally valid ways of encouraging a boy's interest in the priesthood. The essential thing is not to let the seeds God plants die from neglect.

Introductory (Propaedeutic) Course

God calls when He wills. Yet the majority of those entering the seminary do so after completing high school, during college or even later.

Preparation for the priesthood cannot be reduced to ordinary career training. From the first chapter we insisted on the uniqueness of the priestly identity and mission, and we spoke of formation as transformation into Christ, the Priest. It hardly suffices for seminarians to attend fairly complete courses of philosophy and theology. We have to pay attention above all to what we examined when speaking about spiritual formation.

This holds true for the whole period of formation. It remains a priority even after priestly ordination. It is necessary, not to say indispensable, for the seminarian to have a good spiritual base. Some have it when they enter, but not everyone. We then have the problem of how to achieve it. Studying philosophy and theology, however, is a full-time occupation and not all our seminarians have laid an adequate spiritual foundation before entering. The problem is how to assure their spiritual foundation in the midst of other absorbing occupations. In response, more and more seminaries have instituted an introductory period, the *propaedeutic course*.[8]

This course is designed in the first place to facilitate the *vocational discernment* we spoke of at the beginning of this chapter. The candidate is given the chance at the very beginning of his vocational path to reflect calmly and seriously on the existence of a divine call. He can study what priesthood is and what it implies. He is able to analyze his own qualities and defects, trying to listen more attentively to the Holy Spirit. The formators are there to help him do this and at the same time to get to know the candidate more deeply, so that they can make a clear and sure discernment as soon as possible.

The propaedeutic course helps a young man achieve the necessary *adaptation* to the new mentality and lifestyle that the priesthood presup-

---

[8]   OT 14; RFIS 42; Congregation for Catholic Education, *Circular letter concerning some more urgent aspects of spiritual formation in seminaries,* January 6, 1980, (concluding note).

poses. Little experience is needed to realize that the young men entering the seminary, while coming with very good dispositions, are not always ready to go directly into seminary life. Their habits, customs, points of view are often quite distant from the characteristics of someone called to be another Christ for the world. It is not unusual for them at first to feel "out of place." If they are not helped during this initial stage, they run the risk of spending their whole lives trying to find "their place."

One principal fruit of the initiation should be the solid spiritual base mentioned earlier, which will guarantee their interior maturation throughout their whole formation. Therefore, the main occupation of students during this stage should be spiritual growth. It is the time to begin personal prayer (perhaps directed prayer at first) along with a concentrated effort to exercise priestly virtues, the time for a seminarian to engrave a deep love for Christ in his heart. For some, it may be the moment they discover that love for the first time.

The climate of this course must be especially favorable to prayer, silence, dedication to the things of God and personal reflection. The program can include spiritual talks, study of the fundamental structure of Catholic doctrine (possibly insufficiently known by many of them), introduction to Scripture accompanied with frequent personal reading of it, explanation and study of Vatican II and other fundamental documents of the Magisterium... They might spend some time on an introduction to Latin and even to philosophy.

In some places the introductory course spans an entire year. Considering the importance of this formation, a year goes by very quickly. But if even this is not possible, at least a few months should be dedicated to it, for instance, the summer before the first year of philosophy. Experience shows that when an introductory program is well planned and organized, it is never a waste of time.

Philosophy

A large part of priestly formation is devoted to the study of philosophy and theology. Sometimes they are combined. In the section concerned with intellectual formation we have already touched on the reasons that would suggest that philosophy be studied first to ensure an adequate foundation for theology. Following this line of thought, philosophy should be considered a specific stage of formation with its own characteristics. What is said here, though, may be applied to that single stage of formation often called "ecclesiastical studies."

In the first place we have to remember that philosophy is the candidate's first experience of academic life in the seminary. If it has been preceded by the propaedeutic course, the seminarian has an important spiritual base and is generally adjusted to seminary life. When the introductory period has not preceded philosophy, we should find a way to provide the essential elements that the initiation offers (i.e., deep vocational discernment, introduction to the spiritual life, etc.), which seem so important for priestly life.

In any case, the time of philosophy should help to settle the seminarian's fundamental option for Christ and his vocation. It is not good to maintain an indecisive attitude all through philosophy and theology; in addition, the task of interiorizing of which we have spoken on several occasions is also something that cannot be simply left for later.

Experience teaches some typical problems associated with this period. Seminarians begin to alternate activities for their spiritual, human and apostolic formation with studies that absorb a good part of their time, energies, and interest. They should not forget the ultimate meaning behind the academics. No seminarian should allow himself to turn into "just a student," who happens to pray once in a while. We have to think out the programs and schedules of the seminary so that, in addition to an intense dedication to philosophy, seminarians will have the elements to continue their preparation in all the other areas of priestly formation. For instance, opportunities for apostolic work (as we mentioned in the section concerning pastoral formation) are very helpful to keep academics within the context of their priestly-pastoral meaning.

Seminarians often find it difficult to understand why philosophy is important for their priestly formation. They may in fact go along with it simply because it is a requirement. Metaphysics, cosmology, etc., for many seem like dry, difficult subjects. We have to encourage them and explain as far as we can the place of these subjects toward a profound understanding of the world, man and God (so necessary for the apostolate) and their importance as a base for solid theological reflection.

Finally, as we mentioned in the section dealing with intellectual formation, since philosophy is a science that requires rational proof for everything, and since the student is usually in the process of definitive affirmation of his own judgment, it is possible that studying it may provoke certain problems of faith. Professors should show clearly both the power and limits of reason, but the other formators too should help each student personally in the most suitable way when, and if, these problems occur. If we take care to direct each seminarian personally during this period, it will prove to be a decisive stage, benefitting his maturity as a man and a *believer.*

Theology

Entering theology usually helps seminarians to realize how near priesthood is. They have been maturing in their personality and in their vocational option. Now they must consolidate and secure what they have achieved thus far not only as a base for ordination, but also for their whole future as priests.

Theological studies should contribute decisively in this direction. The effort to achieve a deep intellectual appreciation of the richness of the faith should also lead to a deeper spiritual life. Naturally, for this to happen, we have to encourage them to make theology more than an intellectual exercise or enrichment. They should understand that theology, even as a science, is true to itself only when explored *in faith, from a perspective of faith, and in order to comprehend and transmit the faith.*

During theology, seminarians receive the ministries of lector and acolyte. They should not be received routinely or taken for granted, but as authentic milestones on the road to the priesthood. There should be a certain solemnity in their preparation and conferral. New ministers should have opportunities to exercise their ministry in the seminary or in outside pastoral service.

All this applies with more reason to the diaconate. As well as being "the final step" before priesthood, it marks the candidates with the first degree of the ministry of orders. Their intense preparation for it and the way they live it consciously and deeply will be a great help for their priestly consecration and their future priestly ministry.

In some places, after the diaconate, the last year of formation is spent in pastoral work. We commented on this possibility in the section on apostolic-pastoral formation and made some remarks on this period of internship. We should never forget that this is a stage in the formation of a future priest. This means he should use it well to put into practice in this new situation all that he has experienced and assimilated in the seminary. It is anything but an opportunity to grow lax in prayer or the practice of virtue, but rather it is a time to reinforce the habits of priestly living without the help of the formative atmosphere of the seminary.

If a seminarian lives this period in the company of one or more priests outside the seminary, they should help him to continue preparing for priesthood as authentic formators.[9] They should remember that a deacon has acquired many spiritual and cultural resources but as yet lacks apostolic experience. Therefore, they should be understanding with him and not expect him to know how to do everything, they should offer guidance and support that will allow him to learn gradually the art of apostolic effectiveness.

Direct apostolate is at the heart of the pastoral year. But their apostolate is not just "practice." The best way to learn the apostolate is to try to produce concrete results. Even so, full time apostolic work can be enriched with reading and study. It will be very helpful to go more deeply into some themes of pastoral and moral theology which will help him to apply the great principles he studied in philosophy and theology to the concrete work he is engaged in. This actually is something that every priest should do. Encouraging a seminarian to further his integral formation, including intellectual formation, during the pastoral year helps him to understand the meaning of *ongoing formation.*

Ongoing Formation

One of the fundamental principles we emphasized in Chapter Two was "gradual and ongoing formation." The divine call to perfection (Mt 5:48) and the task of becoming like Christ the High Priest imply that our ideal will always be ahead of us. Our formation does not end on the day of

---

[9] Cf. CIC 258.

ordination. It must continue. In a certain sense, then, we may speak of ongoing formation as another stage of priestly formation, the longest one of all.

We do not need to ponder here its importance or draw up a complete syllabus of its content and the methods to effect it. The council and other documents of the magisterium have specified these.[10] We can, nevertheless, make some observations to complete what has been said.

First of all we should say that ongoing formation is not limited to intellectual formation. Progress should continue in everything that defines him as a priest and is the base for his mission. Therefore, we have to consider all four areas of priestly formation and pay special attention to what is the nucleus of the priestly life, that is, his spiritual life as the constant search for holiness in his identification with Christ the High Priest.

Let us also stress that ongoing formation is a personal task of each priest. The principle of "self-formation" is just as valid when we leave the seminary behind. If seminarians do not understand and value ongoing formation while still in the seminary it is unlikely that they will give it importance when absorbed by the pace of pastoral work. It is up to every priest to persevere every day in his quest for holiness and apostolic effectiveness. It is up to him to continue to seek the means of sanctification that helped him in the seminary: frequent confession, spiritual direction, spiritual reading... It is up to him to set time aside on a daily or weekly basis for reading and study.

But, as always, self-formation needs support. Dioceses need to establish programs that will help their priests, especially (but not exclusively) the younger ones. According to the needs and circumstances of the local clergy the program could be made to include such things as courses to update theology or pastoral methods, spiritual exercises, more extended periods of priestly renewal, get-togethers and meetings, etc. As in all areas of diocesan life, the bishop is ultimately responsible. He can seek assistance among seminary faculty or he may choose to name someone to promote and coordinate this area of priestly life. At times coordination with various dioceses and religious institutes could prove useful, espe-

---

[10] Cf. OT 22; CD 16; PO 19. RFIS 100-101.

cially for organizing courses in subjects in which a diocese does not have its own experts. In each case it is necessary to see what is needed and what is possible. Ongoing formation of our priests is a vital element of priestly life and therefore for the whole Christian community, and was clearly proposed and requested by Vatican II. What matters is that it gets beyond theory.

In reality, in all that has to do with the formation of priests, you have to see what is good to do and what is possible in each case. As we said at one stage, education is more a practical art than an exact science. In it there are no dogmas. What really counts is our sincere effort to carry out as best we can the extraordinarily absorbing and important task of forming the future shepherds of the Church.

Throughout these pages I have tried to communicate in an orderly fashion my particular lived experience in this field. As with any experience, it is individual. It is always enriching to receive the diverse experiences and reflexions of all those who carry out this ministry in the broad field of the Lord's vineyard.

Nevertheless, in our exchange of views we would all do well to attempt sincerely and humbly to lend an ear not so much to our own discoveries and opinions, as to the essence of the Catholic priesthood which we can deduce from the Gospel and the centuries-old tradition of the Church under the light of the magisterium. In reality we all are no more than workers in the harvest. We have to try to work as the one who has called us to his service would have us do. He unceasingly calls new workers and entrusts them to our mission as formators. He is the Lord of the Harvest.

Index